George Bullock: Cabinet-maker

Patrons

His Excellency Monsieur Luc de La Barre de Nanteuil,
the French Ambassador to the Court of St James

His Excellency Sir Ewen Fergusson,
the British Ambassador to France

GEORGE BULLOCK

'A Sculptor with a Bust of Mr Blundell'
by Joseph Allen (see p.129)

George Bullock

CABINET-MAKER

Introduction by
Clive Wainwright

JOHN MURRAY
H. BLAIRMAN & SONS

Produced by Edition, 2a Roman Way, London N7 8XG
Published by John Murray (Publishers) Ltd, 50 Albemarle Street,
London W1X 4BD in association with H. Blairman & Sons Ltd,
119 Mount Street, London W1Y 5HB

Printed and bound by Richard Clay Ltd, Chichester, Sussex

First published 1988

Edited and designed by Jill Hollis

British Library Cataloguing in Publication Data

Bullock, George, 1783-1818
    George Bullock : cabinet makers :
    introduction by Clive Wainwright.
    1. English furniture. Bullock, George,
    1783?-1818. Catalogues, indexes
    I. Title II. H. Blairman & Sons
    III. Sudley Art Gallery
    749.22

ISBN 0-7195-4540-4

George Bullock: Cabinet-maker

Exhibitions at:
H. Blairman & Sons Ltd, London
24th February - 19th March 1988

and

Sudley Art Gallery, Liverpool
21st February - 26th March 1988

Contents

LENDERS
Page 7

FOREWORD
Page 9

ACKNOWLEDGEMENTS
Page 11

GEORGE BULLOCK AND HIS CIRCLE
Clive Wainwright
Page 13

GEORGE BULLOCK IN BIRMINGHAM AND LIVERPOOL
Lucy Wood
Page 40

THE SALE OF BULLOCK'S STOCK IN TRADE
Martin Levy
Page 48

THE CATALOGUE
Page 51

GEORGE BULLOCK: SCULPTOR
Timothy Stevens
Page 127

CHRONOLOGY
Lucy Wood
Page 155

BIBLIOGRAPHY
Page 159

Lenders

His Grace the Duke of Abercorn
His Grace the Duke of Atholl
City Museums and Art Gallery, Birmingham
Brotherton Library, University of Leeds
Cheltenham Art Gallery & Museums
The Marquess of Cholmondeley
Mr. & Mrs. Timothy Clifford
Leeds City Art Galleries
Manchester City Art Galleries
Major & Mrs. John Mansel
Mrs. Patricia Maxwell-Scott
The National Trust (Sudbury Hall)
The Earl of Rosebery
James Stirling, Esq.
The Board of Trustees of the Victoria & Albert Museum
The Earl of Wemyss & March and Lord Neidpath
Various private collectors

Foreword

Blairman's and the National Museums & Galleries on Merseyside are delighted to have joined together in organising these major exhibitions of work by George Bullock. This is the first occasion since his workshop was sold up in 1819 that a comprehensive range of his furniture, together with some sculpture, has been presented publicly.

We are privileged that His Excellency Monsieur Luc de La Barre de Nanteuil, the French Ambassador to the Court of St. James, and His Excellency Sir Ewen Fergusson, the British Ambassador to France, have honoured us by becoming patrons of the exhibitions. We should also particularly like to express our gratitude to all those collectors and institutions without whose generosity these exhibitions would not have been possible.

We should especially like to thank Timothy Stevens, now at the National Museum of Wales, for his inspired enthusiasm and support and Clive Wainwright at the Victoria & Albert Museum whose dedication to George Bullock, together with that of Martin Levy at Blairman's, has ensured the success of these exhibitions, which would not have been realised without the untiring energy of Lucy Wood at the Lady Lever Art Gallery.

We hope this publication will re-establish Bullock's position as one of the major cabinet-makers in the history of English furniture.

George J. Levy
H. Blairman & Sons

Edward Morris
National Museums & Galleries
on Merseyside

Acknowledgements

We should like to thank all those people who have contributed in many different ways to the organisation of these exhibitions and the preparation of the catalogue, not least those who replied to our enquiries about their ancestors' purchases at the Bullock Sale of 1819. In particular we are grateful to the following:

Jane Anderson, Andrew Barber, Sir Geoffrey de Bellaigue, Mary Bennett, Roy Boardman, Susan Bourne, Xanthe Brooke, Lady Cholmondeley, Timothy Clifford, Frances Collard, James Corson, Caroline Davidson, June Dean, Ian Dunn, Ian Eaves, Martin Ellis, Mrs. Evetts, Lord Ferrers, Helen Fielding, Terry Friedman, P.J. Gardner, Jonathan Harris, Canon W. Herbert-Bullough, The Rev. J. Higham, Martin Hopkinson, Jana Horak, Nicole Hubert, Professor Michael Jaffe, James Johnston, John Kenworthy-Browne, John Kenyon, Alex Kidson, Lorna McEchern, Michael Maclagan, Anthony Malcolmson, Philip Mansel, Gilbert Martineau, John Morley, Brian Nodes, A.V.B. Norman, Bernard Nurse, Julia Poole, Hugh Roberts, Robert Scott, Jacob Simon, Janet Smith, Michael Snodin, Roger Strong, C.J. Tuplin, Lady Verulam, Adam White, Glennys Wild, Lady Wilson and Canon Yandle.

We should also like to thank: Nancy King, Anita Byrne and the staff of the Walker Art Gallery; also the staff of the following libraries and archive repositories: Birmingham Local Studies Library & Record Office; Cheshire Record Office; The Guildhall Library, City of London; Linnean Society; Liverpool Record Office & Local History Library; Public Record Office of Northern Ireland; Westminster Central Library.

Packing & Transport: Keith Rout, G.& R. Removals
Secretarial Co-ordination: Maggie Williamson-Holland

George Bullock and his Circle

CLIVE WAINWRIGHT

This essay gives a short account of George Bullock's career after he left Liverpool, describes several commissions and discusses the nature of the circle in which he moved. An essay on his career in Birmingham and Liverpool and a factual chronology appear elsewhere in this catalogue.[1] Other publications concerning Bullock are given in the bibliography.

The sources are meagre. It has even proved impossible to trace Bullock's will, though he certainly made one. A few letters survive, notably those concerning Tew, Cholmondeley and Abbotsford, but there is no Bullock 'archive'. None of the records kept by his firm has been discovered, though a number of bills have been found in houses to which he supplied furniture. Nevertheless, it is possible to build up a composite picture of his character and personality from the records left by others in letters and diaries, and from articles in contemporary periodicals.

The most important source regarding his work, however, is the so-called *Wilkinson Tracings*. When they were acquired in 1974 by the City Museum and Art Gallery of Birmingham, the *Tracings* consisted of a scrapbook into which a wide range of tracings and engravings were pasted or loosely inserted. More recently the book has been split into separate sheets. It came with no provenance, but the first page was inscribed, 'Tracings by Thomas Wilkinson, from the designs of the late Mr George Bullock 1820'.

Who Wilkinson was, and how he had access to the original designs (which have since vanished) is unknown. It is possible that he was one of the metal-working dynasty of Wilkinsons in Birmingham. (Interestingly Matthew Robinson Boulton of Tew Park married a Wilkinson and yet another person of the same name was housekeeper at Aston Hall.) Another possibility is that he was Thomas Wilkinson, one of a family of London cabinet-makers, who worked in Brokers Row, Moorfields, from 1812 to 1828.[2] As a practising cabinet-maker, this second Wilkinson might well have recognised the considerable commercial value of Bullock's fashionable designs. As none of Bullock's business papers survive, it has not been possible to establish whether anyone by the name of Wilkinson was actually employed by Bullock. But such a person would have had ready access to all the designs in the office. The date of 1820 in the inscription is interesting, for it points to the time after Bullock's death in 1818 when the firm continued to operate for a while to execute outstanding orders. This phase certainly continued until at least 1819. The remaining

[1] For a concise account of Bullock's whole career, *see* Clive Wainwright, 'George Bullock' in Gilbert and Beard (eds), *Dictionary of English Furniture Makers*, London, 1986.

[2] *Dictionary of English Furniture Makers*, 1986, pp.977-78.

stock of Bullock's ware-rooms was sold in May 1819, and it is likely that by 1820 the cabinet-making workshops themselves had been, or were about to be, closed down. The Mona Marble works, however, seem to have remained in existence into the 1820s (*see* Chronology).

It is possible that Wilkinson made the tracings out of devotion to Bullock's memory, but it is more likely that he thought that they might come in handy in the future – others in the Bullock circle such as Richard Brown and Richard Bridgens were, as we shall see later, probably up to much the same game.

The designs come in a variety of forms and they are certainly not all by Bullock himself. As well as tracings, there are at least one original drawing and a number of engravings of full-size patterns for marquetry or inlay to be executed in wood or metal. The patterns are very crudely engraved; some bear a date and the legend 'Published', and sometimes the name of the client for whom the piece of furniture was made. They may well have been intended for use in the workshop or as a record of work done. The fact that examples of these patterns have been found among the designs of other 19th-century cabinet-makers points to the fact that they did circulate in the trade, at least to some extent. Of course, before the days of the photocopier, tracing was the normal method used by designers and architects for duplicating designs. It would thus seem likely that Wilkinson took a number of engraved designs (of which several copies probably existed in Bullock's workshop) and made tracings of some of the original drawings there.

As well as the names of clients that appeared on the engravings, there are also clients' names and place names on the tracings. These clues on particular designs have revolutionised the study of Bullock's career, though the full story of the tracings has yet to be – and indeed may never be – established. But their discovery has certainly made it possible to document firmly a wide range of Bullock furniture; for this reason there is copious reference made to the *Wilkinson Tracings* in this catalogue, and some examples have been illustrated both here and in the catalogue entries of various exhibits.

To understand the singular character of Bullock's work, it is necessary to introduce several other members of his circle. First J.M. Gandy (1771-1843), the architect and architectural artist, who was for much of his life closely associated with Sir John Soane (1758-1837).

In April 1809, Bullock wrote to James Watt Senior: '. . . my business has so far exceeded my calculations that I have found great difficulty in supplying it . . . I have now called in the aid and assistance of a clever man, Mr Joseph Gandy Architect, whose professional abilities and system of business, will enable me to conduct and accomplish everything I wish in my undertaking . . . '[3] Accompanied by Soane's eldest son, to whom he was tutor, Gandy moved to Liverpool and went into partnership with Bullock, a collaboration that was described as: 'Bullock, George & Joseph Gandy, architects, modellers, sculptors, marble masons, cabinet makers, upholsterers . . . '

Gandy was a rather impractical and eccentric man and it seems that Bullock's high hopes may not have been fulfilled, for on 1st September 1810, Gandy wrote to Soane: 'The affair of the Liverpool Academy . . . took a most serious turn a few days after you left us,

[3]Extract from the Watt Family Archives published by Virginia Glenn in 'Regency Furnishing Schemes', *Furniture History*, Vol. XV, 1979, p.63.

[4]A.T. Bolton, *The Portrait of John Soane*, 1927, p.126.

my partner insisting on one hand that the partnership interest was most deeply hurt by my refusal of joining with him, as one of the members of the Liverpool Academy, which I on the other hand peremptorily refused . . . the consequence was an immediate proposal of separation, and we parted in high words . . . I am preparing every thing to fix my residence in London by Michaelmas . . .'[4]

Gandy was in fact in the right, for he had been elected A.R.A. in 1803, and at this time the Royal Academy did not allow its members to belong to any other rival society. There are indications, though, that he may eventually have patched up his quarrel with Bullock. Not surprisingly, Bullock's name appears prominently in the list of 'Academicians' in the catalogues of the Liverpool Academy of Arts from its foundation exhibition in 1810 and he was President for its first two years. There is of course no sign of Gandy at first, but already in 1813 there was an exhibit (number 209) shown by him: 'A restoration of the East Window of Melrose Abbey from its ruins . . .'

[5]H. Colvin, *A Biographical Dictionary of British Architects*, 1978, pp.328-29.

Whether Gandy designed any furniture while in partnership with Bullock is unknown, though I would suggest that it is likely that he did. He was, however, certainly active as an architect,[5] and as he was actually in partnership with Bullock, they may have been jointly involved in designing and furnishing a number of buildings. For instance, in 1809 Gandy designed and built a Rotunda for the display of panoramic views in Bold Street, Liverpool, and in 1810 the Assembly Rooms in Castle Street. The diarist Farington noted on 12th January 1811 that 'Gandy called . . . He had settled in Liverpool one year & a half, and had been well employed, having built much there . . . He now proposes to reside in London.'[6] At some point Gandy made a design for an Entrance Hall for Ince Blundell (near Liverpool), but the actual date and whether this was executed are unknown.

[6]James Grief (ed.), *The Farington Diary*, Vol. VI, 1922-28 p.227.

As Henry Blundell died in 1810 this design may well date from the period of Gandy's partnership with Bullock, but it is also possible that the design was for Blundell's son – there was clearly a strong Bullock/Blundell tie-up, evidenced by the busts of Blundell made by Bullock and by the fact that one of these appears in the portrait of Bullock by Joseph Allen.

Gandy had been involved as architect on several buildings in the north of England before he and Bullock went into partnership. It is possible that the two had co-operated in the furnishing of some of these buildings, and that this led naturally to the formation of the partnership. From 1806 to about 1810 Gandy was involved in refurbishing the mediaeval house of Bolton Hall in Yorkshire for

[7]Clive Wainwright, 'The Romantic Interior in Britain', *National Art-Collections Fund Review 1985*, pp.85-86.

John Bolton of Liverpool.[7] The antiquarian interiors created here were comparable to work done by Bullock at Cholmondeley Castle. From 1808 to 1811, again for John Bolton, Gandy remodelled Storrs Hall in Westmorland, but on this occasion he was working in the classical style. The nature of the furniture provided for Storrs is not yet known.

It seems likely, then, that the partnership led to Bullock's involvement in both these projects. There is also tentative evidence that Bullock knew Bolton (who came from Liverpool) in that he exhibited a bust of a Colonel Bolton at the Liverpool Academy Exhibition of 1810.

The partnership – and the possible earlier collaboration – with Gandy appears to have marked a significant new phase both in Bullock's career and in his stylistic development. Gandy and young Soane will have brought with them to Liverpool the very latest architectural ideas, and their experience of the advanced classicism that characterised the work of Soane's office at this date must have been a revelation to Bullock. They would also, of course, have been able to introduce Bullock to the sophisticated version of Gothic as recently developed by Soane in his designs for the furniture, and interiors of the Gothic Library at Stowe, 1805-08.

The nature of the connection between Bullock and Richard Brown (active 1804-42) is unclear. Brown, who styled himself 'Architect and Professor of Perspective', was a designer of buildings and author of several works on perspective and architecture[8], notably *The Principles of Practical Perspective*, published in 1815. His office was situated close to Bullock's workshop and on 1st April 1819 it was announced that 'Mr. R. Brown of Wells-Street is about to publish *The Rudiments of Drawing Cabinet Furniture* wherein are contained concise and explicit instructions for enabling cabinet-makers to design and delineate the different articles . . . after the manner of the antique, on twenty-five coloured plates, each accompanied with classical remarks.'[9]

[8]H. Colvin, *A Biographical Dictionary of British Architects*, 1978, pp.147-48.

[9]*The Repository of Arts*, 1st April 1819, p.239.

I have never seen a copy of this edition, but one must presume that it was not a phantom, for the many copies of the 1822 edition that exist all bear the legend 'the second edition, improved'. Several commentators have noted that the book is largely devoted to Bullock and his furniture and many of the plates depict not merely Bullock designs, but actual pieces of Bullock furniture, for example Napoleon's sofa (*see* fig. 33). In his caption to the final plate, Brown wrote of Bullock that:

' . . . some of his designs were certainly too massy and ponderous, nevertheless grandeur cannot be obtained without it; such are the standards of his octagon tables. There was great novelty without absurdity, as well as happy relief, in his ornaments: yet many of his articles were considerably overcharged with buhl; sometimes the

Fig. 1. 'Octagon table'. Present whereabouts unknown.

buhl-work was sunk in brass, and on other occasions the counterpart was of the same wood as the furniture itself, and the whole surface represented a brazen front. He appears to have been peculiarly happy in his mouldings, which were of the Grecian taste, sharp, bold, and well relieved . . . Most of his ornaments were selected from British plants, his woods were of English growth, which were admirably well polished. He has shewn that we need not roam to foreign climes for beautiful ornaments, but that we have abundance of plants and flowers equal to the Grecian, which if adopted, would be found as pleasing as the antique.'

It seems likely that Brown passed on this enthusiasm for Bullock's unique versions of both the Grecian and the Gothic to one of his pupils, the architectural draughtsman and author Michael Angelo Nicholson, for *The Practical Cabinet Maker*, on which Nicholson collaborated with his father, Peter Nicholson, contains a number of plates depicting pieces of furniture in the Grecian and the Gothic styles with very much the look of Bullock designs.

Whether Brown ever actually collaborated with or worked for Bullock is not known. The fact that the publication of his book was announced less than a month before the Bullock Sale in May 1819 could be thought to smack of opportunism, and indeed one wonders whether Brown managed to get at the surviving designs before Wilkinson. But if this were the case, would he have paid such a handsome tribute to Bullock in the text? He certainly publicised Bullock's name and designs and kept them in the public eye well into the 1820s. Nicholson paid no such tribute.

Richard Hicks Bridgens (1785-1846) was perhaps the most important member of Bullock's circle. He emerges as a rather shadowy figure who died in Port of Spain, Trinidad, in November 1846. An obituary in a West Indian newspaper recorded,

'Died – In this Town, on Friday last, aged 61 years, Richard Bridgens, Esq., Superintendant of Public works. Mr Bridgens had devoted his early days to the fine arts and aided by an excellent natural taste acquired a great proficiency in several branches of his studies, particularly that of ornamental architecture . . . the fellow student and intimate friend, in early life of the celebrated Chantrey, who was heard to express repeatedly the highest opinions of this gifted but modest and unobtrusive companion. Mr Bridgens' abilities were almost, if not altogether, lost in this country – that the situation which he filled for many years past, and up to the time of his decease was on one hand unworthy of his genius – and whilst on the other it required a knowledge of the humbler branches of the profession which Mr. B had never studied – and the Artist often committed faults which the humbler mechanic could have seen and avoided. It was as if the high racer had been put to the plough . . .'

This obituary was preserved by the late great grand-daughter of Bridgens who also recalled that 'My grandmother [Richard Bridgens's eldest daughter] told me that he had known a great many artists & architects of the period but sad to say we have no trace left of any of these connections. Any papers & letters that he had up to this period of his life were all burnt in a disasterous fire in Port of Spain . . . his wife inherited a sugar estate in Trinidad B.W. Indies & they must have left England shortly after 1825.'

Bridgens married Mary Ann Shaw at St George's, Hanover Square – a stone's throw from Bullock's workshop – on 5th October 1816. A daughter was born in Chelsea in July 1817, another in Birmingham in April 1819, a son in July 1825 in London, and then three daughters in Trinidad between January 1827 and April 1831.[10]

Of Bridgens's early career we know nothing; for instance, how, when and where could he have been a 'fellow student' of Francis Chantrey when neither man was ever registered as a student at the Royal Academy? We do know that Chantrey went to evening classes at the Academy in 1807 and *if* Bridgens was in London at the time, he might have done the same. Another possibility is that they met when Chantrey was apprenticed to Robert Ramsay – a carver and gilder of High Street, Sheffield. Perhaps Bridgens actually came from Sheffield and they were fellow apprentices? Chantrey completed his apprenticeship in 1802 at the age of 21 when Bridgens was 16; at that time apprenticeships commonly began at the age of 14. No R. Bridgens appears in the Sheffield directories of the time but two people called Bridgens, which is a fairly unusual name, are listed, both in the metalworking trades. Whether Richard Bridgens was connected with either of these is pure speculation, but Bridgens had certainly been trained both as a sculptor and as a furniture designer.

Quite apart from being an important artist and designer in his own right, Bridgens was, without doubt, a key participant in Bullock's business. When and how Bridgens met Bullock is unknown but he was certainly involved with Bullock during the partnership with Gandy: in the catalogue of the first Liverpool Academy Exhibition (in which he showed two designs), Bridgens's address is given as 'At Messrs Bullock and Gandy's'. At the 1811 Exhibition he showed a model of 'A Nymph Attiring', and Chantrey, who was classed as a 'Non Resident Academician', showed four busts. Thus Bridgens might have met him at this time even if they had not known each other before.

Bridgens was certainly involved in work at Abbotsford both before and after Bullock's death and also, as will be shown, at Aston and Battle, but his importance in the context of Bullock studies lies in one in particular of his several books: *Furniture with candelabra and interior decoration designed by R. Bridgens*, published in 1838. A glance at this tall folio with its elegant coloured plates is enough to puzzle any furniture historian or bibliographer for it belongs rather to the world of Regency pattern books such as Hope, Brown, Ackermann, Stafford, Pugin or Nicholson than to the early Victorian period. Not only does the book look very old-fashioned for 1838, but the designs were distinctly so; many of them, such as those for Battle Abbey, date from Bridgens's involvement with Bullock twenty years before.

The first indication I found that there had been an earlier edition of the publication was in an 1833 sale catalogue of the library of A.C. Pugin which included as lot 470 'Bridgens (R.) Furniture with Candelabra and Interior Decoration'. Then my attention was drawn to the existence in the R.I.B.A. Library of two parts of a part issue

[10]I am indebted for much of the information concerning Bridgens to Dr. James Corson, the Honorary Librarian of Abbotsford.

[11] I am indebted to Nicholas Savage for this information.

of an earlier edition[11]. It still carries the original printed wrapper, which reads *Furniture with candelabra and interior decoration, applicable to the embellishment of modern and Old English Mansions. Designed and etched in outline by R. Bridgens . . .* A descriptive sheet informs us that

'In order to make this work as useful as possible a few copies will be introduced from Ancient Examples, and as designs are sometimes called for in the style prevalent in England during the Reigns of Elizabeth and James I. as a specimen of that period will be given – *Details, &c. of Aston Hall, Warwickshire, THE RESIDENCE OF JAMES WATT, ESQ. . . .* It is proposed to deliver this Work Monthly, and [it] will be confined to ten parts, Folio, containing six plates each . . .'

The title page depicts a classical frame, composed of ornaments that frequently appear on Bullock furniture, which surrounds the legend *Furniture with candelabra and interior decoration designed and etched by R. Bridgens.* The twelve plates in these two parts date from September 1825 to October 1826 and are not numbered in sequence, but run from I to LVIII. Though no copy of the whole ten parts is known to exist and it is therefore possible that only two parts appeared, it would seem that at least 36 plates were etched, for a close examination of the 1838 edition reveals that the imprint lines are erased or altered on 36 plates. Of the twelve plates in Parts One and Two, eleven appear in the 1838 edition. Plate LVIII, however, showing details from three mediaeval churches, is absent.

Bridgens claimed on the title page to have both designed *and* etched the plates for the 1825-1826 edition. However, the title page of the 1838 edition must have been re-etched, for though it has the same border as the earlier one it reads *Furniture with candelabra and interior decoration designed by R. Bridgens.* Henry Shaw's name appears on many of the plates in the 1838 edition and that of Bridgens on only a few. Moreover the 1857 edition of Henry Lowndes's *Bibliographers Manual . . .* states that the 1838 edition was 'Published in conjunction with Henry Shaw'.

Shaw is, of course, author of the well-known *Specimens of Ancient Furniture.*[12] It is tempting to speculate that he was a relation of the Ann Shaw whom Bridgens married in 1816. A plate of an ancient chair in St Mary's Hall, Coventry, which appears both in Shaw's book and in the 1838 edition of Bridgens, is further evidence of a close association between the two men.

[12] Clive Wainwright, 'Specimens of Ancient Furniture', *The Connoisseur* Vol. 184, 1973, pp.105-113.

There is certainly more to be discovered concerning the publishing history of this fascinating and important book. And it might uncover more information about a series of as yet inexplicable actions. Bridgens emigrated to the West Indies while his book was being published in part issues. He returned to England in the 1830s. After publishing *West Indian Scenery with illustrations of negro character . . .* , 1836, and the 1838 edition of *Furniture with candelabra . . .* , he returned to the West Indies.

On the basis of the title of the earlier edition of *Furniture with candelabra . . .* I suggest that whilst Bridgens was working for Bullock he specialised in the design of furniture and interiors in the Mediaeval and what he termed the 'Old English' styles. These are the styles in which he certainly worked at Battle and Abbotsford, and at Aston in the mid 1820s.[13] All the designs that he showed at the Liverpool and the Royal Academies during his association with Bullock were in these styles, and as far as we know he never designed in the Classical style for a Bullock commission. In 1822 he showed at the Royal Academy his 'Attempt to improve the Barberini tripod etc', and though candelabra play a part in his book there is no evidence that he ever wholeheartedly embraced classicism.

Of the 60 plates in *Furniture with candelabra* . . . , 25 are stated to be 'Designs in the Grecian Style', but are they actually by Bridgens? Like the other designs in the book, they are certainly for Bullock commissions, but is it possible that Bridgens too, like Brown and Wilkinson, was pillaging the designs left in the workshop after Bullock's untimely death? 27 are 'Designs in the Elizabethan Style' and 7 are 'Designs in the Gothic Style'. Bridgens claimed on the title page that the designs were all his, yet many appear in the *Wilkinson Tracings* as the work of Bullock. Thus the classical designs in *Furniture with candelabra* . . . might well actually be by Bullock or at least by the designer of his classical pieces. The answers to all these questions may never be known, but the complex issues surrounding the authorship of the various designs executed in Bullock's workshop must be appreciated by anyone interested in his work.

Concerning Bullock himself, one obituary gives such a clear impression of how he was viewed by his contemporaries that it is worth quoting in full:

'Died lately at his house in Tenderten [sic] Street, Hanover Square, George Bullock, Director of the Mona Marble Works, who carried taste, in design of furniture, to a higher pitch than it was ever carried before in this country. Mr. Bullock was, in many respects, a man of very remarkable powers; every thing that he thought, or did, or executed, was on a grand and extended scale. He appeared to have entered into his late pursuit from one much higher, and much more elevated, bringing more powers to his task than was merely requisite. He was originally a sculptor and modeller, and carried the taste and feeling of an artist into what he latterly directed. It may appear to some, that designs for furniture are a very inferior branch of art, but they certainly are a branch of it, and any one who carries such designs to a high pitch of excellence, and who contrives to raise the character of the nation in such respects, is certainly entitled to be noticed in a journal devoted to the Fine Arts, like our own. His borders were generally designed from nature with exquisite taste, and his eye for the harmony of colour, was excessively remarkable, as the rooms which he adorned with his furniture will amply prove. He was a man of unbounded liberality of sentiment in private life, ever ready to sacrifice his own comfort, his own convenience, his own time, and his own interests to the comfort and happiness of others. He was, in every respect, an Englishman, and ambitious of his country's reputation. To him was entirely owing, our possession of the casts from Shakespeare's bust at Stratford, which bears the internal marks of its being a portrait. To the nobility and gentry his loss is very great, and to his friends quite irreparable; they will long

[13]Virginia Glenn, 'Regency Furnishing Schemes', *Furniture History*, Vol. XV, 1979.

[14] *Annals of the Fine Arts*, VIII, 1819, pp.321-322. I am indebted to Frances Collard for this reference.

[15] I am indebted to Robin Sanderson of the Geological Museum for showing me their samples of Mona Marble.

[16] *The Repository of Arts . . .* XIII, 1815, p.278.

[17] *The Repository . . .* IX, 1813, p.338.

[18] Angharad Llwyd, *A History of Mona or Anglesey . . . the prize essay to which was adjudged the first premium at the Royal Beaumaris Eisteddfod . . .*, 1833, pp.260-261.

remember, with melancholy satisfaction, the many happy evenings they have spent at his hospitable house. He was in the vigour of life, and a few weeks since, seemed as likely to live as any of his younger friends. His death was sudden and lacerating. – Peace to his shade!'[14]

An important aspect of Bullock's business was his involvement in the mining of Mona Marble.[15] In 1815 this account appeared:

'An interesting discovery was made in Anglesea a few years since by M.G. Bullock of Liverpool. He found, in the centre of that island and about seven miles from Paris mountain, some marble quarries, containing two beds of rocks, the one resembling, in colour and effect, the Oriental porphyry, and the other the *verd antique* . . . some of the blocks which these quarries have produced, vie with the richest specimens of those valuable materials of the ancient sculptors . . .'[16]

The exact date when Bullock acquired the quarry has not yet been established, but it is clear from Liverpool newspapers of the time that he owned it as early as 1806. Anglesey was only a short sea voyage from Liverpool, but the transport of Mona Marble from Anglesey to London after Bullock's move there must have been far more expensive and lengthy.

Bullock was not the only person to promote native minerals, for in June 1813 his friend the publisher Rudolph Ackermann noted,

'Indeed our native marbles are deserving public cultivation and, many of them approach to the perfection of the antiques. With much plausibility, though not with evidence amounting to conviction, the late Sir George Wright maintained that the verd antique was of British origin, having opened a long neglected quarry in Wales. As the country where this precious marble was produced, is not known by the virtuosi of the present, he deemed this tacit corroboration of his hypothesis . . . The chimney-pieces of Mr. Ackermann's Great Room, are specimens of the Devonshire marble.'[17]

The theory that the Romans quarried *verd antique* on Anglesey is not as far-fetched as might at first appear. In the early 19th century the site of the original quarries was still unknown. It was only later that they were re-discovered in Greece. The Romans certainly had the technology to quarry and import marble from Britain had they chosen to do so, and in fact they did import large quantities of certain minerals from Britain – for example, lead was mined in the Mendips and then exported. (It was also believed in Bullock's time that the Phoenicians had imported tin from Cornwall.)

After repeating the Roman story, a commentator of 1833 described the actual location of Bullock's quarry: 'Llanvechell is in the hundred of Talybolion . . . besides a mineral spring, near Cevn Coch and the fallen cromlech, there is in this parish, a quarry of curious and beautiful marble, called verd antique, intersected with asbestos. Some few years ago, £1,000 was given for the lease of a small quarry, by Mr. Bullock of London who brought the Mona marble into celebrity.'[18]

The material in question was not, in fact, marble but 'Serpentine, or Mona marble . . . a stone which, when polished, has a near resemblance to marble, is of dark green colour, or reddish, variously streaked, and spotted with lighter green, brown and yellow . . . of

the serpentine obtained from the Island of Anglesea a great pro-
portion is sent to London by Messrs Bullock and Co. who have a
large warehouse and polishing rooms for it in Oxford Street . . .
The quarries are worked by them to a considerable extent, though
this is necessarily attended with very heavy expenses. They manufacture it into chimney-pieces, slabs, columns and other articles . . .'[19]
Several of the pieces of furniture in this exhibition have Mona Marble
slabs for which this description is most appropriate.

[19]William Bingley, *Useful
Knowledge* . . ., Vol. I, 1816,
pp.88-89.

It would seem that Bullock did not actually discover the quarry
but purchased it and exploited the 'marble' from it. Whether he
believed the *verd antique* story or simply made use of it as an advertising
ploy is not clear, but he certainly did not go out of his way to deny
it. The mere possibility that Mona Marble *might* be the veritable Roman
material could be quite enough to persuade an ardently Neo-Classical
client. Quite apart from any Roman associations, the island of Mona
had also been important to both the Ancient Britons and the Druids,
so there were other historical links to enhance further the selling
potential of the marble. Sir Walter Scott frequently called Bullock
the 'Prince of the Black Marble Island' in an allusion both to the
island of Mona and to the character of that name in *The Arabian Nights*.

In 1786 an immense quantity of copper ore was discovered at Parys
mountain, and Anglesey vied with Cornwall for the title of Britain's
main producer of copper. Matthew Boulton, the pioneer industrialist,
had an important part in the copper mining and it is possible that
Bullock's attention was originally drawn to the Mona Marble a few
miles outside Parys through his being acquainted with Boulton.

Did Bullock's enthusiasm for British marbles, and also, as we saw
in Brown's description, his keen use of native woods and ornament,
stem from a genuine sense of patriotism or was it largely opportunism? Certainly at the height of the Napoleonic Wars, foreign woods
and marbles were difficult to obtain. In any case, during time of
war, nationalism tends to become a more prevalent mood, which
might well encourage a taste for indigenous materials, so perhaps
Bullock was capitalising both on the availability of British materials
and on their popularity.

Bullock, more than almost any cabinet-maker of his day,
demonstrates in his choice of ornament and form an awareness of
contemporary developments in France. He would certainly have
known that the British blockade had made the use of native woods
and marbles fashionable in France. Marbles such as 'Porphyre vert
des Vosges' and 'Marbre Napoleon' from Boulogne were frequently
used where foreign ones might previously have been chosen. Native
French woods such as walnut, beech, oak and elaborately figured
burrs of elm, ash and yew replaced mahogany, particularly after the
importation of mahogany was banned by Imperial decree in 1806.
In 1811 the 'Société d'encouragement pour la fabrication de meubles
en bois indigènes' was founded and further encouraged this trend.
Quite possibly Bullock realised the potential for creating a similar
fashion in England. A nice irony is that Bullock was finally to supply
furniture made from British woods to Napoleon himself.

In terms of design the results of Bullock's use of native materials
are remarkable, as seen in the figured oak and holly in the Tew pieces

(nos. 25-29), the Mona Marble slabs on the Palmella commodes (no. 10), the Glen Tilt marble slabs and the larch for the Blair commodes (no. 9) and Morritt's yew for the Shakespeare pedestal (no. 15). Bullock's – or his designers' – adaptation of Classical forms to an English context is masterly, for instance in re-designing the Classical thyrsus by replacing the Roman grapes with British hops; this motif appears both on the table (no. 50) and on the Palmella commodes (no. 10). Many other British plants are incorporated in his ornament, so successfully transformed into flat pattern that one has to agree with Brown's observation that ' . . . we have abundance of plants and flowers equal to the Grecian which, if adopted, would be found as pleasing as the antique.' These designs can fairly be seen as the most successful application of natural forms to flat pattern until those published by A.W.N. Pugin in 1849 in *Floriated Ornament*.

As will be noted elsewhere in this catalogue Bullock's brother William was the first of the two to move to London. His Museum was established at The Great Room, 22 Piccadilly, and was open to the public by January 1810. By the beginning of May that year Ackermann's *Repository* could report,

'We never remember any public exhibition having met with the universal patronage and approbation as Mr Bullock's celebrated museum has done since opening in the metropolis . . . We are assured that upwards of forty thousand persons have examined this place of rational amusement and delight . . . her Majesty, her Royal Highness the Princess Charlotte of Wales, Sir Joseph Banks, and many other persons distinguished either for rank or science, have marked their approbation of the proprietors exertions, by presenting him several valuable and curious articles.'

A month later the *Repository* published a view of the interior and noted that the number of visitors had risen to eighty thousand.

The whole story of William Bullock's museums and various other business ventures and his spectacular foreign travels is a fascinating one that well deserves to be told in full. A good survey has recently been published,[20] and the story of his important ethnographical collections has also been fully covered.[21]

Whether the finances of George and William were connected and to what extent their business enterprises were interdependent is unclear, though there is some indication that they were closely linked. The brilliant success of William's London Museum, where George repeated the concept of the Grecian Room that he had pioneered in Liverpool, certainly provided an ideal foundation for his move to London. George Bullock first appears in the London directories of 1813, listed at his brother's address: 'Bullock George, upholsterers, Grecian Rooms, Egyptian Hall Piccadilly'. In the 1812 exhibition of the Liverpool Academy, Richard Bridgens showed a 'View of the entrance of the Ware Rooms of Mr Geo. Bullock's Egyptian Hall, Piccadilly, London'. Whether this was a design for the entrance, or a topographical view of it as it existed, is impossible to tell. The entrance illustrated in fig. 2 could again be a design or a view, and might be the one by Bridgens, but to complicate matters further it could be for the Grecian Rooms in either Liverpool or London. However

[20]Richard Altick, *The Shows of London*, 1978.

[21]A. Kaeppler, 'Cook voyage provenance of the "Artificial Curiosities" of Bullock's Museum', *Man*, Vol. IX, 1974, pp.68-92.

as fig. 2 is an illustration from the *Wilkinson Tracings*, and these designs in the main represent post-Liverpool work, it is likely that this particular illustration represents the London Grecian Rooms.

Quite how long George Bullock remained in Piccadilly is unclear, but making his debut as a cabinet-maker in William's Museum, with its 'passing trade' of thousands of visitors, was probably an astute commercial move. It is tantalising to speculate on the contents of the Piccadilly Grecian Rooms: was there perhaps a mixture of furniture, Mona Marble and sculpture? It would seem that the rooms could not have been furnished with furniture brought from Liverpool for that had been auctioned in Liverpool in August 1812. If new furniture was made, where were the workshops? Where was the Mona Marble finished? Were both furniture and marble still made and finished in Liverpool and shipped down to London?

In 1814, the following listing appeared in the London directories for George Bullock: 'Sculptor, 4, Tenterden Street, Hanover Square; Mona Marble and Furniture Works, Oxford Street'. The premises in Oxford Street included 'a large warehouse and polishing rooms' for marble in addition to the furniture workshops.[22] Nothing further is documented about how many people were employed there or the form that these premises took, but the premises must have been extensive for by the end of 1817 (when they would have been in existence for less than three years) they and their contents were insured for the considerable sum of £3,800. At 4 Tenterden Street, which runs west off the north west corner of Hanover Square, was a further workshop which may have adjoined the one in Oxford Street. In Bullock's day Tenterden Street boasted six houses, numbers 1-5, on the northern side, all of whose gardens stretched up to the rear elevation of 313 Oxford Street, which apparently had a long frontage.[23] In 1819 (after Bullock's death) the London directory gave the Oxford Street address for the first time, listing 'Bullock & Co. Mona Marble & Furniture Works 313 Oxford Street'. It is reasonable to assume that this was on the same plot of land as 4 Tenterden Street and was literally at the bottom of Bullock's garden.

The house was certainly grandly furnished, as indicated by the sale catalogue of its contents: *A CATALOGUE OF The Superb Furniture, AND SCULPTURED ARTICLES OF BEAUTIFUL MONA MARBLES, A COSTLY DOOR-CASE AND DOOR, Inlaid With Designs in Brass, from Antique Greek Paintings; AND A Noble Pair of Columns of Mona Marble, AND DOORS, Suited for a Library, Ball or Concert Room, or any distinguished Publick Building, BEING THE WHOLE OF THE FINISHED STOCK of that highly ingenious Artist, Mr GEORGE BULLOCK, Dec. Which will be Sold by Auction, BY Mr. CHRISTIE, ON THE PREMISES, No. 4, Tenterden Street, Hanover Square, on Monday, the 3d of May, 1819, And Two following Days . . .'

Several rooms were listed by name: 'Bow room Second Floor, Marble Room, Entrance Hall, Bow Room Adjoining Long Room, Bow Room Entrance from Garden, Inner Hall, Gothic Room and Long Room.' It would seem that the Bow was at the back, as the Bow Room was entered from the garden and thus the Long Room must have also been on the ground floor, as of course were the two Halls. Which floor the Marble Room and the Gothic Room were on is not clear, but as there was a second-floor Bow Room, it is reason-

[22]William Bingley, *Useful Knowledge*, Vol. I, 1816, pp.88-89.

[23]Clearly shown on Richard Horwood's *A Plan of the Cities of London & Westminster . . .* , 1813.

able to assume that the bow ran – as is often the case in London – at least three stories up the garden elevation of the house.

No documented illustration of the interior of the house is known but among the *Wilkinson Tracings* is one of an un-named room (*see* fig. 3) which may conceivably be a representation of the 'Inner Hall' at Tenterden Street. Could the rather dandified figure leaning languidly on the balustrade be Bullock himself? Among the contents of the 'Inner Hall', sold on the second day of the sale, was lot 30: 'A noble and lofty candelabrum, the center shaft covered with foliage bronzed, and terminated by a cluster of 3 deers heads: on a triangular pedestal; the panels embellished with bronzed scenick masks and devices in relief from the antique; the corner columns shaped as chimeras, bronzed on a circular base.' A slightly modified version of this singular object appears in the part issues of *Furniture with candelabra* . . . labelled: 'Designed and etched by R. Bridgens' and it also appears in the 1838 edition.

It would seem that Bullock lived on the premises, for it was here that he died, and his obituary talks of it having been 'his house' and refers to the 'hospitable evenings' that took place there. He presumably entertained his important clients in the house, while the marble works and furniture works were just a short step out of the garden door of the Bow Room and down the garden for anyone who wished to inspect them. The house also seems to have had another function, for in 1817 the *Annals of the Fine Arts* record that paintings by Benjamin Robert Haydon, 'The Macbeth, Judgement of Solomon, and the Death of Dentatus, by the same excellent historical painter, are again assembled in London, being hung on the magnificent staircase of

Below: *Fig. 2. Entrance to the 'Grecian Rooms', probably from 1812/14 at William Bullock's Museum, The Egyptian Hall, 172 Piccadilly; front and side elevations,* Wilkinson Tracings, *p.184. (City Museums and Art Gallery, Birmingham.)* Right: *Fig. 3. The 'Inner Hall' at 4, Tenterden Street,* Wilkinson Tracings, *p.1. (City Museums and Art Gallery, Birmingham.)*

Mr. G. Bullock, in Tenterden Street, who with great liberality, permits amateurs and others to view them. We have been indulged with a sight of them and certainly think they never looked so well; the tints are mellowed, and the situation and light assist them . . .'[24]

The house thus seems not only to have been a place of entertainment for Bullock's friends and clients, but also to have acted as an informal art gallery. Certainly Haydon, with his legendary lack of luck in finding exhibition space, would have been grateful to Bullock for the opportunity to show in central London. After Bullock's death Haydon rented exhibition space from William Bullock who seems, from a comment by Haydon, to have been as dynamic a personality as his brother: 'We concluded the bargain, and I took the room for a year at £300 without a shilling in my pocket, my capability to pay depending entirely on my success. But my landlord was a fine fellow and loved the game of ruin or success – Westminster Abbey or victory – as well as myself.'[25]

Annals of the Fine Arts was edited by a close friend of Haydon, the architect James Elmes, and Haydon was a frequent anonymous contributor to the publication. It seems likely that Haydon was the anonymous author of the obituary of Bullock quoted above. In a diary entry of December 1818, Haydon wrote, 'George Bullock was one of those extraordinary beings who receive great good fortune & are never benefitted by it, and suffer great evils, and are never ruined, always afloat but never in harbour, always energetic, always scheming, who should have had a frame of adamant, money without end, & a world that was boundless.'[26]

A few other details concerning Bullock's business can be gleaned from the events following his sudden death on 1st May 1818. His friendship with Sir Walter Scott is already well known,[27] but a letter of 15th May 1818 written to Scott by Daniel Terry, who knew both him and Bullock well, is of great interest:

'Mrs Bullock is, I understand, very ill her health was always precarious & her condition broken and rickety . . . by a former will made nine years ago Mrs Bullock is left sole executrix a task she is little fit for . . . I do not see how a large concern which owed its existence its conduct & its peculiar excellence entirely to the personal talent and activity of poor Bullock can be continued longer than the impetus which he had given to such an immense machine remains in force – whenever the orders which he left in design and arrangement are finished I fear the establishment must either stop or dwindle down into a commonplace character for it is a hopeless expectation that a man of equal originality and will will be found to supply his place – It will however take two years to execute the orders at present upon their books. I have no doubt that George's fate was something accelerated by the rapid & enormous increase in business beyond capital perhaps and by money affairs being thrown by some leasing perplexity by the damnable conduct of the monied partner Colonel Frazer an old crackbrained east indian jackass . . . George had more in his own department to attend to than almost any head could stand under and was surprized into confusion and anxiety by the tricks and quirks of a proud and puzzlepated madman.'[28]

[24]*Annals of the Fine Arts*, I, 1819, pp.106-107.

[25]*The Autobiography and Memoirs of Benjamin Robert Haydon*, 1926, p.280.

[26]W.B. Pope (ed.), *The Diary of Benjamin Robert Haydon*, Vol. II, 1960, p.209.

[27]Clive Wainwright, 'Walter Scott and the Furnishing of Abbotsford', *The Connoisseur*, Vol. 194, 1977, pp.3-15; *The Antiquarian Interior In Britain 1780-1850*, PhD. Thesis, University of London, 1987.

[28]National Library of Scotland, Scott Manuscripts, Mss 3889.f.94.

[29]I am indebted to Major J.M.A. Tamplin of the Army Museum Ogilby Trust for this information.

[30]National Library of Scotland, Scott Manuscripts, Mss.3890.f.128.

[31]I am indebted to Miss J.M. Tatton of the Royal Bank of Scotland for searching their records.

[32]The work at Tew Park has been covered in detail in a scholarly essay by Hugh Roberts in the Christie's Tew Park sale catalogue, 1987.

This letter raises several questions. No trace of a will can be found. And who was the singular 'Colonel Frazer'? We know from the insurance records for Bullock's premises that a man called Charles Fraser was involved in the business. There was a Charles Mackenzie Fraser who, after distinguished service in the Peninsular War, retired in 1814 and became Colonel of the Ross, Caithness & Cromarty Militia in 1815.[29] Assuming that this is the right Fraser, what was the East Indian connection? His army career hardly fits with him being described as old in 1818, though the wound he received before Burgos in 1812 might have made him 'puzzlepated'! Boyle's *Court Guide* lists a Colonel Fraser as living at 28 Montague Place in Bloomsbury in 1813, 1814 and 1815. But whoever 'Colonel Frazer' was, it seems likely that he provided at least some of the capital needed to set up and run what must have been fairly extensive workshops at Tenterden Street and Oxford Street.

The workshops certainly continued in operation for some time after Bullock's death: furniture was still being delivered to Blair and Abbotsford well into 1819, although, interestingly, an 1819 London directory lists Bullock & Co. (instead of Bullock, G.) for the first time. On 18th June 1819 Daniel Terry wrote to Scott, 'The concern is entirely sold off and the accounts closing – your other articles are making under Mr Atkinson's direction by workmen formerly employed at Bullock's.'[30]

It is obvious from letters in the Tew Archive that at the time of Bullock's death the firm had no separate bank account; the only account was a personal one held by Bullock at the London bankers William, Moffat & Burgess, but sadly no record of this survives.[31] Most cabinet-makers of the time – indeed most tradesmen – were quite seriously undercapitalised. There were frequent bankruptcies precipitated as often by bad debts as by poor management. It is clear from a letter in the Tew Archives, for example, that a cheque to Bullock from Sir Godfrey Webster of Battle Abbey for £1000 worth of work was bounced by Webster's bank.

The recent discovery at Tew Park of the complete set of bills for the supply of the Bullock furniture, which had itself survived *in situ*, established this as Bullock's largest surviving commission. Matthew Robinson Boulton, son of Matthew Boulton, the famous industrialist and entrepreneur, purchased the Tew Park estate in the village of Great Tew in Oxfordshire in 1815. From 1816 to 1818, Bullock's workshops provided all the furniture and upholstery for the main reception rooms and bedrooms at Tew and oversaw their decoration. Bullock's final bill amounted to more than £4,000; it was not until after his death, however, that the last pieces of furniture were supplied and the account settled. The furniture (*see* nos. 25-29) is not of the grandeur and elaboration of pieces made for Blair Castle or indeed those for the Duke of Palmella (*see* nos. 10 and 11), but in its studied simplicity (in terms both of design and of choice of materials) and in the variety of pieces (ranging from sofas and cabinets to towel racks and night stools), it provides an unusually clear indication of the range of furniture produced by Bullock's workshop at the height of its reputation.[32]

A house for which Bullock may well have produced work, although this has so far proved impossible to document, was Hafod. This was originally a spectacular Gothic Revival house built by Thomas Johnes in the depths of Wales towards the end of the 18th century; it has been frequently discussed in print, although most accounts, both contemporary and modern, confine themselves to the architecture, the paintings and sculpture and the celebrated library of books and manuscripts. The grandeur of the Cardiganshire countryside, which surrounded the house, inspired George Cumberland's *An Attempt to Describe Hafod*, 1796, and then, in 1810, *Tour of Hafod* by Sir James Edward Smith (whose portrait bust was sculpted by Bullock, *see* no. 62). The original house at Hafod was largely destroyed by fire in 1807 which caused damage estimated at £70,000, and it was during the rebuilding that Bullock made his appearance.

Johnes and Bullock had at least three mutual friends in William Roscoe, Francis Chantrey and Sir J.E. Smith. On 15th March 1808 Johnes wrote to Roscoe, 'I parted on Saturday with a protege of yours Mr Bullock – a very clever fellow, and who is to fit up my house when ready for it. He will I trust give you such an account of my wilderness that you may be tempted to come & see it.'[33] Bullock may well have been involved there until at least October 1810 when Johnes wrote to Anthony Ramilly of Sloane Square, 'From the very great line of business that Mr Bullock is engaged in, I have neither heard him, nor seen him since I sent him your last letter.'[34] It has proved impossible to discover who supplied the furniture to Hafod or indeed what became of it – the several sale catalogues provide little help.

Extensive use was made of Mona Marble, however:

'The octagon library contains busts of Mrs. and Miss Johnes, by Banks, a bust of Mr. Johnes by Chantrey . . . This library is ornamented by eight pictures from Monstralet, by Stothard, to imitate bassi-relievi. Both doors have columns of Mona marble . . . In the Hall, which is paved with Mona marble, is a statue of bacchus, which is of the heroic size, which was formerly at Pain's Hill . . . The whole of the furniture in these apartments is in a style of elegant simplicity. Some of the marble chimney pieces which are enriched with sculptured devices, touched by a masterly hand, were brought from Fonthill; as were also three magnificent French mirrors in the long library; having been bought at Mr. Beckford's sale.'[35]

The sale referred to was the one held by Beckford when he was demolishing his father's house, Fonthill Splendens. One wonders whether the furniture described as 'in a style of elegant simplicity' might perhaps have been made by Bullock? And might it still exist somewhere?

As far as Bullock's work in Scotland is concerned, one is on safer ground. Much of the history of the Scottish commissions has been recorded in Anthony Coleridge's pioneering articles.[36]

Abbotsford has been internationally famous since well before 1820 as the home of Sir Walter Scott. Over a period of almost twenty years until his death in 1832, Scott transformed a small Scottish farmhouse into what he regarded as a suitably romantic setting for his growing collection of antiquities and for his family (descendants of

[33]Liverpool Public Library, Roscoe Mss 2223.

[34]Dalaucothi Correspondence V22/6. I am indebted to C. Lloyd Morgan and other colleagues at The National Library of Wales for information concerning Hafod.

[35]Thomas Rees, *The Beauties of England and Wales . . .* Vol. XVIII, 1815, pp.422-423.

[36]Anthony Coleridge, 'The Work of George Bullock cabinet-maker in Scotland', *The Connoisseur*, Vol. 158, 1965.

whom live there to this day). Working in close collaboration with Scott and Scott's two architect friends, Edward Blore and William Atkinson, Bullock spent a considerable part of the last two years of his life helping to create the interiors at Abbotsford: he supplied furniture (*see* nos. 15 to 17) and furnishings, advised on the disposition of the ancient armour in Scott's collection (*see* fig. 4) and, using his talents as a sculptor, helped to translate the medieval carvings from nearby Melrose Abbey into suitable ornaments for the Armoury ceiling. As a result of this association, Scott drew Bullock into his circle and they became firm friends. Indeed after Bullock's premature death, several of Scott's friends wrote letters expressing their shock at his demise (which, incidentally, contain vital clues concerning Bullock's business).

Blair Castle, seat of the Duke of Atholl in the highlands of Scotland, represented a far grander commission than Abbotsford. Bullock worked at Blair from 1814 until his death, during which time he supplied some particularly fine furniture (*see* nos. 7, 8 and 9). Here,

Fig. 4. Design for the armoury at Abbotsford. Watercolour. Signed and dated by Richard Bridgens, 1818. (Mrs. Patricia Maxwell-Scott.)

DESIGN FOR THE ARRANGEMENT OF AN ARMOURY NOW ERECTING AT ABBOTSFORD
THE SEAT OF
WALTER SCOTT ESQ.

as at Abbotsford, where pollard oak from Drumlarig was used for the dining table, he was able to exploit and enhance the Scottish character of his interiors by an imaginative use of native materials, in this case larch and Glen Tilt marble. While working at Blair, Bullock established a firm friendship with the Duke of Atholl. Indeed, at one point the Duke sent him a stag's head, a quintessentially Scottish item, from which Bullock took plaster casts. These may have been the models for the stags' heads on the monumental candelabrum that stood in Bullock's hall at Tenterden Street. One letter in particular shows how enthusiastically Bullock embraced the Highland stag-hunting ethos, a trait which would naturally have endeared him to his Scottish patrons. Bullock wrote to the Duke of Atholl on 8th December 1817,

'I had the honor to receive a letter from your Grace yesterday enclosing a shipping note of a fine Roe Buck I shall not content myself by having it moulded only but have engaged a person to stuff it also . . . I have taken every means of seasoning the Larch as expeditiously as possible it came also safe with the Roe bucks horns which prove an excellent ornament for my study combined with the cast of the Bucks Head which forms a very conspicuous feature in it . . . I have turned several snuff boxes one of the handsomest of which I have sent to Rundell & Bridge to put a gold lining in it . . . on the lid inside I propose to have engraved a description of the tree as shewn on the *card* given to me by your Grace any *further* account I shall be happy to add that your Grace may be pleased to favour me with. I flatter myself that this Box independent of the peculiar interest it must have with all those connected with its growth cannot fail to be hereafter thought a Great curiosity as being made from a Wood first used in the *Kingdom* for the purposes of its Navy . . .'[37]

Another letter reveals that the snuffbox was also of larch.[38]

It is obvious from those commissions for which letters survive, notably Tew, Blair and Abbotsford, that Bullock was able to establish a more cordial relationship with his clients than was usual for a cabinet-maker of his day. There is evidence of further Scottish commissions in the *Wilkinson Tracings*, and it must surely have been the influence of Bullock's friend Walter Scott that led to the inclusion of the two figures in Highland dress in the design for the Dining Room at Armadale Castle, on the Isle of Skye (*see* fig. 5). This was an important commission; Armadale was designed for Lord Macdonald by the celebrated Scottish architect James Gillespie Graham and built between 1814 and 1822. The interiors were completed and furnished by 1819,[39] but nothing is known about what Bullock supplied.

The *Tracings* also show that Bullock was working at Biel in Berwickshire which was extended by William Atkinson, between 1814 and 1821.[40] A strong Bullock/Atkinson link existed as result of work both in Scotland and England. They both worked at Abbotsford, Bowhill, Biel, and probably at Scone and Panshanger, and were involved in work for St Helena.

As mentioned above, Abbotsford has already been documented, but it is worth noting that as well as providing furniture, joinery,

[37]Blair Castle Archives, Charter Room 68(7)319.

[38]As this catalogue was going to press, this snuffbox was discovered at Blair Castle; *see* no. 9A.

[39]James Macaulay, *The Gothic Revival 1745-1845*, 1975, pp.240-241.

[40]James Macaulay, *The Gothic Revival 1745-1845*, 1975, p.223.

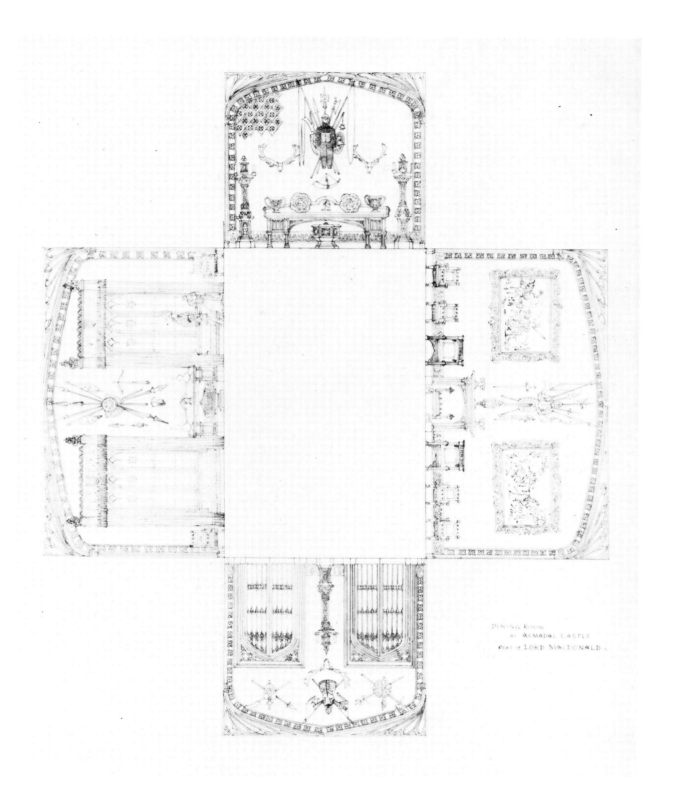

Fig. 5. 'Dining Room at Armadal
[sic] Castle, seat of Lord Macdonald',
elevations, Wilkinson Tracings,
p.13. (City Museums and Art Gallery,
Birmingham.)

chimneypieces and plaster details for the ceilings, Bullock and Bridgens helped to arrange Scott's collection in a suitable 'Old Scotch'
way. A watercolour of the scheme for the Armoury was painted by
Bridgens and shown at the Royal Academy in 1818 (*see* fig. 4).

One other English commission should be mentioned: that for
Battle Abbey, the celebrated mediaeval building on which extensive

Gothic Revival works were carried out between 1812 and 1822 for Sir Godfrey Vassal Webster. As we have seen, Webster was a bad payer whose life reads like that of a character in a novel by Thomas Love Peacock. Besides the extravagance manifested by the grandiose nature of the works he commissioned at Battle, he was an inveterate gambler who once wagered and lost £6,000 on a race between two wood-lice which inhabited the arm of his chair at his London club. Webster eventually fled abroad, dying in exile in 1836 and leaving nearly £30,000 in debts. The only documentation of the Bullock work which survives are three designs in the *Wilkinson Tracings* of interiors at Battle and others of furniture (some of which were also published by Bridgens as designs for Battle). Several of the Battle pieces are in the exhibition (nos. 12-14). Also, several Victorian guidebooks to the mediaeval buildings mention the Webster works.

Finally I should like to mention the furniture made by Bullock which was recently discovered in Portugal and auctioned in London. Several of those pieces can be seen in this exhibition (nos. 10-11). The full-size template for the brass inlay on the commodes (no. 10) exists in the *Wilkinson Tracings*, but this is the only record of its kind. This furniture was made for Don Pedro de Sousa e Holstein, First Duke of Palmella (1781-1850), one of the most celebrated Portuguese of his day: he fought under Wellington in the Peninsular War, was several times Ambassador to London, held a number of ministerial posts in Portugal, and represented his country at both the Congress of Vienna in 1815 and the Coronation of Queen Victoria.

Palmella was in London for much of the period 1812 to 1820, was Ambassador for part of this time, and lived up to January 1819 at the Portuguese Embassy, a grand Georgian house that still survives, at 74 South Audley Street. He is mentioned in many contemporary diaries and letters, but most interestingly in those of William Beckford where he is portrayed as rather a character. The two had formed a close friendship when Beckford was in Portugal and Palmella was a very young man. Beckford habitually called Palmella by the pet nick-name 'Fulibus', which he invented.

In June 1817, Palmella became Secretary of State for Foreign Affairs and War which meant that he had to give up the Ambassador-ship and was supposed to move to Rio. But he preferred the social life in London and did not actually leave until May 1820, despite the fact that by January that year he had been forced to move from the Embassy to a rather dubious hotel in Berkeley Square. It was here that Beckford visited him on 19th January 1819:

'I found Fulibus in his accustomed glory amongst old papers, mo-rocco folders and secretaries, mixing in a queer kind of way the useful and the agreeable, in his new diplomatic palace (Thomas' Hotel). There he was between two or three fine fat boys, half secre-taries, half *valet de chambre* – one or two dough-coloured and another rose-and-lily (after four days of scrubbing of course).'[41]

[41]Boyd Alexander, *Life at Fonthill . . .* , 1957, p.270.

A few days later on 22nd January Palmella returned the visit:

'Fulibus, faithful to all his customs, came to pay me a visit last night at half-past eleven. I was already in bed, but I heard the voice of

[42]Boyd Alexander, *Life at Fonthill* . . . , 1957, p.272.

a punchinello on the stairs proclaiming "Fort bien, je reviendrai bientôt" . . .'[42]

It is obvious from these letters that Palmella was friendly with everyone who was anyone; he dined at Apsley House and stayed at Brighton with the Prince Regent. Nothing is known about when or why Palmella patronised Bullock, but it is possible that the furniture he ordered was either for the Portuguese Embassy itself (and later taken to Portugal) or made for a house in Portugal and sent there immediately. What is known is that Palmella's stay in London spanned the years of Bullock's greatest fame and that he commissioned the most elaborate suite of Bullock furniture that has yet been discovered. There is even the bizarre possiblity that if Bullock's partner was the Fraser who had fought in the Peninsular War, he and Palmella were old comrades-in-arms!

In many ways, however, the most exciting Bullock commission is the one that has been discovered most recently, which is also the work that made the greatest impact on his contemporaries: the furniture and furnishings supplied to Napoleon on St Helena. Several of the pieces of furniture and some ceramics are included in the exhibition (nos. 18-21 and 30) and a number of relevant designs and illustrations appear in this catalogue. The first clue I found to the existence of this commission was in Angharad Llwyd's *A History of Mona or Anglesey*, 1833, which refers to ' . . . the late Mr. Bullock who manufactured a magnificent table of green marble, which was sent to Buonaparte when at St Helena.'[43]

[43]Llwyd, as note 18 above, p.14. I shall publish more information on this aspect of Bullock's work in due course.

Longwood House exists on St Helena to this day. It is open to the public and, no doubt like many others, I assumed that this was the place to which Napoleon had been sent to spend his last days. Many of the books about Napoleon reinforce the impression that the British had confined him and his retainers to this quite unsuitable small house. The truth is much more interesting. Old Longwood, as it should correctly be called, was intended only to be a temporary home. As soon as Napoleon had been dispatched to St Helena, plans were quickly made for a residence of suitable grandeur to be provided for him. It was soon realised, however, that the island was so barren that all the building materials and furnishings would have to be shipped from England. On 24th October 1815 a newspaper reported that:

'The rumours that B[uonaparte] had on the eve of his departure for St. H., provided himself with a variety of costly articles of furniture for future use, are totally unfounded. The exiled captive sailed from England with few accommodations . . . It was at length specially determined by express order of the Prince Regent, that B. should be furnished in his banishment with every possible gratification and comfort . . . an order was last month issued by Earl Bathurst [Secretary for War and Colonies], to one of the most tasteful and ingenious artists of the metropolis – this order comprised every species of furniture, linen, glass ware, clothes, music and musical instruments . . . the whole work to be made up in a style of pure and simple elegance, with this only reservation that in no instance should any ornament or initial creep into the decorations, which would be likely to recal [sic] to the mind of B. the former emblematic appendages

Fig. 6. New Longwood House, St Helena. Hand-coloured aquatint. English, early 19th century.

of Imperial rank. The order was to be completed within six weeks, and by the indefatigable exertions of four hundred men it has been finished in the given period, and in greater part packed up for immediate conveyance to Plymouth . . . the architect for the Ordnance department has nearly completed at Woolwich, not a wooden house, as has been mentioned, but a timber frame work, for a building to be erected on the island, in the cottage style. It will consist of 24 rooms, the general size of each will be about 25 feet by 18; and this architectural skeleton will accompany the furniture already mentioned . . . some ornaments composed of green Anglesey marble are, also in preparation. It is right to add, that the extraordinary man for whom this extensive order is fitting up has no knowledge whatever of the preparations which are furnishing for him.'[44]

The press report described every detail of the house and its furnishings and furniture:

'The front is 120 feet in length, containing fourteen windows and a fine open corridor . . . The drawing-room is coloured in various shades of green. The curtains are Pomona green, made of light silk taboret, bordered in full green velvet, and edged with a gold coloured silken twist or gimp . . . the centre table is formed out of one piece of exquisitely veined British oak, polished in the highest degree of perfection. The pier table is of the same timber and quality, inlaid with a slab of the *verd antique* marble of Mona . . . The chairs in this apartment correspond with the tables. There are two Greek sofas . . . enriched with highly finished *or-molu* ornaments . . . Dining Room . . . the wine-cooler is of bronze and rich wood and shaped after the fashion of Greek Baccanalian vases . . .'[45]

[44] *The Times*, 24th October 1815.

[45] *The Times*, 25th October 1815.

It is no surprise to learn that the Architect of the Board of Ordnance was none other than William Atkinson, with whom Bullock was at this very date working at Abbotsford. The Public Records help to complete the story, and plans survive for the house. The scale of the operation to transport the house and contents was huge; one incredulous letter of 14th September 1815 reads, '. . . I have just learned there will be about 2,000 tons of material for Bonaparte's house and the barracks for the Ordnance Corps . . .'[46] Then on 23rd September, ' . . . two thirds of the fir timber and one third of the deals and battens have been forwarded to Woolwich . . . 23,000 slates are now furnished, and the remaining 52,000 are expected in three weeks . . .'[47]

After a long sea voyage to St Helena these materials had to be manhandled a considerable distance up to the site of the house, then erected by craftsmen sent out from England by the Ordnance Corps. The house was finally completed early in 1821 (*see* fig. 6), but Napoleon hardly occupied it and died on 5th of May in his bedroom in Old Longwood (*see* fig. 7). Some of the furniture was removed from New Longwood by the Governor Sir Hudson Lowe and the rest auctioned. The two houses fell into disrepair. In 1858 Old Longwood was purchased by Napoleon III and restored. It still contains several pieces of Bullock furniture. New Longwood, however, has entirely disappeared.

In all the documentation, the only mention of Bullock is in connection with the supply of ceramics. I have not found any bills for the furniture. But fortunately there are, among the papers of Sir

[46]Public Record Office: WO 1/796 f.241.

[47]Public Record Office: WO 1/796 f.253.

Fig. 7. 'Intérieur', engraving after Louis Marchand, depicting Napoleon on his deathbed; several examples of Bullock's furniture are shown. (Cliché Musées Nationaux – Bois Préau, Musée de Malmaison.)

Hudson Lowe in the British Museum, designs in Bullock's hand for the furnishing of seventeen of the rooms at New Longwood and one design for a 'Wardrobe for Gen Bonaparte'. Examples are shown in figs. 8, 34, 40 and 43. An alternative design for the Drawing Room occurs in the *Wilkinson Tracings* (on p.70), and several others, dated November 1815, illustrate a large number of pieces of furniture as well as documenting the curtains and other furnishings of this important and interesting commission.

Already a number of these pieces have been traced and several appear in this exhibition, including one of the chairs and sofas mentioned above. One of the single chairs is at the Château de Bois-Préau at Malmaison (*see* fig. 9), and another is at Longwood. A wine cooler is now in the Russell-Cotes Museum in Bournemouth along with a table also from Longwood. Fig. 7, which shows Napoleon on his deathbed in Old Longwood, demonstrates that he was able to use at least some of his splendid Bullock furniture in his old house. One of the chairs (*see* fig. 9) and two of the Grecian sofas are at the foot of the bed and there are two chairs similar to those in the exhibition (*see* nos. 21, 23 and 24) also in the room.

Fig. 8. 'Dining Room for St Helena', plan and elevations. (British Library. Add. Mss. 20,222, Lowe Papers, folio 216.)

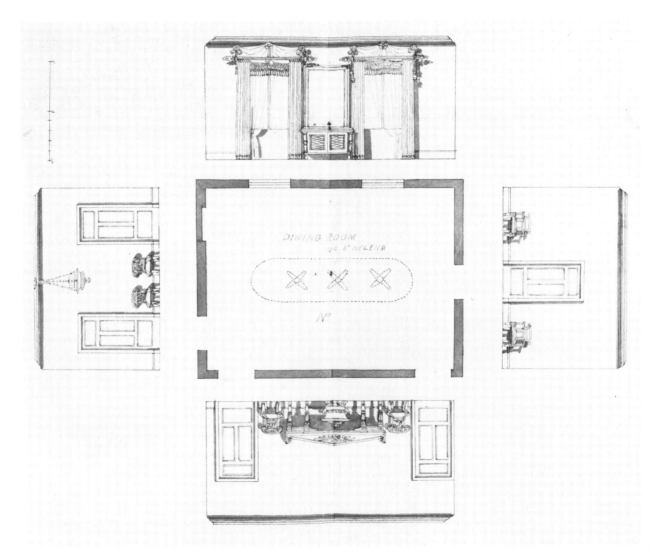

I have dealt with this commission at some length not only because anything to do with Napoleon is of perennial interest, but because it was certainly one of Bullock's most important commissions. It will have provided splendid publicity for his business. One wonders whether it was a coincidence that exactly the same metal mounts were used on the arms of both Napoleon's and Palmella's sofas?

Many questions remain concerning Bullock, his friends and his career. Where are the splendid light fittings (*see* fig. 10) and the elegant plate (*see* fig. 11) illustrated in the *Tracings* and who manufactured them? Do pieces of furniture such as the richly ornamented table-top cabinet (*see* fig. 12) shown in the *Tracings* still exist, and if so, where? Did Bullock work for the royal family? There is no mention of Bullock in the Royal Accounts nor any record of correspondence with the Prince Regent, but there is a tantalising reference in the Tew letters to his being held up at Windsor – was this the castle or the town?[48] Certainly Queen Charlotte owned at least one Bullock piece, for the sale of her collection of curiosities in 1819 included 'A very sumptuous circular ink stand, of the late George Bullock's Buhl manufacture, with richly cut glass'[49], and one wonders whether she

[48]I am indebted to Sir Geoffrey de Bellaigue for this information.

[49]*A catalogue of the remaining part of a valuable collection of curiosities . . . Christie . . . May 24, 1819 . . .* I am indebted to Clare Graham for bringing this to my attention.

owned more. It is possible, however, that, as an early benefactor of William Bullock's Museum, Queen Charlotte had merely purchased a single piece on show in the Museum's Grecian Rooms.

Finally, there is no clear evidence as to how much of the furniture, marble objects and furnishings and textiles produced and supplied

Fig. 10. Design for chandelier, Wilkinson Tracings, p.50. (City Museums and Art Gallery, Birmingham.)

Fig. 11. Designs for plate. Bullock had contacts with Rundell & Bridge as well as with the Boulton family, Wilkinson Tracings, p.182. (City Museums and Art Gallery, Birmingham.)

by the firm was actually designed by Bullock himself. There certainly were a number of trained designers and architects like Gandy, Bridgens and Atkinson who *did* design for the firm. Bullock's training as a modeller and sculptor would have given him more idea of the principles of design than it was usual for a cabinet-maker to possess, but it also appears that he was constantly involved in travelling to see clients, organising the workshops and finance for his business, in general, managing the firm, so that even if he were a talented designer he would have had little time actually to sit at a drawing board. It is therefore as yet impossible to come to any clear conclusion concerning how many of the remarkable and pioneering pieces made by his firm were actually designed by its presiding genius.

Those involved in this exhibition and its catalogue expect a spate of discoveries to follow in its wake and greatly look forward to this. Perhaps Bullock's friend Sir Walter Scott should have the last word concerning Bullock's unique place in the world of Regency cabinet-making: 'He is in his way a great loss to the public for he had a taste rarely found in that profession in which such sums of money are expended to make more barbarous and costly monstrosities . . .'[50]

[50]H.J.C. Grierson, *The Letters of Sir Walter Scott 1817-1819*, 1933, p.157.

George Bullock in Birmingham and Liverpool

LUCY WOOD

Mystery still surrounds the circumstances of George Bullock's early life; even the year and place of his birth remain unresolved. The statement at the time of his intended departure from Birmingham in August 1798, that 'his age does not exceed twenty',[1] has always been taken as a pronouncement of his actual age, and indeed on 24th August 1778, a son of William and Elizabeth Bullock was christened George at All Saints Church, West Bromwich.[2] However, the record of his burial on 8th May 1818, 'aged 35',[3] would place his birth in 1782 or 1783, in which light his early career appears remarkably precocious, even by the standards of the time. It is of course possible that he chose a form of words in 1798 specifically to conceal that he was only 15 or 16 at that time; and the same 1798 announcement speaks of his 'returning to London', which suggests that his origins may not have been in the Birmingham area.[4]

His mother's first recorded appearance in Birmingham also gives the impression of a newcomer to the town. While nothing is known of Bullock's father (beyond the possibility that he was called William) his mother emerges as a colourful figure, from whose enterprises both of her sons drew inspiration. On 26th May 1794, an advertisement placed in *Aris's Birmingham Gazette* announced:

'Mrs. BULLOCK presents her most respectful Compliments to the Ladies and Gentlemen of Birmingham and its Vicinity, and begs leave to inform them, that she is just arrived with a most beautiful Cabinet of WAX FIGURES, which are all of the full size of life . . .'

The waxworks exhibition was to open the following day 'in a commodious Room, in Mr Mansell's late Tea Warehouse, nearly opposite the corner of New Street'.[5] Two years later the exhibition reappeared 'in the House lately occupied by Mr. Hodgkins, No. 87, Bull Street;'[6] and, after a period in Lichfield,[7] Mrs. Bullock announced in November 1796 that it was ' . . . again opened for the Inspection of the Public, at her House, No. 29, Bull-street, Birmingham, near the Bank . . . as she has preferred Birmingham for the place of her Residence, she presumes her Friends will deem weekly Advertisements totally unnecessary.'[8]

Mrs. Bullock continued to advertise her exhibition from this address – periodically taking it to other towns – until 1798.[9] Among the figures she exhibited were members of the British Royal Family (including the Duke of York 'dressed in a Suit of Regimentals which have been worn by himself' and the 'unfortunate Royal Family of France . . . done from original Models, taken in Paris, in the Beginning of the late Events, by the celebrated Monsieur Oudon . . .'; also 'A very capital Representation of Tippoo Sultan, and his two Sons . . . Catherine, Empress of Russia . . . the late Earl of Chatham' and 'A fine Figure of the late Dr. Franklin, of America'[9] (probably also by or after J.-A. Houdon).[10] In 1797 she began to diversify her activities, announcing on 27th March the opening of a modelling class at 'Bullock and Son's Modelling and Statuary Warehouse, No. 29, Bull-street, Birmingham.' On 29th May it was reported that 'Mrs Bullock and Son' had been 'for a considerable Time busily employed in modelling new Figures for the Exhibition', including 'LIKENESSES of the PRINCE and PRINCESS of WIRTEMBERG, of the POET FREETE of this Town, and several Others.'[11] To judge by George Bullock's earliest independent activities (discussed below), it seems very likely that he was the son taken briefly into partnership at this time. But a year later Mrs. Bullock was offering a range of services that foreshadow the activities of both George and his brother William[12] in Liverpool: 'Likenesses modelled from one to twenty Guineas each, Miniature[s] painted. All Kinds of Statue Figures for Halls, Stair-cases, and Pleasure Grounds; Figures with Lamps, Girandoles for Side-boards, &c. in Plaister of Paris, Hard Metal, Lead &c. Modelling in all its Branches.'[13]

One of Mrs. Bullock's new acquisitions at about this time marks a further new departure: 'a Likeness of GENERAL BUONAPARTE, Commander in Chief of the French Armies, dressed in the National Uniform of France. This figure is modelled in Rice Paste (from an original Painting taken from Life) and is allowed to be one of the first Productions of the Kind.'[14] Over the next few years, George Bullock was to make extensive use of rice paste, although it was also used by other artists, including apparently Houdon,[15] who, as noted already, was well represented in Mrs. Bullock's wax collection. A number of 19th-century manuals of instruction, most of which seem to rely on a single original source, refer to this versatile medium as 'rice glue' or 'Japanese cement'. The earliest account so far discovered is that of William Pybus in *A Manual of Useful Knowledge*, published in 1810:

'To make Japanese Cement, or Rice Glue, which may be formed into Busts, Statues, Basso Relievos, etc.

This elegant cement is made by mixing rice flour intimately with cold water, and then gently boiling the mixture. It is beautifully white, and when dry is semi-transparent. Papers pasted together with this cement will sooner separate in their own substance than at the joining. It is in every respect preferable to flour paste, for the purposes to which the latter is applied. It answers well, in particular, for pasting into books the copies of writings taken off by copying machines, on unsized silver paper.[16]

With this composition, made with a comparatively small quantity of water, that it may have a consistence similar to plastic clay, models, busts, statues, basso relievos, and the like may be formed. When dry, the articles made of it are susceptible of a high polish; they are also very durable. The Japanese make quadrille fish of this substance, which so nearly resemble those of mother of pearl, that the officers of our capital East Indiamen are often imposed on.'[17]

The material's reputation for durability would appear to have been undeserved, for not a single example of Bullock's rice-paste sculpture has been identified, although he apparently turned it out in large quantities. Mrs. Bullock advertised for portraits to be 'modelled in wax or rice paste' in July 1798,[18] by which time George had apparently become well-practised in the art, for he must surely have been the artist whose work was admired by a traveller passing through Birmingham in 1797, and coming upon a shop in Bull Street:

'The first thing that caught my eye was a most beautiful little figure, in rice paste, of a dying Saint, of exquisite workmanship, and enquiring who was the artist, I was answered by a curious looking fellow in a white jacket [William Bullock?] who said if I would not think the worse of it, it was the work of an Englishman, who was yet a boy . . . I was highly entertained with the great variety which surrounded me, such as miniature paintings, models in wax, rice paste, and plaster of Paris, which for delicacy of finishing surpassed any thing of the kind I had ever seen; landscapes and devices of different kinds, which formed such a pleasing variety I never before found in any shop of the kind. I was equally gratified with the

sight up stairs, which was an exhibition of Wax Figures, in such perfection as we have never seen in London'.[19]

The traveller gave a five-minute sitting for his portrait, and received a few days later 'that which is universally allowed to be a good likeness'.

Bullock was not slow to dispel his anonymity. By August the following year he was recognised as 'Mr. Bullock, the young artist who has gained such great repute in Birmingham', and was said to be 'returning to London, the statue business not answering his expectation. He now intends giving his whole attention to the modelling and painting of likenesses.'[20] He may have thought better of the projected move to London, for which there is no further evidence, since by September 1799 he was again (or still) in Birmingham, independently established as 'G. Bullock, Modeller in Rice Paste' at no. 12 Ann Street;[21] and in 1800-1801 he was listed in the Birmingham trade directories as 'Bullock George, Miniature-painter and Portrait-modeller in Rice-paste, Ann-street'.[22]

It is possible that Bullock was married during this period, although this cannot as yet be verified because of the doubt surrounding his date of birth. On 24th March 1799 (when he would have been either 16-17 or nearly 21), a George Bullock was married in Birmingham to a pawnbroker's widow, Elizabeth Mansell of Coleshill Street; his occupation was identified as that of 'glass picture-frame-maker'.[23] If this was the same George Bullock, then the marriage may well have contributed, at least financially, to the rapid advance of his career.

Whether he was also helped by an influential local patron has not been ascertained, although there are circumstantial grounds for speculating that the pioneer industrialist, Matthew Boulton, may have fulfilled this role. The pointers are chiefly from Bullock's later career, when he had professional connections at Tew Park with Boulton's son, Matthew Robinson Boulton (*see* nos. 24-31), and at Thornhill with his daughter Anne Boulton, as well as James Watt, the son of Boulton's former partner.[24] In addition to these links, both men had mineralogical interests in Anglesey: Boulton in the Parys Copper Mines and Bullock, later, in the 'Mona Marble' quarries. It is possible that further research will throw light on their early association.

Bullock may also have received assistance from his brother (apparently the older of the two), in whose premises his first recorded independent work, a portrait of Mrs. Siddons (no. 73), was exhibited in September 1800.[25] William Bullock had opened his Museum, or 'Cabinet of Curiosities' in August that year, at Portugal House, New Street (which stood next to the Theatre), and put out an extended advertisement describing its attractions.[26] It included 'Likenesses of some of the most conspicuous Characters of the present Age modelled in Wax' and 'A Collection of capital

Models in Rice Paste', some of which were quite probably inherited from his mother's Exhibition.[27] Other exhibits may well have come from the Cabinet of Curiosities of Mr. Curtius, which was shown in Birmingham from September 1796 to February 1797,[28] and contained 'Busts in Wax, and Figures in Rice Paste', as well as a glass model of a man of war which almost certainly reappeared in William's Museum.[29] Curtius was presumably connected with the Swiss wax modeller of the same name, who was the uncle and adoptive father of Marie Tussaud. In February 1797, Curtius had advertised for a partner who could expect shortly to inherit the business,[30] and it is possible that William Bullock took up this opportunity. By the time he opened in Portugal House he had also acquired material from other collections, including one of the celebrated 'Mechanisms' from James Cox's Museum,[31] and 'the whole of the ARMS & ARMOUR of the LICHFIELD MUSEUM' [the collection of Richard Greene of Lichfield, who died in 1793; William Bullock bought the armour from his son in 1800[32]]. This collection formed part of the display in a room 'fitted up in the Manner of an ancient Armoury', and gave George Bullock ideas for his first essay in baronialism a few years later.

On 13th October 1800, William Bullock announced that his Museum would remain open in Portugal House 'a short Time longer'.[33] In March the following year he re-opened in Liverpool, at 24, Lord Street, describing himself as 'Silversmith, Jeweller, Toyman, and Statue Figure Manufacturer' and claiming that the Museum had already been 'honoured with the approbation of the first amateurs in the Kingdom'.[34] His advertisement ends: 'Likenessess Modelled in Rice Paste from Ten to Fifteen Guineas each. – Specimens of which may be seen', which suggests that he was providing a Liverpool outlet for his brother's work (see also no. 77). George himself, last recorded in Birmingham in 1801, is not known to have been permanently based in Liverpool until 1804,[35] although his portrait wax of Henry Blundell (one of his principal Liverpool patrons) is dated 1801 (no. 58); and he is presumed to be the 'Mr. Bullock' referred to in Roscoe's correspondence of August and September 1803 (see no. 62).

At his first certain appearance in Liverpool, Bullock lodged with his brother in Lord Street, and described himself as a 'Modeller and Sculptor'.[36] His career in cabinet-making seems to have grown out of his partnership with William Stoakes, of which he gave advance notice in June 1804:

'G. Bullock . . . has taken pains to improve his acquaintance with the present state of the Arts in the Metropolis; and has selected from the various articles of taste in Bronze, now so prevalent in the fashionable circles, a few of the choicest Specimens; and in order to display them to advantage, intends to remove from the Museum to the Large Room at Mr. Stoakes's, next door to the Athenaeum . . .'[37]

A more particular motive for moving out of the Museum may have been a desire quite literally to distance himself from his brother, who had a prior stake in the business of retailing ornamental wares. There are periodical signs of intense competition between them, for William Bullock also moved, some six weeks later, to larger premises in Church Street, which he styled the 'Museum and Bronze Figure Manufactory', and from where he sold 'every article in the Bronze Figure and Ornamental Business'.[38] Both brothers claimed the patronage of the Duke of Gloucester,[39] and on 13th March 1805 they advertised rival busts of 'Master Betty, the Young Roscius' in the *Liverpool Chronicle*.[40] George's answer to the opening of William's 'Egyptian Hall' was to give his showrooms the grandiose title 'Grecian Rooms',[41] and on eventually dissolving his partnership with Stoakes in October 1806, and moving to no. 13 Bold Street, he announced:

'As frequent mistakes have arisen, in consequence of Mr. Bullock, of the Museum, being of the same

Fig. 13. Advertisement by William Bullock, Liverpool Chronicle, *13th March 1805, p.1, col. 1.*

BUST OF THE YOUNG ROSCIUS.

THE inhabitants of Liverpool and its vicinity, are respectfully informed, that a Bust of MASTER BETTY in ACHMET, taken since his late illness by Mr. Gahagan, Sculptor, will in a few days be published, under the patronage of the DUKE of CLARENCE.

Subscriptions of 3 guineas each, are received by W. H. BETTY, Esq. No. 12, Bedford-street, Bedford-square; Mr. Jaques, 14, High Holborn; Mr. Gahagan, 5, Bentick-street, Soho, London; and Mr. W. Bullock, at the Museum, Liverpool, where the Bust may be seen.

** A Bust of Sir FRANCIS BURDETT, from the Life, just finished, is likewise open for public inspection, at the Museum in Church-street.

(One Property.)

Fig. 14. Advertisement by George Bullock, Liverpool Chronicle, *13th March 1805, p.2, col. 3.*

name, George Bullock takes this opportunity of observing, that he has no connection whatever with Mr. Bullock's Business or Shop; he therefore intreats the favour of his friends to direct particularly for George Bullock, Grecian Rooms, Bold Street.'[42]

However it was during the Stoakes partnership that Bullock moved into the line of business in which he was to establish his major reputation, and in which William was never a serious competitor.[43] Until Bullock joined him, Stoakes's establishment consisted of a 'Looking Glass Manufactory' in Church Street,[44] but in 1805 the partnership professed to be 'Cabinet-makers, General Furnishers, and Marble Workers'.[45] A vivid description of the shop is given in *The Picture of Liverpool*, published in 1805, in which Stoakes's part is wholly subordinated to Bullock's (and the distinction from William Bullock's business is reiterated):

'In a Picture of Liverpool it would be unpardonable not to notice, with commendation, the splendid *SHEW ROOMS of Mr. GEO. BULLOCK*, Sculptor and Modellor, next door to the Athenaeum, in Church-Street. Here the admirers of the fine arts will receive much gratification. Visitors are gratuitously admitted to a suite of rooms, in which a variety of the most fashionable and elegant furniture, in a stile of exquisite taste, is constantly displayed, as well as an extensive collection of statues, figures, monuments, tripods, candelabras, antique lamps, sphinxes, griffins, &c. &c. in marble, bronze, or artificial stone; Egyptian, Grecian, and modern chimney-pieces, in the various species of marble, in bronze, &c.; and a number of curious mosaic, inlaid, and marble tables, comprising fine specimens of porphyry, verd antique, and Egyptian green. Mr. G. Bullock has also a great collection

of ancient and modern busts; – among the latter are many portraits of the most distinguished characters in Liverpool and its neighbourhood, modelled by himself, and exhibited at the Royal Academy during the last two seasons.

The effect of these rooms is much heightened by the mirrors, pier, and chimney glasses of Mr. Stoakes, which are exhibited on the same premises; together with a quantity of ancient stained glass.

It may not be improper to add, that this establishment is wholly distinct from the Museum of Mr. W. Bullock, already mentioned.'[46]

Bullock's lack of experience in 'general furnishing' at this date was shown up in his earliest known commission, at Cholmondeley Castle, when he supplied unseasoned wood and unfathomable drawings for the use of the craftsmen employed there, and clearly had minimal oversight of the execution of his designs (*see* no. 1). But his remarkable inventiveness is already revealed in the same commission, by the armour he supplied to baronialise the hall (no. 4), and over the ensuing years he seems to have cultivated a high reputation as an interior designer.

At the same time he assumed increasing responsibility for the design and manufacture of the goods he offered for sale. On removing from Stoakes's rooms to Bold Street in 1806, he assured his customers that he 'continue[d] to manufacture,

Fig. 15. Advertisement by George Bullock, Liverpool Chronicle, *12th February 1806, p.2, col. 4.*

from the most approved original and antique designs,'[47] marble, bronze and other furniture and ornaments of the kind described in *The Picture of Liverpool*; whereas in 1804 his boast had been to have brought back a choice selection from the 'Arts in the Metropolis'.[48] One aspect of his practice is dimly illuminated by the account he held with the Herculaneum Pottery from 1807 (shortly after its foundation) to January 1811.[49] Bullock bought examples of their manufacture on a small scale, presumably to retail in his shop, and also procured small quantities of clay from there for his own use (about 3½ hundred weight a year), which no doubt was transformed into the 'Leaves', 'lion's heads and claws', 'figures' and one mysterious 'tablet', that he periodically had fired in their kilns. Conversely, he was paid by them on three occasions for 'bronzing' [wine coolers and unspecified objects], and on 30th April 1808 was credited with £1.11.6d. 'for designing the arrangements of the Rooms' at their new warehouse in Duke Street, which had been 'fitted up in a superior stile of elegance'[50] in 1807. At such a low fee, this would not appear to have been a very significant commission, however.

By 1806 Bullock had also gained control of the Mona Marble quarries in Anglesey,[51] for whose much-vaunted virtues his workshop came to be uniquely distinguished; and by the time he moved to no. 13 Bold Street he was running a separate marble works in Church Street, producing 'an extensive assortment of the most fashionable and elegant Sculptured and Plain Chimney Pieces, of pure statuary and variegated marbles'.[52] He acquired additional premises in Hanover Street, as 'furniture rooms', in about 1809, and by 1811 had a separate manufactory at 79 Bold Street, no. 39 Hanover Street having become his counting house (which in itself would seem to imply a sizeable establishment).[53] At the sale of his furniture stock in 1812 it was alleged that 'the whole of the modern articles are manufactured by Mr. Bullock, in the best manner.'[54]

This rapid expansion, which culminated in Bullock's moving to London, again invites speculation as to whether he had a local backer. He was certainly associated in various contexts with the cabinet-maker and antiquarian Matthew Gregson (1749-1824), especially in the furnishing of Speke Hall (no. 5),[55] but their connections are perhaps no more than one would expect to find between two enterprising men in the same line of business. A more substantial case can be made for William Roscoe (1753-1831), the man who contributed more than any other in Liverpool's history to the town's cultural development. He was one of Bullock's principal patrons, taking considerable tutelary interest in his career, as was observed by another early patron, Thomas Johnes of Hafod (*see* nos. 6 and 61). Roscoe was involved in the foundation of many of Liverpool's artistic and literary institutions, including the Society for Promoting the Arts in Liverpool in the 1780s; this was later (in 1810) re-established as the Liverpool Academy, with Bullock as its first President and himself as Treasurer. Roscoe was apparently instrumental in securing the patronage of the Prince Regent after the death of the Academy's first Patron, Henry Blundell of Ince (*see* no. 59); but the letter which Bullock and the artist J.W. Faulkner wrote to him on this subject suggests that Bullock himself was the driving force behind the enterprise:

'We have great pleasure in sending you the copy of a Letter from the Prince Regents Sec.ʸ to Mr Creevey expressing in the most gracious & obliging terms, his Royal Highnesses assent to our wishes of his becoming the Patron of the Liverpool Academy.

We are at a Loss how to describe the Gratitude we feel to You for the Kind & friendly assistance You have at all times afforded us, in our arduous undertaking; under your counsel & direction, Success has smiled upon our efforts, & we trust that our future exertions will render the Academy worthy the Honor of so distinguished a Friend & patron of Genius. It is our intention to wait now upon the principal Nobility & Gentlemen, who are the Promoters of modern Art, for the purpose of soliciting their Patronage & Support, & we have every reason to flatter ourselves with success. Mr Creevey has behaved in the most Kind & Gentlemanly manner to us whenever we have called upon him. With every sentiment of Respect & Gratitude . . .

Geo Bullock
J W Faulkner'[56]

It was over the issue of the Liverpool Academy that Bullock's second short-lived partnership, this time with the architect Joseph Gandy, came unstuck in September 1810, when Gandy refused to join the new foundation (as he was obliged to do by virtue of being an Associate of the Royal Academy).[57] During its brief existence, the partnership was comprehensively styled 'architects, modellers, sculptors, marble masons, cabinet-makers and upholsterers'.[58] Only one of their collaborative ventures has so far been identified: Storrs Hall, near Lake Windermere, which was enlarged by Gandy for John Bolton in 1808-11 and retains several characteristic Bullock features, including two doors bordered with one of his most common inlay patterns (*see* no. 10).[59] It is likely that Bullock also contributed to Gandy's work at Bolton Hall for the same patron, whose bust he showed at the first Liverpool Academy (*see* no. 88), and conversely Gandy may possibly have been involved with Bullock at Speke Hall (*see* no. 5).

In 1812 Bullock resigned the Presidency of the Academy, and ceased to exhibit there after that year, although he remained a member until its dissolution in 1814. This was presumably due to

EXTENSIVE SALE OF
ARTICLES OF MODERN TASTE.

By Messrs. WINSTANLEY & TAYLOR,

On Monday the 3d of February next, and following days, at eleven o'clock precisely each day, at the large Rooms in the Exchange, Manchester,

A NUMEROUS and elegant selection of MARBLE CHIMNEY PIECES, formed of the finest Verd Antique, Bloodstone, and Porphry Marbles of Mona, pure Statuary, Egyptian and the various Italian Marbles, and fitted up with classic correctness of taste and design to various dimensions and different qualities, from the chamber to the ornamented drawing-room purpose.

Rare specimens of the above mentioned Marbles elegantly mounted in scarce valuable wood, as Tables, Cabinets, Commodes, &c. of the most tasteful forms.

Splendid Lustres and Lamps of the Grecian, Roman, and French forms, richly ornamented with brilliant cut Glass.

Elegantly ornamented and useful Furniture, manufactured of Mahogany, Zebra, Topaz, and other Woods in Cabinets, Cabinet Bookcases, Superb Library Bookcases inlaid, Library Tables, exhibiting specimens of various Fancy Woods, Sideboards, Sarcophagus-shaped Wine Coolers, splendid Sofas in the modern fashion, with a great variety of useful articles of Cabinet Work of every description.—The property and manufacture of Mr. George Bullock, of Liverpool.

The whole may be viewed the week preceding the sale and Catalogues had of Mr. Zanetti, Market-street, lane, Manchester; of Messrs. Broster and Son, Chester; of Mr. G. Bullock, Bold-street, Liverpool; at the place of sale; and of Messrs. Winstanley & Taylor, Church-street, Liverpool, price 1s.

Fig. 16. Advertisement by George Bullock, Liverpool Mercury, *31st January 1812, p. 244, col. 2.*

his decision to move to London in the wake of his brother, who had taken the Museum to Piccadilly in 1809. Clearance sales of his stock were held in Manchester and Liverpool in February and August 1812, as well as a sale of his art collection,[60] and for two years in 1813-14 he based his 'Grecian Rooms' at William's Egyptian Hall in Piccadilly, before establishing his business permanently in Tenterden Street.[61] During this transitional period he maintained reduced premises in Liverpool,[62] presumably in order to fulfil his long-term commitments there, which may have been quite considerable, for the comprehensive range of his stock at this date, and indeed his major commission at Thornhill from James Watt Junior begun in 1808,[63] show that he was already in the business of complete house furnishing, of the kind later undertaken at Tew Park. The announcements of the 1812 sales make it plain that by the time he moved to London, the upholstery and cabinet-making business had, with the Mona Marble works, become his predominant concern, and that many of the characteristics of his London workshop style were fully established: among the pieces offered for sale were a 'beautiful Cabinet and Pier Tables, enriched with ebony [and] Brass, and Mona Marble Slabs; a pair of elegant Cabinets of English Oak, with Drawers for Coins or Shells; two Cabinet Bookcases of Peach Wood, richly ornamented with Ebony and Brass work; an elegant Zebra Wood Library Bookcase',[64] and other similar pieces (see also figs. 13, 14, 15 and 16).

Bullock's small remaining stock and his property in Bold Street were sold late in 1814, apparently signalling his final departure from Liverpool.[65] After his death, however, an auction was held in Liverpool of 'The late Mr. Bullock's Library, Pictures, &c. with Shares in the Public Institutions', namely the Athenaeum, Lyceum, Union Rooms and Botanic Garden.[66] The pictures and books (which included the works of Bartolozzi, Piranesi and Thomas Hope, a catalogue of 'Boydell's splendid Shakespeare',[67] or 'Woodburn's Gallery of Ancient Portraits',[68] and 'beautiful Plates of the Marriage and Coronation of Napoleon Buonaparte') may have been brought from London in the hope of reaching higher prices where Bullock was locally celebrated; or they may possibly indicate that Bullock maintained a house in or near the town up to his death. Either way, it is clear that he never totally severed his Liverpool connections.

NOTES

1) *Aris's Birmingham Gazette* [hereafter *ABG*], 27th August 1798, p.3, col. 3 (quoted in J.A. Langford, *A Century of Birmingham Life . . . 1741-1841*, Birmingham, 1868, Vol. II, p.118).

2) *International Genealogical Index*. The parents were perhaps William Bullock and Elizabeth Smallwood, whose marriage at the same church is recorded on 7th September 1769. Two other possible marriages are those of William Bullock to Elizabeth Ward on 10th February 1777 at Gnosall; and William Bullock to Elizabeth Corbet on 8th April 1777 at Stoke-on-Trent. No plausible birth date has

been found for George's (older?) brother William Bullock, to parents of the same name (see note 12 below).

3) Westminster City Libraries, Archives Department, Buckingham Palace Road, London SW1, parish records of St George's, Hanover Square, burial register 4, No. 388. This date is compatible with his being considered 'yet a boy' in 1797, but scarcely with his being the George Bullock who married in 1799 (see p.41).

4) Bullock was, however, quite a common name in and around Birmingham, and a number of Bullocks were involved in the metal-working trades there in the later 18th and early 19th centuries.

5) *ABG*, 26th May 1794, p.2, col. 5. Benjamin Mansell's Tea Warehouse in High Street is in fact recorded in the Birmingham trade directories from 1785 (or earlier) to 1798, although he died on 18th August 1794 (*ABG*, 25th August 1794). He may have been connected with Bullock's wife (see p.41).

6) *ABG*, 16th May 1796, p.2, col. 5.

7) *ABG*, 29th August 1796, p.2, col. 4.

8) *ABG*, 14th November 1796, p.3, col. 5.

9) *ABG*, 27th March 1797, p.2, col. 5 (at Stourbridge); 29th May 1797, p.3, col. 3; 28th May 1798, p.3 col. 5; 2nd July 1798, p.3, col. 5; 16th July 1798, p.3, col. 5 (at Wolverhampton); 30th July 1798, p.3, col. 5 (at Dudley). She also exhibited at an unknown date in Manchester (see E.J. Pyke, *A Biographical Dictionary of Wax Modellers*, Oxford, 1973, p.21).

10) *ABG*, 26th May 1794, p.2, col. 5; 16th May 1796, p.2, col. 5. For Houdon as wax modeller, see E.J. Pyke, *A Biographical Dictionary of Wax Modellers*, Oxford, 1973, p.70.

11) *ABG*, 27th May 1797, p.3, col. 3.

12) William is identified as George's brother in a letter from Sir Walter Scott to Daniel Terry of 18th April 1819, published in H.J.C. Grierson (ed.), *The Letters of Sir Walter Scott, Vol. V, 1817-1819*, London, 1933, p.364.

13) *ABG*, 28th May 1798, p.3, col. 5.

14) As note 13 above.

15) William Bullock's Museum contained in 1807 'An exquisite Model of the Death of Voltaire, done in Rice Paste, by Mons. Querrin of Cologne . . .' (*Companion*, 5th edition, 1807, p.14, no.12); in 1810 it listed apparently the same figure . . . by Mons. Oudon, of Paris' (*Companion*, 8th edition, 1810, p.12) and several unattributed rice paste figures.

16) See Eric Robinson and Keith L. Thompson, 'Matthew Boulton's Mechanical Paintings', *Burlington Magazine*, August 1970, p.498, for possibly related 'silver pictures' mentioned in the correspondence of James Watt and Josiah Wedgwood.

17) William Pybus, *A Manual of Useful Knowledge*, Hull, 1810, p.103. William Bullock's 'Persian Cement', sold in bottles from his Liverpool Museum 'for Ladies' Work, and joining Glass, Stone, Shells, Ivory, Wood, Paper, &c.' (*Liverpool Chronicle*, 11th September 1805, p.1, col. 4) may have been essentially the same substance. A closely derivative version of Pybus's account was given by James Smith (not the subject of no. 62), in *The Panorama of Science and Art*, Liverpool, 1815, vol. II, p.787. James Smith was apparently Liverpool-based, and a friend of the Liverpool architect Thomas Rickman, so he may have seen some of Bullock's work.

18) *ABG*, 2nd July 1798, p.3, col. 5.

19) *ABG*, 27th November 1797, p.3, col. 4: letter to the Editor from 'J.P.L.' who had been 'Passing some time since through Birmingham . . .' (the whole letter quoted in J.A. Langford, *A Century of Birmingham Life . . . 1741-1841*, Birmingham, 1868, Vol. II, p.118).

20) *ABG*, 27th August 1798, p.3, col. 3 (see note 1).

21) *ABG*, 16th September 1799, p.3, col. 4.

22) *Chapman's Birmingham Directory*, 1800 and 1801 editions.

23) Birmingham City Record Office, parish register of St. Martin's Church, Birmingham, 24th March 1799; *ABG*, 1st April 1799, p.3, col. 3. Mrs. Mansell's former husband, Samuel Mansell, may have been related to the Benjamin Mansell in whose house Mrs. Bullock had first exhibited her waxes; he died on 20th August 1798 (*ABG*, 27th August 1798, p.3, col. 2), but the business was still recorded in his name in trade directories up to 1801. After her marriage his

widow also appeared as Elizabeth Bullock, Pawn-broker, Coleshill-street in *Chapman's Birmingham Directory* for 1800 and 1801, the same years for which George Bullock was listed as miniaturist and modeller.

24) Virginia Glenn, 'George Bullock, Richard Bridgens and James Watt's furnishing schemes', *Furniture History Society Journal*, XV, 1979, pp.54, 63-64. Two designs among the *Wilkinson Tracings* (pp.51 and 73) are inscribed 'Miss Boulton Thornhill'.

25) *ABG*, 22nd September 1800, p.3, col. 4.

26) *ABG*, 11th August 1800, p.2, col. 4; repeated 18th August, p.2, col. 3. Further advertisements in *ABG* on 22nd September 1800, p.3, col. 4 (repeated 29th September, p.3, col. 3) and 13th October 1800, p.3, col. 3. The August advertisements refer to 'Descriptive Catalogues' of the collection, but no catalogue of the Museum while shown at Birmingham is known. The 3rd edition of the *Companion* was dated 1801; James Drake, *The Picture of Birmingham*, 1825, p.38, mentions that Portugal House was 'so called by its original proprietor who had gained a fortune in the Portugal wine trade' and in a later edition (1837) a partial view of the building was included (facing p.93) – information kindly provided by Stephen Price. For William Bullock's career, especially after his move to London in 1809, *see* R.D. Altick, *The Shows of London*, London, 1978, pp.235-252. Altick gives no evidence, however, for the claim that William first opened his Museum in Liverpool in 1795 (p.235).

27) It is possible that Mrs. Bullock died in 1798, since her recorded advertisements cease abruptly after 30th July that year (*ABG*, p.3, col. 5). She gave no hint of retiring, apart from announcing a sale of plaster figures four weeks earlier, 'as she intends to decline that Part of her Business' (*ABG*, 2nd July 1798, p.3, col. 5).

28) *ABG*, 5th September 1796, p.3, col. 4; 12th September 1796, p.3, col. 5; 27th November 1796, p.2, col. 5; 16th January 1797, p.3, col. 5; 30th January 1797, p.3, col. 4; 6th February 1797, p.3, col. 4; 13th February 1797, p.3, col. 3; 20th February 1797, p.3, col. 4.

29) *ABG*, 5th September 1796, p.3, col. 4; 27th November 1796, p.2, col. 5; William Bullock, *Companion to the Liverpool Museum*, 5th edition, 1807, p.12, no. 2. An annotation in the *Fascimile London Museum Sale Catalogue* of 1819 states that this was made by William Bullock, but there is perhaps a confusion with the glass model of a fountain at St. Cloud which William Bullock did claim to have made himself (*Companion*, 4th edition, 1807, p.13, no.7).

30) *ABG*, 13th February 1797, p.3, col. 3. Philippe Guillaume Mathé (or Johann Wilhelm Christoph) Creuz or Kurz or Curtius, said to have died (been poisoned?) at Vitry-sur-Seine in 1794. Mme Tussaud and her husband carried on Curtius's Cabinet de Cire under his name until 1800, but the Birmingham advertisements of 1796-97 are clearly placed by a real Mr Curtius, who makes reference to his wife and youngest child and mentions his own advanced age.

31) R.D. Altick, *The Shows of London*, London, 1978, pp.69-72.

32) *ABG*, 11th August 1800, p.2, col. 4; R.D. Altick, *see* note 31 above; J.W. Whiston, 'The Lichfield Clock', *South Staffordshire Archaeological and Historical Society Transactions*, Vol. 18, 1976-77, p.79; *A View of the Lichfield Museum from the Gentlemen's Magazine*, 1788, is reproduced in Clive Wainwright, 'The Romantic Interior in England', *National Art Collections Fund Review*, 1985, p.84.

33) *ABG*, 13th October 1800, p.3, col. 3.

34) *Billinge's Liverpool Advertiser*, 16th March 1801, p.3, col. 3.

35) *Chapman's Birmingham Directory*, 1801; *Gore's Liverpool Directory*, 1803 (in which Bullock does not appear); *Woodward's New Liverpool Directory*, 1804. Bullock is also listed in James Bisset's *Poetic Survey Round Birmingham . . . [and] Magnificent Directory . . . .*, 1800, plate J and index.

36) *Woodward's New Liverpool Directory*, 1804.

37) *Liverpool Chronicle* [hereafter *L.C.*], 27th June 1804, p.1, col. 4.

38) *L.C.*, 8th August 1804, p.1, col. 1; 24th April 1805, p.1, col. 5; 22nd May 1805, p.2, col. 4,

39) *L.C.*, 8th August 1804, p.1 col. 1; 11th September 1805, p.1, col. 4 (W.B.); 15th January 1806, p.1, col. 1, and elsewhere (G.B.)

40) *L.C.*, 13th March, p.1, col. 1 (G.B.); and p.2, col. 3 (W.B.; repeated 20th March 1805, p.1. col. 5). *See* nos. 81 and 85.

41) *L.C.*, 26th June 1805, p.1, col. 3; 17th July 1805, p.2, col. 5; 4th September 1805, p.1, cols. 2-3.

42) *L.C.*, 22nd October 1806, p.1, col. 2.

43) At William Bullock's establishment, furniture could be 'bronzed and altered to the present taste' (*L.C.*, 11th September 1805, p.1, col. 4); and the articles offered for sale in the Egyptian Hall included 'marble tables . . . consoles, glasses and mirrors,' while 'The various fashionable articles for supporting lights are here manufactured on the premises' (*The Picture of Liverpool*, 1805, p.129): this sounds like a relatively minor sideline.

44) *Gore's Liverpool Directory*, 1803.

45) *Gore's Liverpool Directory*, 1805.

46) *The Picture of Liverpool* 1805, pp.130-131. For William Bullock's Museum, *see* pp.128-130. A shorter but derivative account of Bullock's Grecian Rooms in Bold Street was published in successive editions of the *Stranger in Liverpool*, 1st edition, 1807, p.118; 2nd edition, 1810, p.130; 3rd edition, 1812, pp.138-139.

47) *L.C.*, 22nd October 1806, p.1, col. 2.

48) As note 37 above.

49) Liverpool Public Library: Herculaneum Pottery Records, 380 MD 48, Ledger, 1806-17, p.161; William Bullock also held a small account there (Herculaneum Pottery Records, as above, p.137).

50) Liverpool Public Library: Herculaneum Pottery Records, 380 MD 48, Ledger, 1806-17, p.161 (the fee was paid on the Duke Street Warehouse account, p.346); Minute Book, 1806-22, pp.19-20, annual report of the committee for 1807 (Bullock's name is not mentioned).

51) *L.C.*, 22nd October 1806, p.1, col. 2.

52) As note 51; *Gore's Liverpool Directory* for 1807 gives the address of his 'yard' as 55 Church Street.

53) *Holden's Triennial Directory*, 1809-11; *Gore's Liverpool Directory*, 1811.

54) *Liverpool Mercury* [hereafter *L.M.*], 28th August 1812, p.68, col. 2.

55) Gregson also owned the building in Duke Street leased by the Herculaneum Pottery for their warehouse, whose 'arrangement' was designed by Bullock (Liverpool Public Library: Herculaneum Pottery Records, 380 MD 47, Minute Book 1806-22, pp.19-20; 380 MD 48, Ledger, 1806-17, p.161); and in 1812 he became an honorary member of the Liverpool Academy, founded in 1810 under Bullock's presidency.

56) Liverpool Public Library: Roscoe Papers, 920 ROS, 571, n.d. [1810/11].

57) A.T. Bolton, *The Portrait of Sir John Soane, R.A.*, London, 1927, p.126.

58) *Gore's Liverpool Directory*, 1810.

59) Timothy Clifford kindly drew this to the writer's attention.

60) *L.M.*, 31st January 1812, p.244, col. 2, announcing sale on 3rd February by Winstanley and Taylor, Exchange, Manchester; *L.M.*, 28th August 1812, p.68, col. 2, announcing sale same day by Winstanley and Taylor, on the premises, Bold Street; *L.M.*, 11th September 1812, p.84, col. 2, announcing sale same day by Winstanley and Taylor, Church Street, Liverpool.

61) *London Post Office Directory*, 1813, 1814, 1815.

62) *Gore's Liverpool Directory*, 1813 and 1814 (G.B., modeller, sculptor, &c. Troughton Street; counting house & cabinet manufactory, 79 Bold St.)

63) *See* note 24 above.

64) *L.M.*, 24th August 1812, p.68, col. 2.

65) *L.M.*, 18th November 1814, p.164, col. 3, announcing sale on 21st November by Winstanley and Taylor, on the premises, Bold Street.

66) *L.M.*, 19th March, 1819, p.201, announcing sale on 24th-25th March by Branch & Sons, Hanover Rooms, Liverpool.

67) Josiah Boydell's edition of *The Dramatic Works of Shakespeare*, revised by G. Steevens, 1802, is in the British Library. He and John Boydell, engraver and printseller at the Shakespeare Gallery, also published several catalogues of their stock from 1790 to 1803.

68) Presumably Samuel Woodburn, *Woodburn's Gallery of Rare Portraits . . .*, 1816.

The Sale of Bullock's Stock in Trade

MARTIN LEVY

As this exhibition catalogue was going to press, a major new source of information was discovered. Preserved among the archives at Christie's London is:

'A CATALOGUE OF ALL THE VALUABLE UNMANUFACTURED *Stock in Trade*, OF Mr GEORGE BULLOCK, Dec. CONSISTING OF Brass work; viz Mountings for Cabinets, and Moulds for the same; Buhl Arabesque Bordering of Ebony, Rose Wood, Holly Oak and Brass . . . prepared for Inlaying; a large Quantity of Veneering, of Rose Wood, light and dark Oak, Elm and Holly; Planks of Spanish and Honduras Mahogany; 500 yds of new Brussells Carpeting; 20 pieces of new Bed Ticking; strong Twilled and Shawl Pattern Furniture; the Original Tinted and other Designs for Upholstery, by Bullock, &c.'

All this was offered for auction sale 'BY Mr CHRISTIE ON THE PREMISES, No 4, Tenterden Street, Hanover Square . . . On Thursday 13th of MAY, 1819', and two following days. The title page concludes, 'At the same Time will be Sold the LEASE of the MANSION and Modern PILE OF WORKSHOPS'. This sale (referred to in this catalogue as the Bullock Stock in Trade Sale, 1819) commenced eight days after the conclusion of the now well-known sale of 'THE WHOLE OF THE FINISHED STOCK' (referred to here as the Bullock Sale, 1819).

The various lots in the Stock in Trade Sale were subdivided into groups under the following headings:

Day 1.

'Printed Cotton Bordering for Bed Furniture and Window Curtains, &c.' (lots 1-47)

'Chased Pattern Brass Bronze ornaments, Mouldings for Cabinets, Sofas, Sofa Tables, Chimney Pieces, &c.' (lots 48-71)

'Buhl Bordering of Brass, Ebony, Oak and Rose-Wood for Tables, Cabinets, Sofas, &c of elegant Designs' (lots 72-94)

'THIRD SHOP. Spanish and Honduras Mahogany in Planks' (lots 95-106)

'WAINSCOT' (lots 107-122)

'SATTIN WOOD' (lot 123)

'NUTMEG WOOD' (lots 123-155)

'OAK, ELM AND HOLLY VENEERING' (lots 156-182)

Day 2.
(un-headed, but comprising miscellaneous fabrics – lots 1-12)

'NEW BED TICKING' (lots 13-21)

'BRUSSELS CARPETING' (lots 22-29)

'Chased-pattern Brass Mouldings and Ornaments for Cabinets, Sofas, Tables, &c.' (lots 30-62)

'Bulh [sic] Bordering in Ebony, Brass, Rosewood, and Holly, for Cabinets, Sofa Chairs and Tables' ots 63-86)

'SPANISH AND HONDURAS MAHOGANY' (lots 87-95)

'Dark and Light Oak, Elm and Holly Veneers' (lots 96-134)

'LOGS OF EBONY, &c. &c.' (lots 135-206)

Day 3.
[un-headed, including miscellaneous workshop equipment – lots 1-12]

'No. 9. *Drawing Room*' (lots 13-19)

'CASTS FROM ARMOUR IN THE TOWER OF LONDON, &c.' (lots 20-35)

'Coloured Drawings and Outlines, designs by the late Mr GEORGE BULLOCK for Drawing-room, Dining-room and Bed-room Furniture, and for Ornamental Articles, of elegent and superior taste' (lots 36-65)

'Spanish and Honduras Veneers, Rosewood, Gold, Camphor, and other Woods' (lots 1-81)[1]

'LOGS OF EBONY' (lots 82-94)

[Various miscellaneous items are written into the end of the sale, lots 95-107.]

It is intended that this hitherto unrecorded sale catalogue will be fully published in due course. In the meantime, this note is to record its existence and extract several of the more important details from its pages – particularly where these relate to matters discussed elsewhere in the present publication.

The range and quantity of items offered for sale together with the lease of the 'mansion' and workshops surely bear out the fear expressed by Daniel Terry when he wrote doubting that ' . . . the large concern which owed its existence . . . to the personal talent . . . of poor Bullock can be continued longer than the impetus he had given . . .'[2]

Terry described Bullock's concern as 'large' and this sale catalogue offers a few specific details. Lot 178 (on Day 1) is described as 'Three cabinet-maker's work benches'. These are followed by six more of the same and also by six 'carpenters' benches; twelve further benches were included in the third day of the sale. We also learn from the Stock in Trade catalogue something of how the workshops were divided. Two 'Upholsterers Rooms' are mentioned (No. 6 and No. 7) and there was also a Brass Room (No. 2, second floor), Calico Room (No. 5) and Stone Room (No. 4).[3] A Drawing Room (No.9) and THIRD SHOP are mentioned in the catalogue sub-headings.

A slightly clearer picture of Bullock's premises is beginning to emerge from this list particularly when the information it provides is coupled with the references to rooms in the catalogue of the Bullock Sale, 1819. However, it is still uncertain precisely how the accomodation was apportioned between living quarters, workshops and showrooms.

Given the quantity of finished objects described in the catalogue of the Bullock Sale, 1819, it seems likely that these were displayed around 4, Tenterden Street. The 'PILE of WORKSHOPS' referred to in this catalogue may well have been at the end of the garden, a part of the Oxford Street works.

Among the workshop equipment disposed of at the Stock in Trade Sale were, on Day 3, lot 19, 'Sundry large shop glue pots, and sundry painters pots, stone bottles, tin oil cans &c.' as well as a 'copying machine, with Lever' (Day 3, lot 85), 'Masons Tools' (Day 3, lot 99) and a 'Weighing Machine' (Day 3, lot 106). The dispersal of such items together with partly made-up furniture and large quantities of timber and veneers, metal mounts and inlays must have marked the final closure of Bullock & Co.

On 1st July 1819 *The Times* reported that several of George Bullock's workmen had been engaged by E.T. Cox. A person named 'Cox' had been one of the names recorded as a buyer (of five lots) at the Stock in Trade Sale.

As one might expect, the list of buyers at this sale reads like an extract from a compendium of contemporary cabinet-makers, with names such as 'Snell' (11 lots), 'Robins' (1 lot), 'Mower' (3 lots), 'Baker' (41 lots) and 'Balls' (18 lots). The last-mentioned, probably John Balls (active 1809-40), is recorded in the *Dictionary of English Furniture Makers*,

1986, as having made a rosewood dwarf bookcase 'inlaid with brass . . . a frieze inlaid with scrolling foliage . . .'[4] Among the purchases made by Ball at the sale was lot 92 on Day 2: '118 feet of stamped border, brass and ebony, of two patterns'. These two facts may be a coincidence, but if they are connected, they indicate one of the ways in which the Bullock style might have been disseminated during the 1820s.

Perhaps the best-known cabinet-makers who purchased at the sale were Morel & Hughes. On Day 2 they purchased lot 67, 'Fourteen feet of 2-inch foliage border'. 'Morel' (presumably Nicholas Morel, formerly of Tenterden Street before his partnership with Robert Hughes) made a further six purchases, including 'Seventeen patterns engraved on copper . . . ornamental designs for cabinets, sofa tables, sofas, candelabra &c' (Day 3, lot 48).

Among other names listed are 'Atkinson' (the architect William Atkinson?), 'Mrs Terry' (the wife of Sir Walter Scott's friend, the actor-manager Daniel Terry?) and 'Swaby', probably the dealer of that name who was to supply Scott with furniture during the 1820s.

One final purchaser must be mentioned here. The name 'Wilkinson' occurs 21 times. His acquisitions included decorative panels, mounts and borders as well as 40 drawings (Day 3, lot 40) and some engraved copper plates. Could this be the same Wilkinson who was responsible for the *Tracings*? If so, the range of purchases he made would seem to suggest that he was actively involved in the cabinet-making trade (*see* Introduction, p.13).

Both the title page and the sub-heading of the Stock in Trade catalogue state that the designs being offered are by Bullock. There is no suggestion that they are by others such as Richard Bridgens or Richard Brown, and this represents the clearest evidence to date that Bullock was personally responsible for at least part of the design output.[5] There were seven lots of designs (Day 3, lots 36-42) making up a total of 290 'Coloured drawings, designs for canopy and other bedsteads, sofas, sofa tables, cabinets, candelabra, chimney pieces &c. &c.' Only one pen, ink and wash design, that may have come from this group, has been discovered so far (*see* no. 55). Lot 43 on Day 3 is described as 'A folio scrap-book, containing tracings from nearly all the designs of the late Mr George Bullock'. These were sold for £43.11.6d to 'Johnstone' (who acquired a further 24 lots at the sale). This was a considerable price when one considers that lot 41 in the same part of the sale, a group of forty coloured designs, fetched only £3.12.0d (bought by 'Elliott' – the cabinet-maker Charles Elliott?). It is tantalising to consider whether these tracings were in some way related to the *Wilkinson Tracings*? Did 'Johnstone' allow Wilkinson to copy them?

This same section of the sale included various

'parcels' of working drawings, together with engraved copper plates for ornamental patterns. These were presumably for the printing of templates to be used in the workshop (or to be published and sold to other cabinet-makers?). Some samples of these printed patterns survive, unbound, and, like the *Wilkinson Tracings*, now belong to the City Museums and Art Gallery, Birmingham.

Finally, under the 'Drawings' heading in the catalogue of the Stock in Trade Sale, 1819, there were various items such as lot 50, 'A swan neck and center patterns, in wood' and lot 52 'Patterns carved in wood for moulding in brass'. These descriptions suggest close in-house attention to the design of the distinctive metalwork found on Bullock's furniture. The existence of a 'Brass-Room' seems to imply that castings were executed on the premises. It is tempting to wonder whether the 'lamb's tongue pattern moulding' (Day 3, lot 51) might be the same as that around the lower part of the Tew Park fenders (*see* no. 31 in this catalogue).

Lots 20-26 on the third day of the Stock in Trade Sale are evidence that Bullock's interest in making castings of such items as armour, busts and vases continued throughout his career. No 'cast' vases have been discovered so far, but several busts made at different stages of his life are noted in this exhibition catalogue. Among the earliest recorded works of 'sculpture' is an Equestrian model of Edward the Black Prince (*see* no. 77). In the sale, lot 20 (on Day 3) was 'A suit of armour of Edward the Black Prince, cast from the original in the Tower' (sold for £2.11.0 to 'Atkinson'). The following two lots were casts of part of the same armour and lot 23 was 'The complete moulds . . .' Lot 15 on the same day included 'Four painted wooden shields . . . two battle axes . . . four carved morning stars, 7 pair of stags horns'. Bullock was clearly involved with arms and armour both real and imitation throughout his working life; for instance at Cholmondeley (1804-05) and Abbotsford (1816-19). Were the pieces in lot 15 left over from some similar commission? Were they part of the decoration of his own house (*see* fig. 3) or were such examples available from him 'off-the-peg'?

The textiles included in the sale, particularly lots 1-47 on Day 1, together with the 'Brussels Carpeting' should prove to be most worthy of investigation. In the past, the main evidence for Bullock's interest in textiles has been from the plates in Ackermann's *Repository*, where details of upholstery and sophisticated window hangings are shown. More recently the bill for the furnishings supplied to Tew Park[6] has provided more information (*see* no. 25). The detailed descriptions and quantity of material in stock are evidence that Bullock was seriously involved with the provision of textiles. As has been mentioned above, Bullock's premises included a 'Calico room' and lots 28-34 on Day 3 comprised 108 'blocks for printing calico, of rich and elegant patterns'. The only textiles with possible Bullock connections that have been identified to date are a selection of fragments found in a basement store at Tew Park. These were generously presented to the Walker Art Gallery by Mr James Johnston. At least two borders from this group should now be confidently attributed to the Bullock workshop.

The Stock in Trade Sale is important both because of the range of material offered and also for the list of buyers, many of whom are extremely likely to have been cabinet-makers. The sale indicates a probable explanation for the appearance of furniture with distinctive Bullock features made by various cabinet-makers during the 1820s. The detailed descriptions of the lots offered emphasise the extreme caution which is needed when making stylistic attributions to Bullock based solely on the evidence of his familiar inlaid patterns. More positively, the catalogue enables us to build up a more comprehensive impression of the scale and nature of Bullock's business.

NOTES
1) After lot 65, the lot numbers start again at 1 and run through to the end of the sale.
2) Letter from Terry to Sir Walter Scott, 15th May 1818. (Quoted by Clive Wainwright in 'Walter Scott and the Furnishing of Abbotsford', *The Connoisseur*, January 1977.)
3) Stock in Trade Sale catalogue: Day 3, lots 1, 2 and 4.
4) Christie's London, 28th April 1983, lot 107 (not illustrated).
5) Stock in Trade Sale catalogue: Day 3, lot 12 included 'A painted deal drawing desk [and] 3 deal tracing boards'.
6) Tew Archive. There are also significant references in the Boulton/Bullock correspondence. In addition, the report 'House and Furniture for Buonaparte', *The LONDON PACKET; And Lloyd's Evening Post* (23rd-25th October 1815) describes some of the curtains and carpets intended for Longwood House.

The
Catalogue

CHOLMONDELEY CASTLE

The Gothic castle at Cholmondeley was built by the first Marquess of Cholmondeley (the 4th Earl as he then was) between 1801 and 1805, to what were essentially his own designs.[1] His consultant architect was William Turner of Whitchurch, and the progress of the work is recorded in detail in a surviving letter book kept by Lord Cholmondeley's agent, George Yerbury.[2] The correspondence is chiefly between Lord Cholmondeley and Yerbury himself, with a few letters from William Turner. Near the beginning, Yerbury noted, 'General Directions from Lord Cholmondeley. Sep. 22. 1801,' which makes the latter's relationship with his architect quite explicit:

'Lord C. has sent his Idea of a Front, & if Mr Turner will make a Sketch or two in pencil to accompany the Plan to be drawn by Mr Hill, he will be glad; they must accord with his Idea.'

His other instructions register the same attention to every architectural aspect. But most significant of all is his principal specification:

'It is intended that the new Hall shall in every Respect have the appearance of an old Gothic Castle, as much as possible consistent with neatness, & peremptorily to exclude both from without & within every thing that is new fashioned.'[3]

It was apparently not until the latter part of 1804, when the house was nearing completion, that Lord Cholmondeley discovered a sympathetic spirit in George Bullock. He is first mentioned in the correspondence on 1st December 1804, after a hiatus of three months, during which time Lord Cholmondeley had been in residence and had evidently engaged him. Bullock's principal contributions were the design of the Gothick drawing room (*see* no. 1) and the arrangement of the baronial hall with sculpted armour (*see* no. 4). Of the 'Rich Gothic Furniture' supplied by Bullock (*see* no. 4) no details are forthcoming from the letter book, although a coherent group of delicate Gothick furniture remains at Cholmondeley, which may be tentatively attributed to him. But it is clear that the house had been substantially fitted out both with new furniture from London, and with furniture made on the spot by Mr. Cliff (*see* no. 2), before Bullock was involved at all.[4] Bullock's furniture is mentioned only twice in the correspondence (which again comes to a temporary halt immediately afterwards). Yerbury (whose reports to Lord Cholmondeley show increasing impatience at Bullock's failure to meet his commitments) wrote on 29th August 1805 that they had 'not reced the Bed for new Room [*see* no. 2], nor any Furniture from Mr Bullock.' Part of the delay was caused by Bullock's wish to show off the furniture in his newly-opened showrooms at Stoakes's Church Street premises, where he announced on 4th September that it could be seen

for one day only, before being despatched to Cholmondeley.[5] Bullock and Stoakes also supplied glass for Lord Cholmondeley's bedroom,[6] and possibly some of the fire furniture, for Yerbury wrote to Lord Cholmondeley that a fender, five foot wide, would be wanted for the drawing room 'unless ordered from Mr Bullock.'[7] Eighteen months after the furniture had been delivered, Yerbury (having overcome his former exasperation) proposed ordering the chimneypieces for the two bedrooms over the dining room from Bullock, as a cheaper and better alternative to having them made on the estate; but it is unclear from the correspondence whether these were in fact supplied by Bullock.[8]

NOTES
1) *See* Gervase Jackson-Stops, 'Cholmondeley Castle, Cheshire – II', *Country Life*, 26th July 1973, pp.226-230.
2) Cheshire Record Office, DCH/X/20. The letter book is unpaginated, and the extracts given below are identified by their date.
3) To this end (as well as for economy's sake), many of the materials from the old house were re-used in the new, and furniture and chimneypieces were also brought from 'Charlton' – a house [?] as yet unidentified – and from Devon.
4) Cheshire Record Office, DCH/X/20. Letters dated 3rd July-30th August 1804. This included furniture for the drawing room (letter dated 30th July 1804).
5) *Liverpool Chronicle*, 4th September 1805, p.1, cols. 2-3.
6) Cheshire Record Office, DCH/X/20. Letters dated 20th July and 10th August 1805.
7) Cheshire Record Office, letter dated 3rd August 1805.
8) Cheshire Record Office, letters dated 27th March, 25th May and 23rd June 1807.

1. *The Drawing Room*

Although Bullock was involved only at a late stage in the creation of Cholmondeley, the Drawing Room appears to have been reserved for special treatment from the beginning. While the decoration of the rest of the house was well under way during 1803, work in the drawing room was confined to structural matters; and against the estimate of December 1803 for the work due for completion by 1st April next year, Yerbury noted: 'No Charge is made . . . for the Drawing Room Ceiling.'

Bullock's name first occurs in the letter book[1] in Yerbury's report of 1st December 1804:

'We have put up the Frames for Tapestry in Drawing Room, and have heard nothing from Mr Bullock, can we go on awhile, but unless we receive Directions from him or your Lordship respecting the framing of Shutters and Dado in the course of a fortnight, Wilkinson[2] will be obligd to go home again, for want of work.'

A week later Yerbury wrote:

'We only want the Drawings for Dado, and front of Shutters, which I suppose we shall receive in time, as your Lordship has written to Mr. Bullock; if they are sent from London you will be pleased

to direct that they may be made, at least half an Inch to a Foot, for if the Scale is too small, the Workmen will find more difficulty in following them.

We are in no want of the Drawing for Cornice and Ornament in Center of ceiling, as the first coat of Plaster is applyed, and I do not expect it will be sufficiently dry to receive a Second in less than three Weeks if so soon.'

Yerbury's apprehension about Bullock's drawings was only too well founded, for on 24th December he had to report:

'On Saturday I rec̄ed the Model of Cornice and Sketches for Dado &c in Drawing Room, and being wholly at a loss to understand the latter, as are the Workmen to execute them, I should have gone over to Liverpool for Mr Bullock's Explanation, but as your Lordship mentioned his Meeting you in London, was uncertain whether I should find him at home . . . [Mr. Stephens] has directd me to inclose the Sketches, and take your Lordship's Directions respecting them. What I wish to ask is, whether the Pannels marked P are to be framed sunk below the Stiles marked S, or projecting forwards, or whether we are to frame the whole of the Dado, Door, and Shutters, of one level Surface, and take no Notice, of the Ornaments, which may be applyed afterwards, and appear to me, to be rather the work of a Carver, than that of a Joiner. The Dado &c might certainly be framed in Gothic Pannels, resembling Mr. Bullocks Sketches without much additional Trouble, either with sunk or raised Pannels; the former of which would be easiest executed, and of which I have inclosed a Sketch for your Lordship's Inspection.

The Cornice was settled at Cholmondeley, not to come down more than 4 Inches on the Wall; and the upper Margin above the Frames for Tap-

estry was set out accordingly. The Cornice Pr Model comes down 8 Inches; but this we can accommodate, by lowering the upper part of the Frame, and reducing the Height of the Tapestry 4 Inches.'

He made regular progress reports in the following weeks:

11th January 1805
'I have taken Mr Bullock's Explanation of his Sketches for Drawing Room, and hope the work there, will now proceed without further Delay.'[3]

26th January 1805
'We have floated the Walls and Ceiling of Drawing Room, and prepared the Moulds for casting the Cornice.'

9th February 1805
'Burd is employed in casting the Cornice for Draw-ing Room.'

By 9th March 1805, Burd had 'compleated three fourths of the Cornice in Drawing Room'; in April and May they were laying the Drawing-Room floor, and on 1st June Yerbury sent to Lord Cholmondeley 'A Pattern for the painted Glass in Drawing Room Windows.' It does not appear that Bullock supplied the glass, although Bullock and Stoakes had 'a quantity of ancient stained glass' for sale in this period (see p.43).[4] In the same report Yerbury wrote:

'In case Mr Bullock does not wait upon your Lordship soon have marked the Size of Drawing [Room] Door on the inclosed Paper, in order that your Lordship may get some other Person to make a Drawing for it, it being absolutely necessary we should receive it soon. We have laid down the floor in Drawing Room, and have began [sic] to put up the Dado there . . . '

On 15th June Bullock had failed him yet again:

'We are now fixing up the Chimneypiece in Drawing Room,[5] and hanging the Shutters &c there; we have cut out, and are now working upon the new Door, but the Timber Mr Bullock sent proves so green, that I am in doubt whether it will take the Glue, shall consult him, when he comes here, as to the propriety of hanging it this Season.'

The door as completed is attached to the back of one of the standard panelled doors used in the principal rooms of the house.

Progress was further impeded by the fact that many of Turner's workmen, who were employed to make the window-sashes and frames, had volunteered for the corps. And a further delay was threatened, as Yerbury informed Lord Cholmondeley on 27th July:

'Mr Bullock was here on Thursday giving Directions respecting the painting of Drawing Room, he proposed some Alterations in the Dado, Shutters &c, by cutting Mouldings in the edge of the Sinkings, but as this was not the original Design, and foreseeing that if the Alterations were adopted, the Painting must be delayed some Weeks I submitted to him as your Lordship was very desirous of finishing the Room, whether the Alterations ought not to be postponed – to which he has consented: if he fulfills his promise in sending the Patterns for the Colours in time, the Painters will begin on Monday Aug. the fifth . . . '

Bullock's failure to 'perform his Promise', and then his 'having made an alteration in the Painting of the Pannels in Drawing Room' meant that Yerbury could not finally report the job completed until 24th August.

It is clear from this correspondence that Bullock did not oversee the execution of his designs particularly closely, but the finished work nonetheless shows much greater vigour and sophistication than the otherwise comparable Gothick

decoration of the hall (see fig. 18). The account by J.A. Hanshall in about 1817 (perhaps not an eyewitness report) describes the drawing room as well as the hall as decorated with 'ancient military trophies' (see no. 4).[6] One imagines that any trophies introduced to the drawing room would have been of a less awesome character than the armour in the hall, perhaps more comparable to the trophies shown between the window arches in Bullock's later design for a dining room (published in Ackermann's *Repository* in August 1816; see no. 56). They may have been removed as early as 1820-21 when the windows were altered, new curtains made, and other repairs and unspecified work carried out in the drawing room;[7] or they may have been sacrificed in the alterations of the later 1820s. There is no reason to assume that the character of the plasterwork and panelling has been affected, although it is unfortunate that no record survives of Bullock's original paint scheme.[8]

NOTES
1) Cheshire Record Office, DCH/X/20, from which all the following quotations are extracted.
2) Benjamin Wilkinson of Nantwich, joiner (see no.2).
3) A record in Yerbury's hand of expenses at Cholmondeley up to 6th April 1805, includes £2.5s under the head of sums 'not estimated for' which related to 'Expenses of Journey to Liverpool, taking Mr. Bullock's Directions, Letters &c from him'. Cheshire Record Office, DCH/K/I/5.
4) Stained or painted glass was being installed in other rooms during the summer of 1804, before Bullock was involved at Cholmondeley. According to Hanshall, that in the hall, library and 'saloon' was purchased by the Marquess in France (J.L. Hanshall, *History of the County Palatine of Chester*, Chester, 1817, p.336, see note 6). Much of this has now been removed to the chapel. The character of the glass supplied by Bullock and Stoakes for Lord Cholmondeley's [?] bedroom is not made clear.
5) This was the larger of two chimneypieces brought from Exeter (by ship to Liverpool and from there by canal), which Lord Cholmondeley initially intended for the ante room. He was persuaded, however, that the smaller chimneypiece was more appropriate for the ante room, 'and the other [this one] with Gothic Pillars well adapted to the Size of the Drawing Room.' (George Yerbury to Lord Cholmondeley, letter book, 18th and 23rd June, 7th and 21st July, 1804.).
6) J.H. Hanshall, *History of the County Palatine of Chester*, Chester, 1817, p.336. Although dated 1817 on the title page, the dedication to the Bishop of Chester is dated 1823. But Hanshall's reference to a new wing being 'projected' in 1819 suggests that this may have been his cut-off date.
7) Cheshire Record Office, DCH/K/1/5. But see note 6.
8) Evidence of the treatment of the ceiling comes from a later report in the letter book of 2nd August 1806, when Yerbury undertook 'to get the Ornament in Drawing Room Ceiling Regilt'.

Reproduced by kind permission of the Marquess of Cholmondeley, Cholmondeley Castle.

2. Ornaments for Lord Cholmondeley's bed

'Bronzed' (painted) walnut.
Lion's heads, 35.5 cm (height).
Lion's feet, height, 33 cm (height).

A number of beds were brought in pieces from 'Charlton' (as yet unidentified) to be reconstructed at Cholmondeley in 1804, and others were made

new by Mr. Cliff (probably Washington Cliff of Nantwich), which he described as being 'exactly agreeable to [Lord Cholmondeley's] Directions, tho' not precisely of the same Dimensions &c, as those from Charlton . . . '[1] On 1st December 1804, George Yerbury wrote to Lord Cholmondeley:

'I had sent away the Bedsides and Feet before the Receipt of your Lordship's Letter of Tuesday last. There will be no difficulty in applying the Lion's heads and feet in the way your Lordship mentions, provided the heads are made with proper Tenons, and the Feet with Nuts and Screws to fasten them to the sides, which I suppose the Workmen will do of course.'

The correspondence continues, on 9th February 1805:

'Wilkinson wishes if it is convenient that your Lordship would order the Lion's heads and Feet and Ornaments for Bedstead to be sent down, as it will enable him to have the whole ready for Inspection against your Arrival . . .

If the Lion's heads &c, are sent, they should be directed to Ben. Wilkinson, Joiner Nantwich.'

Apparently nothing was done, however, for on 20th July Yerbury wrote again to Lord Cholmondeley in London:

'Feet & Heads for your Lordship's Bed, must be sent down, unless as you intimated you have ordered them from Mr Bullock.'

On August 10th, he reported:

' . . . we have also recēd the Glass from Mr Bullock and fixed it up, but not the Feet and Posts for your Lordship's Bed.'[2]

The 'Bed for new Room', which had still not arrived by 29th August, may also have been this one. Benjamin Wilkinson, who seems to have been responsible for fixing the ornaments to the bed, is mentioned several times in the letter book, but his name is not known to have been recorded elsewhere.[3]

The 'Bronzed Figures' for supporting 'LIGHTS, TRIPODS, VASES, LAMPS . . . ' etc., which Bullock had 'constantly on sale' at this period[4] (together with actual bronze equivalents), must have resembled these ornaments in their dark green finish. This particular commission recalls William Bullock's recurring advertisement for furniture to be 'altered and bronzed to the present fashion' in his establishment.

NOTES
1) Cheshire Record Office, DCH/X/20, letter of 4th August 1804 from George Yerbury to Lord Cholmondeley. In another letter (30th July 1804), they were said to be of similar form to the Charlton beds, but larger, with the canopy fixed higher.
2) Cheshire Record Office, DCH/X/20, dates as stated in note 1 above.

Reproduced by kind permission of the Marquess of Cholmondeley, Cholmondeley Castle.

3. Chandelier

Brass.
190.5 cm (height) × 109 cm (diameter).

This chandelier, or another identical one, appears in a late 19th-century photograph of the dining-room at Cholmondeley (now the kitchen) which was added to the castle in 1817.[1] Its attribution to Bullock is based on two designs for chandeliers in the *Wilkinson Tracings* (pp.48 and 50; here fig. 10) and a design for a standing oil lamp (*Tracings*, p.163). However, even allowing for the innovator in Bullock it is remarkably advanced for 1805 when he supplied a quantity of 'Rich Gothic Furniture' to Cholmondeley, and, since other furniture remaining at Cholmondeley is closely paralleled

in Bullock's mature output, one is tempted to speculate that he may have been called in again at a later date – perhaps in connection with the new dining room – although no documentary evidence for this has so far emerged.

The design of this chandelier is fundamentally classical, thinly disguised by applied Gothic elements, including the Gothic lantern housing the central oil reservoir, where a vase might typically appear in a purely classical example.

Another chandelier of similar design, with six arms instead of eight, appears in a 19th-century photograph of the library (now the dining room).

NOTE
1) J.H. Hanshall, *History of the County Palatine of Chester*, Chester, 1817, p.336.

Provenance: Cholmondeley Castle, Cheshire.

Lent by the Marquess of Cholmondeley, Cholmondeley Castle.

Exhibited at Sudley

4. Armour from the hall at Cholmondeley

The armour supplied to decorate the hall[1] is the subject of just one oblique reference in the Cholmondeley letter book.[2] It is from Bullock himself that we learn of his responsibility for this remarkable early exercise in baronialism. It was the main attraction at the re-opening of his Grecian Rooms (Bullock was not at all perturbed by the mixture

of styles), which he announced on 4th September 1805, after the show rooms had undergone 'considerable alterations and improvements. The advertisement continues:

GEORGE BULLOCK takes this opportunity of acquainting his Friends, and more particularly those Ladies and Gentlemen who have expressed a desire to see the *Rich Gothic Furniture, Armour, &c*, WHICH HE HAS DESIGNED AND EXECUTED FOR LORD CHOLMONDELEY, That they may be seen until *TO-MORROW*, THURSDAY, the 5th inst. previously to their being removed to Cholmondeley Castle.[3]

It is clear from the Cholmondeley letter book that the decoration of the hall was completed long before Bullock was involved,[4] and the lack of any reference to the armour suggests that it may have been an afterthought, perhaps proposed by Bullock to Lord Cholmondeley after he was engaged to decorate the drawing room. His brother's Museum (which from its Birmingham days had included a room 'fitted up in the Manner of an ancient Armoury'[5]) may well have inspired the idea, and certainly provided plentiful source material (*see* nos. 4a and 4f).

In the absence of evidence to the contrary, it seems likely that the arrangement of armour existing in 1850 when the hall was engraved by Augustus Butler (*see* fig. 17),[6] and later in the century when it was photographed (*see* fig. 18) had not been disturbed since it was put up by Bullock

Left: *Fig. 17. 'Entrance Hall, Cholmondeley Castle'. Lithograph by Augustus Butler, from Edward Twycross's* The Mansions of England and Wales, *(Liverpool Public Libraries.)*

Below: *Fig. 18. The Entrance Hall at Cholmondeley Castle, from a late 19th century photograph. (The Marquess of Cholmondeley, Cholmondeley Castle.)*

in 1805.[7] Besides the 'armour' manufactured by Bullock from wood and some form of fired clay, the arrangement also incorporated some genuine but wholly modern arms, including numerous boarding pikes stacked either side of the fireplace and on the facing wall, and swords of the pattern issued in 1796 for the British Light Cavalry. While on the one hand the scheme is a fascinating precursor of the Abbotsford armoury and other more antiquarian interiors, its sheer inventiveness is still very much in the spirit of the 18th century. It would appear, however, that Bullock continued to execute comparable schemes even after his move to London, since similar imitation armour remained in his stock up to his death (see p.50).

Nos. 4a to 4j are a selection from the surviving pieces, and can all be identified in figs. 17 and 18.

NOTES
1) The documentation on Bullock's sources and inspiration for the design of nos. 4a-4j has kindly been provided by Mr A.V.B. Norman, Master of the Royal Armouries.
2) George Yerbury's report of 24th August 1805: 'We have not reçed any Furniture &c from Mr. Bullock since my last.' Cheshire Record Office, DCH/X/20.
3) *Liverpool Chronicle*, 4th September 1805, p.1, cols. 2-3.

4) Letters dated 10th April 1803 to 26th May 1804.
5) *Aris's Birmingham Gazette*, 11th August 1800, p.2, col.4.
6) Edward Twycross, *The Mansions of England and Wales: The County Palatine of Chester*, 2 vols., London, 1850, Vol. I, facing p.19.
7) The armour was removed from the hall after World War II and the panelling and wooden fire surround were dismantled. The letter book gives no information about the treatment of the hall fireplace in 1803-04: the wooden surround, if original, was perhaps one of '2 Large Chimney Pieces' brought from the hall and dining room of the old house (estimate dated 31st August 1801, from William Turner to Lord Cholmondeley).

Provenance: supplied in 1805 to the first Marquess of Cholmondeley, Cholmondeley Castle, Cheshire; by descent to the present owner.

Lent by the Marquess of Cholmondeley, Cholmondeley Castle.

Exhibited at Sudley

4a. Helmet

Painted ceramic.
38 × 27.2 × 25.5 cm.

The source for this helmet is part of the suit of armour known as the Tong Crusader (see fig. 19), believed until the mid-19th century to be Norman, but subsequently identified as oriental.[1] The

Left to right. Top: *4b. Helmet (see fig. 21); 4d. Helmet (of heraldic inspiration); 4b. Helmet.* Bottom: *4c. Helmet (representing 16th-century Italian burgonet); 4e. Breastplate (based on 17th-century model); 4a. Helmet (see fig. 19).*

Fig. 19. Helmet from the 'Tong Crusader' armour. (The Royal Armouries, H.M. Tower of London.)

Fig. 20. The 'Tong Crusader' (2, 4, and 5) and another suit of armour engraved by J. Hamilton in 1785, and published in Francis Grose, A Treatise on Ancient Armour and Weapons, *London, 1786, Plate 21.*

suit was among the armour collection bought by George's brother, William Bullock from Richard Greene's Lichfield Museum in 1800 (*see* p.42). While the armour was in Greene's collection it was engraved by J. Hamilton and published in Francis Grose's *Treatise on Ancient Armour and Weapons*, 1786 (*see* fig. 20). William Bullock illustrated the armour in the frontispiece to the 6th edition of the *Companion to the Liverpool Museum*, 1808, showing its Gothick setting in the Museum. In a lengthy and evocative description, he recorded the publication of this armour by Grose, and noted that 'This venerable relic of antiquity came originally from the Castle of Tong, in Shropshire, and was presented by the Rev. Mr. Buckridge to the Museum of the late Richard Green Esq. of Lichfield, from whence it was purchased by the present Proprietor.'[2]

Although Bullock had access to the original, it is obvious that he relied heavily on Grose for his own rendition. William Bullock evidently possessed a copy of Groses's *Treatise* (to which he refers more than once in the *Companion*), and indeed it was George's sole source for another helmet (no. 4b).

4b. Helmet

Painted ceramic.
36.5 × 38 cm. Diameter of top: 28 cm.

Bullock based the design for this helmet on an engraving by J. Hamilton in Grose's *Treatise* (*see* fig. 21), described as 'Plate IV. Taken from the

Fig. 21. Designs for helmets including (12) that from the Great Seal of Edward I, engraved by Hamilton, 1785, and published by Grose, 1786, Plate 9, see fig. 20 above.

NOTES
1) Alan Berg, 'A crusader in borrowed armour', *Country Life*, 18th July 1974, pp.168-169; Thom Richardson, 'The Tong Crusader', *Country Life*, 2nd April 1987, pp.98-99.
2) William Bullock, *A Companion to the Liverpool Museums*, sixth edition, Hull, 1808, pp.86-87. The same account appears in earlier editions.

Great Seals of the following Kings and ancient Barons . . . Fig. 12. King Edward I. from Sandford.'

4c. Helmet

Painted ceramic.
28.5 × 23.8 × 44 cm.

This represents an Italian burgonet of c.1550.

4d. Helmet

Painted ceramic.
62.5 × 41 33.5 cm.

The inspiration for this visored helmet is purely heraldic, with no real basis in life. There is also a larger version of it (73.5 × 49 × 36.5cm.).

4e. Breastplate

Painted ceramic with gilt details.
37.5 × 31.5 × 16.3 cm.

Derived from a mid-17th century English(?) model.

4f. Round shield

Painted pine.
19 (depth without support) × 39.5 cm. (diameter)

This is a copy of a Tudor Welsh buckler[1], which, like the Tong helmet (see no. 4a), was acquired by William Bullock from the collection of Richard Greene. While in the Lichfield Museum, it was published in Grose's *Treatise*, Plate 34, Fig. 1 and described as 'A concave Roundel, in the collection

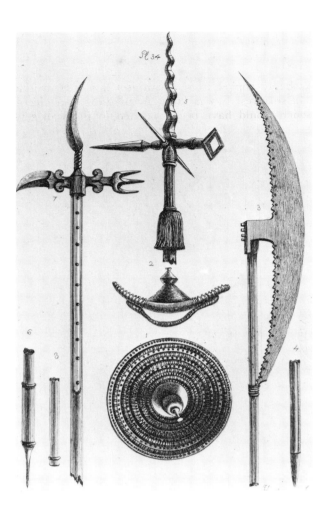

Fig. 22. A 'Welsh Buckler' (1 and 2) with other arms, engraved by Hamilton, 1785, and published by Grose, 1786, Plate 34, see fig. 20 above.

of Mr. Green of Lichfield, Staffordshire, to whom I am obliged for the drawing.' William Bullock illustrated it in the frontispiece to the sixth edition of the *Companion to the Liverpool Museum*, 1808, and identified it as 'A ROUNDEL, RONDACHE, OR NORMAN SHIELD' (see fig. 22). This no doubt accounts for George Bullock's arrangement of the present shield with the 'Tong helmet' (no. 4a), the prototype for which was also thought to be Norman, in the hall at Cholmondeley (see fig. 18).

NOTE
1) Ifor Edwards and Claude Blair, 'Welsh bucklers', *Antiquaries Journal*, vol. LXII (1982), pp.74-115); this example listed no. 7 on p.104.

4g. Shield

Painted pine.
91.5 × 43.5 × 3.1 (depth excluding support).

The design invented. The front carved with a Latin cross.

4h. Lance

92.5 cm.

Probably copied from a carousel lance. Only one half survives. It was probably made in two pieces, which would have been attached to the wall separately and concealed behind one of the shields.

4i. Spear

Pine.
263 × 7.7 cm.

Copy of a 16th-century partisan.

4j. Shield

Painted pine.
68.5 × 39.8 × 6 cm.

The design invented. The three wheatsheaves on the front are probably intended for the arms of Randolph de Blundeville (or Blondeville), Earl of Chester (died 1232).[1]

NOTE
1) Information kindly supplied by Michael Maclagan, *Richmond Herald*.

5. Speke Hall

In 1795, Speke Hall, one of the great 16th-century timbered houses of Lancashire, was acquired by Richard Watt (died 1796), a Liverpool merchant in the Jamaican trade. He bought the house from Charles George Beauclerk, whose family had inherited it from its builders, the Norris family. Watt's acquisition of the much decayed Hall marked a turning point in its fortunes. His nephew, also Richard Watt, inherited Speke and had begun its refurbishment by 1809. In that year he paid £231.4s.11½d, to Matthew Gregson (1749-1824), the Liverpool upholsterer and cabinet-maker, for 'sundries for Speke', which were presumably among the items later included in the 1812 sale (*see below*). Watt made several other purchases from Gregson but there is no indication as to whether these were for Speke or for Bishop Burton, his house in Yorkshire.[1]

It was probably in 1811 that Bullock was called in to undertake the first of several programmes of antiquarian refurbishment which were such a feature of Speke in the 19th century. Richard Watt's death in 1812 brought this first campaign to an abrupt end and the contents of the house were sold in a three-day sale, announced with characteristic flourish in the *Liverpool Mercury* on 14th August 1812 (p.53, col. 4):

'EXCELLENT FURNITURE ON SALE

The last week in August, or the first week in September, of which timely notice will be given. The whole of the FURNITURE of that ancient Mansion SPEKE HALL, and of that admired large Antique Baronial Hall, the Furniture of which is quite new, and but just finished in great taste, and never has been used.

A very eminent Artist and Architect has been called in to assist Mr. Geo. Bullock, and to restore and furnish this ancient British Hall, suitable to the style of the Building and Baronial Costume of former times. This Hall stands an unrivalled specimen (on this side of the country) of the chivalry of our ancient gentry and their grandeur. The walls of the Hall are decorated with the spoils of war, brought from the Royal Palace of Scone, in Scotland, and taken from thence at the same time the Coronation Stone was carried to Westminster Abbey (after the battle of Flodden Field) by Sir Edward Norris, 1513, when under the Earl of Surrey. Sir Edward Stanley and Sir William Molineux, of Sefton, and the owner of this mansion commanding the Lancashire Archers, and their tenantry, came in timely aid to turn the fate of the day, to the honour of themselves and the Lancasterians.

The furniture of the HALL is comprised in a large set of curious Oak Dining Tables, with a Sideboard to correspond in a grand novel style, and a large Sarcophagus with Bronzed Ornaments of peculiar beauty and Design, Gothic Lamps, suspended from the ceiling, and elegant Candelabra, with Patent Lamps, Antique Fire Dog (admirable design) light elegant Armed Oak Chairs, Stuff Backs, covered with crimson and black, Antique Couch, Crimson Curtains, and Cushions round the seats of the Hall, Footstools, &c. &c.

Designed after much study and attention to suit the Antique Costume in true Baronial Magnificence, has been executed by, and under the direction of Mr. GEORGE BULLOCK.

Together with a large Assemblage of *useful* Bed Room, Eating Parlour, and Drawing-Room Furniture, both *convenient* and *valuable*, of the best quality and construction: comprised in handsome Four-post and Tent Beds, with Morine and other Hangings, very *choice seasoned* Goose Feather Beds, Mattresses, Blankets, Counterpanes, Cabinet Work, in Wardrobes, Chests of Drawers, a set of excellent Telescope Dining Tables, and Mahogany Chairs, a Drawing Room Suit of Chairs, black and gold, new Turkey Carpets, Brussels and best Scots Carpets, and a Collection of most excellent Kitchen Utensils and Braziery Goods, of superior workmanship, and other useful Requisites; as will be expressed in the Catalogue, which may be had FOUR DAYS before the sale.

And to prevent the intrusion of improper Company, no person can be admitted to view or sale without a Catalogue, which may then be had at

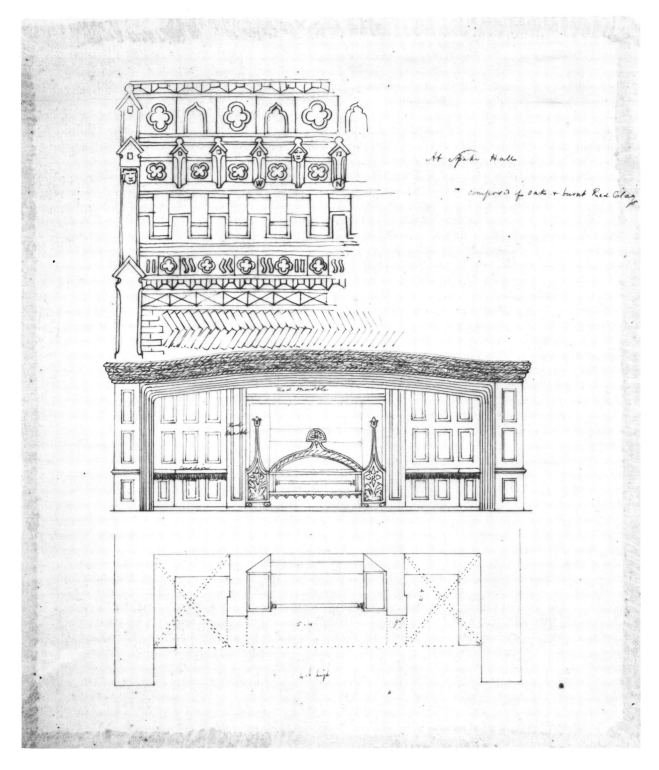

At Speke Hall

composed of oak + burnt Red Clay

Red Marble

Fig. 23. Design for chimneypiece in the Great Hall at Speke, Wilkinson Tracings, p.164. (City Museums and Art Gallery, Birmingham.)

One Shilling each, to be returned to Purchasers at the Sale, from
Mr. MATTHEW GREGSON, Paradise-Street,
Liverpool, Aug. 6, 1812.'

None of the lots auctioned by Richard Walthew on 1st-3rd September 1812 can now be traced. The sale catalogue does not differentiate Bullock's contribution from Gregson's or that of other cabinet-makers.

The identity of the 'eminent artist and architect' mentioned in the advertisement as Bullock's helper cannot now be ascertained. One possible candidate

is Joseph Gandy, with whom he had recently been in partnership (*see* no. 88).

How much of the house was refurbished by Bullock is now uncertain. Undoubtedly, his outstanding contribution was the repair of the Great Hall. Richard Watt II (died 1855) wrote from Bishop Burton, Yorkshire, on 15th December 1827 to William Robert Whatton of Manchester:

'In answer to your enquiries respecting the wainscot at Speke, I am sorry I can give no satisfactory information, having no writings in my possession that throw the least light on the question. Ever since I can remember, it has been said that the wainscot was brought from the palace of Holyrood by Sir Edward Norres, after the battle of Flodden; but this rests entirely on tradition as far as I know. The large carved panels, in common with the rest of the wainscot in the hall, were much broken and defaced, one half of them being split down the middle and taken out. They were renewed, as well as I can recollect, with some sort of composition when the room was restored, fourteen or fifteen years since, under the directions of the late Mr. Bullock of Liverpool; but very many among them are quite perfect. With respect to the library, there were no books at Speke since it came into my family. The interior of the house was very much destroyed by the people (farmers and others) that the Beauclerk family allowed to live there; all the tapestry and an inlaid oak floor belonging to what is called the stucco parlour being taken to

pieces, the one for firewood and the other for horse sheets, as I have always been told.'[2]

An examination of the Hall panelling confirms the accuracy of Watt's letter, for the panels have been extensively repaired. Many of the low-relief figures have had new heads and clothes added in 'composition'. Bullock's *tour de force*, however, was a very ambitious new 'Gothic' overmantel complete with the initials 'WN' for William Norris, the man thought to have built Speke. Although some authorities have regarded this piece as genuine 16th century,[3] the documentary evidence points to its being Bullock's own invention. The relevant *Wilkinson Tracing* (p.164; here fig. 23) is sufficiently different from the overmantel to make it clear that it records a design for, and not a drawing after. For instance, the top register pattern of niche/quatrefoil/niche of the tracing is reversed in the overmantel to quatrefoil/niche/quatrefoil. The next register down in the tracing has only one crocket with a head but this register as executed has every crocket with a head. Possibly the drawing 'Chimney Piece, at Speke Hall', which Richard Bridgens (listed as 'at Mr. Bullock's') showed at the Liverpool Academy in 1811 (number 229), was the design for this splendid new invention.

Speke Hall, coming between Bullock's more decorative Gothic work at Cholmondeley Castle and his later work for Walter Scott, reveals him not only as a sensitive conservator, but also a decorator with a flair for creating a powerful, romantic historical atmosphere much in tune with the sensibilities of his generation.

NOTES
1) Liverpool Public Library, Gregson Papers, 920 GRE 1/27,

Ledger, f.1476. Information kindly supplied by Mrs. June Dean, 1987.
2) 'An inquiry into the probability of a tradition connected with the library and furniture of James IV of Scotland, and of their having been carried off after the battle of Flodden, and set up at Speke Hall, in the County of Lancaster, *Archaeologia Scotica*', Vol. IV, *Transactions of the Society of Antiquaries of Scotland*, p.9.
3) Richard Haslam, 'Speke Hall', *Country Life*, 23rd April 1987, p.99.

6. *Pair of cabinets*

Ebony veneer and mouldings with brass inlay.
99 × 103.7 × 53.2 cm.

Bullock apparently had connections with William Roscoe from at least as early as 1803 (*see* no. 62), and was described in 1808 (by Thomas Johnes of Hafod) as his protegé.[1] The two men were both involved in the establishment of the Liverpool Academy in 1810, Bullock as President and Roscoe as Treasurer. Roscoe evidently set great store by these cabinets, and in the catalogue of the 1816 Roscoe sale Bullock's authorship was noted: 'A

beautiful Cabinet of Ebony, inlaid with Brass, with four Doors, and Divisions for Drawings, and Drawers above and below for Medals, &c; made by Mr. George Bullock.'[2] They were later among the furniture of his sitting room at 180 Lodge Lane, Toxteth Park, which his son described as it was around 1827:

'The . . . Apartment was one which he had fitted up for his own use, and which bore in every part of it the marks of his peculiar tastes . . . On each side of the fire-place stood an ebony cabinet, manufactured from wood presented to him by one of his sons, and containing a few drawings and prints, chiefly the portraits of his friends, together with the drawings belonging to his botanical work.'[3]

These very plain cabinets, although not recorded before 1816, presumably date from Bullock's Liverpool career. They also indicate an early date for a cabinet of very similar form (*see* fig. 24), veneered in rosewood and mahogany: more conventional Regency woods than ebony, although unconventionally treated, with partly bleached

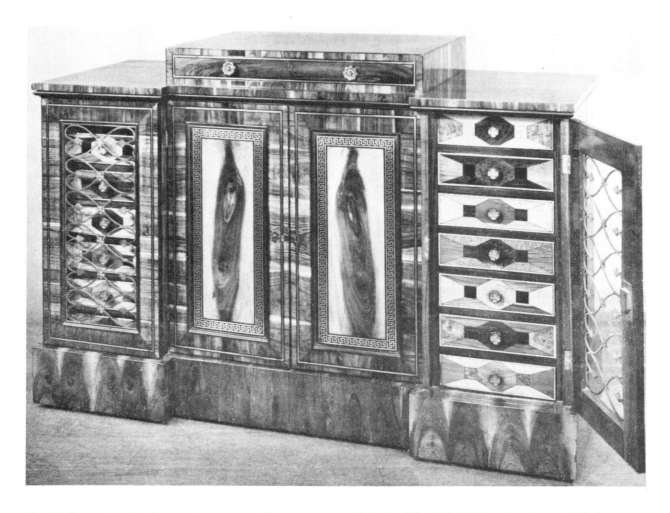

Fig. 24. Rosewood and mahogany cabinet, stamped G. Bullock *on each of the drawer-fronts; whereabouts unknown.*

mahogany door-panels. This cabinet is reported to have been stamped *G. Bullock* on each of the drawer fronts, the only piece known to have been identified by him in this manner.[4] The Greek key inlay seen on this and the Roscoe cabinets recurs on the base of no. 7. The same basic design, though slightly more elaborated, is to be seen in nos. 40 and 41. *See also* no. 61.

NOTES
1) Liverpool Public Library, Roscoe Papers, 920 Ros. 2223; letter from Thomas Johnes to William Roscoe, 1st March 1808.
2) The drawer 'below' is in the centre section of the plinth.
3) Henry Roscoe, *The Life of William Roscoe*, London, 1833, Vol. II, pp.378-379. A watercolour, 'William Roscoe's Study', after Samuel Austin, which is in the Walker Art Gallery's collection (inv. no. 2520), shows the room as Henry Roscoe describes it. One of these cabinets is clearly intended by the piece shown on the near side of the fireplace (the other is out of sight), but it has been radically misunderstood (presumably in the copying of Austin's original). *See* Edward Morris, *Early English Drawings and Watercolours*, Walker Art Gallery, Liverpool, 1968, no. 8 (as inv. no. 2250).
4) Brian Reade, *Regency Antiques*, 1953, p.63 (plate 60) and p.101. The cabinet's present whereabouts are unknown. *See also Country Life*, CLXXXI, 2nd July 1987, p.2000.

Provenance: William Roscoe, Allerton Hall; sale of his drawings and pictures, Winstanley, Liverpool, 23rd-27th September 1816,

4th day, lots 633 and 634 (withdrawn), and later at 180 Lodge Lane, Toxteth; one cabinet bequeathed to the Walker Art Gallery by Mrs. A.M. Roscoe, 1950 (WAG 3449); the other purchased from Mr. John Roscoe, 1961 (WAG 6100).

National Museums and Galleries on Merseyside (Walker Art Gallery).

Exhibited at Blairman's and Sudley (one cabinet each)

7. *Stand*

Ebonised beech with brass inlay and ormolu mounts; specimen marble top.
85 × 71.4 cm.

In Bullock & Co.'s account to the Duke of Atholl for work done between 1814 and 1819, the first item, against the date 3rd November 1814, is:

'An Ebony stand enriched with inlaid Brass and Bronze ornaments for specimens of marble . . .   18.18'[1]

This presumably refers to the present stand, despite the somewhat inaccurate recollection (five years on) of the materials used in its manufacture.[2] The Greek key pattern inlay on the base was also used in the ebony cabinets made for William Roscoe (no. 6). The feet are similar to those (executed in

perhaps not too fanciful to see an allusion to the three Legs of Man (which are still incorporated in the present Duke's arms) on the table's tripod support. The formal foliate inlay in the top is found on a straight line rather than a curve in the *Wilkinson Tracings* (p.137). *See also* no. 37 for an undocumented table of similar form.

painted metal) on ·the wine cooler supplied by Bullock for Napoleon's dining-room at Longwood House, St. Helena, now in the Russell-Cotes Art Gallery, Bournemouth (*see* fig. 8); and also to several that occur in the *Wilkinson Tracings* (for example, p.31; here fig. 31). *See also* no. 49.

NOTES
1) Blair Castle Charter Room, Bundle 699.
2) It was first identified as such in Anthony Coleridge, 'The Work of George Bullock, cabinet-maker, in Scotland: 1', *The Connoisseur*, April 1965, p.249, Fig. 1.

Provenance: made in 1814 for John, 4th Duke of Atholl, at Blair Castle, Perthshire; by descent to the present owner.

Lent by His Grace the Duke of Atholl, Blair Castle, Perthshire.

Exhibited at Sudley

8. *Tripod table*

Bog oak with brass inlay and ormolu mounts.
70.7 × 74.7 cm (diameter).

Together with no. 7, this table was itemised in the Bullock account under the date 3rd November 1814: 'A Circular table of Bog oak from the Isle of Man enriched with inlaid Brass . . .'[1]

Manx bog oak held particular significance for the Duke of Atholl, whose ancestors had been Lords of Man since the 15th century. In 1765 his parents had relinquished their sovereignty but he had personally fought to re-establish through Parliament his manorial rights in the Island.[2] It is

NOTES
1) Blair Castle Charter Room, Bundle 699; first published in Anthony Coleridge, 'The Work of George Bullock, cabinet-maker, in Scotland: 1', *The Connoisseur*, April 1965, Fig. 2. Also on 3rd November 1814, Bullock supplied 'A Work Table of Bog oak enriched with inlaid Brass, blue velvet bag' for £14.14s (*see* Coleridge, as above, Fig. 3).
2) Hannah Ann Bullock, *History of the Isle of Man*, London, 1816, pp.140-146 and 192-200. The author was the wife of Stanley Bullock of the Hague Farm on the Isle of Man, who was imprisoned for debt in 1812 (*Manx Advertiser*, 25th August 1810, 11th June 1812, 14th May 1818; *Isle of Man Gazette*, 9th December 1812. Information kindly supplied by Ann Harrison, Manx Museum & National Trust.) From 1817 to 1819/20, Stanley Bullock appears in the London trade directories as a wine merchant. No connection with George Bullock has been established.

Provenance: Made in 1814 for John 4th Duke of Atholl at Blair Castle, Perthshire; by descent to the present owner.
Lent by His Grace the Duke of Atholl, Blair Castle, Perthshire.

Exhibited at Sudley

9. *Pair of cabinets*

Larchwood, ebony and ebonised wood with brass inlay and ormolu mounts; Glen Tilt marble tops.
110 × 154.8 (and 155.8) × 52.8 cm.

These cabinets, which with nos. 7 and 8 were

is used for all the black wood parts, with the possible exception of the hidden bands of veneer behind the columns.[2] The running mechanism of the drawers on channelled side-grooves shows a most unusual reversion to 17th-century techniques: possibly a conscious revival, as the use of oyster veneers on the door-panels may be also.

Like the bog oak used for no. 8, the materials incorporated in these cabinets had personal associations for the 'Planting Duke' of Atholl, the larchwood being taken from his eponymous plantations, and the marble from his local quarries at Glen Tilt. Bullock also provided other larchwood furniture to the Duke, of which two circular tables and a sofa-table, together with three larchwood snuffboxes, remain at Blair. The letter he wrote to his patron on 8th December 1817 about one of the snuffboxes (*see* no. 9A) is an illuminating record of their shared interest in indigenous materials.

Bullock was presumably referring to the present pieces when he noted in the same letter that 'the Cabinets for Dunkeld are proceeding with a[s] expeditiously as the wood will permit.'[3] On

among the earliest rediscoveries of Bullock's furniture,[1] represent the grandest production of his workshop. The use of larchwood extends to the carcase (for the back and sides), while the doors and drawer linings are of mahogany and the interior is finished with Bullock's characteristic all-over dark stain. On the outside real ebony

Fig. 25. Larchwood and ebony cabinet, with Glen Tilt marble top. (Fitzwilliam Museum, Cambridge.)

11th January 1818, he wrote again: 'I hope to have the Cabinets and Table in a state of forwardness by the time your Grace arrives in Town.'[4] They were itemised in the firm's account (sent to the Duke after Bullock's death) against the date 12th February 1819:

'2 Larch wood Cabinets very richly
ornamented and inlaid with Brass
handsome Brass wreath moulding
round the Top . . . 60 £ . . .   120.--

Sawing Landing working & polishing 2
Glen Tilt marble slabs for do 18.1 @ 12/-
sent to Mr. J. Drummonds[5]   10.17-

At the end of the bill, however, are noted:

Deductions
off of two cabinets to be charged
40 Gins each instead of 60 £ . . .   36. 0. 0.[6]

The implication that the Duke disputed the charge is probably explained by an earlier entry in the same account, dated 12th July 1817, for a single cabinet, proportionally much cheaper than the pair:

'A Cabinet with Drawers of Larch wood
the panels of Door of Brass and ebony
two columns enriched with Brass
ornaments and Brass wreath
moulding round the Top . . .   45 - -

A slab of Glentilt marble at top . . . 6.2 @ 12/- 3.14.-'[7]

The single cabinet does not survive with the pair at Blair, but should almost certainly be identified with a smaller cabinet (87.6 × 120 × 46 cm) in the Fitzwilliam Museum, which is made of the same materials, uniquely indicative of the Duke of Atholl (*see* fig. 25).[8] This identification has hitherto seemed doubtful, because of an apparent discrepancy in the dimensions, but this is due to a misinterpretation of the figures in the bill. The dimensions of the marble slabs cannot be taken for the width of the tops on either the pair or the single cabinet: they may indicate the surface area of the amount of marble required to cut the slabs.[9]

The Blair cabinets are thoroughly documented in the *Wilkinson Tracings*, with designs for the foliate inlay pattern on both the frieze and the door panels (pp.150 and 153 and duplicates for both, unbound numbers 251 and 214), the floral ornament on the bottom edges of the doors (p.121), the pattern at top and bottom of the columns (p.145 and an unbound duplicate, number 219), and the ormolu border to the top (p.126); as well as several variations on this cabinet-model, with its peculiarly distinctive plinth (pp.68, 79, 101, 102, for example). The *Tracings* also include the design for the Fitzwilliam cabinet (p.86; here fig. 26), surmounted by a pier glass (which was not supplied with the Duke of Atholl's cabinet), and two records of the pattern on its doors (one p.99; here fig. 12; the other, unbound number 219; here fig. 47) which is inscribed 'For Mrs Barrons [Barrows?] Oak Book Commode Pub.ᵈ Aug.ᵗ 1816.'. Almost exactly the same angle mounts as those used here and on numerous other Bullock cabinets are depicted in the plate of 'Grecian Furniture' from Bullock's showroom, published in Ackermann's *Repository of*

Arts for May 1816, and the inlaid frieze pattern is used there as the border for the curtains; the same inlay pattern is also indicated in Bullock's design for 'An English Bed', published by Ackermann in November of the same year.

Among other furniture of related form and ornament are the closely contemporary cabinets made for the Marquess of Abercorn (no. 23), a cabinet formerly in Queen Mary's possession at Marlborough House,[10] and a remarkable sideboard in an American private collection, which is nearly identical to a design in the *Wilkinson Tracings* (p.89).[11] An untraced cabinet of the same basic model as the Blair group had plain quasi-Tuscan columns of marble (or serpentine or scagliola?) in place of the familiar carved and mounted 'Persic pillars';[12] similar columns of serpentine appear on another comparable sideboard (also authenticated in the *Tracings*, p.95), formerly at Wateringbury Place.[13]

NOTES

1) Anthony Coleridge, 'The Work of George Bullock, cabinet-maker, in Scotland: 1', *The Connoisseur*, April 1965, Figs. 4 and 5. *See also* E.T. Joy, *English Furniture 1800-1851*, 1977, pp.167-169.
2) The woods have kindly been identified by Mr. George McIntosh at Blair Castle. Mr. Robert Williams at the Fitzwilliam Museum has also identified pine in the base of the related cabinet there and mahogany as its principal carcase-wood.
3) Blair Castle Charter Room, 68(7)319. Letter from George Bullock, London, 8th December 1817, to the Duke of Atholl.
4) Blair Castle Charter Room, 68(8)4. Letter from George Bullock, 4 Tenterden Street, Hanover Square, London, 11th January 1818, to the Duke of Atholl.
5) Blair Castle Charter Room, Bundle 699. James Drummond was married to a daughter of the 4th Duke, Amelia Sophia, but it is not known whether they lived at Dunkeld at this time. Among the purchasers at the Bullock Sale, 1819, were 'Drummond' (1st day, lots 59 and 70) and 'Cap. Drummond' (2nd day, lot 101; 3rd day, lot 10).
6) Blair Castle Charter Room, Bundle 699. Further deductions were also made on all the marble and larchwood supplied by the Duke for Bullock's use.

Fig. 26. Design for a cabinet and looking glass, front and side elevations and plan of plinth, Wilkinson Tracings, p.86. (City Museums and Art Gallery, Birmingham.)

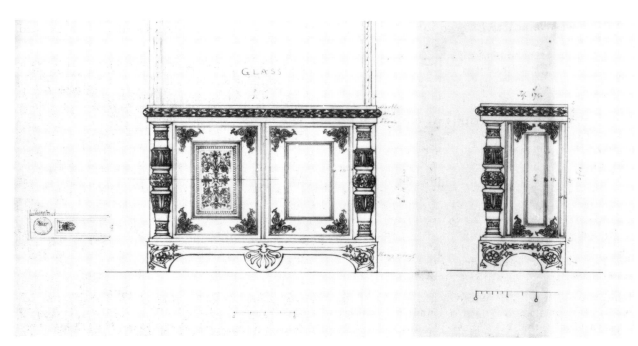

7) Blair Castle Charter Room, Bundle 699.

8) This suggestion was first made by E.T. Joy, in 'Identifying a Regency Cabinet', *Country Life*, 21st August 1980, pp.646-668.

9) The bill seems to imply that the marble was charged at 12 shillings per square foot. However the actual surface area in each case is slightly less than is indicated by the figure in the bill, which suggests that the Duke was expected to pay for the wastage in sawing the slabs. The same principle was apparently applied in the bill for one of the cabinets from Great Tew (Tew Park sale, Christie's, 27th-29th May 1987, lot 35).

10) Marlborough House sale, Christie's, 1st-2nd October 1959, lot 45, bought by Shafloe for £231; later sold by Sotheby's, 28th February 1969, lot 144. *See* J.F. Hayward, 'Documented English Furniture', *Art at Auction 1968-69*, London, 1969, pp.428-429, illustrated.

11) Helena Hayward (ed.), *World Furniture*, 1965, Fig. 768.

12) F. Lewis Hinckley, *A Directory of Antique Furniture*, New York, 1953, p.217, No. 671.

13) Wateringbury Place sale, Christie's, on the premises, 1st June 1978, lot 527; this piece reputedly came from Blenheim Palace.

Provenance: Made in 1817-18 for John, 4th Duke of Atholl, originally for Dunkeld, Perthshire; Blair Castle, Perthshire; by descent to the present owner.

Lent by His Grace the Duke of Atholl, Blair Castle, Perthshire.

Exhibited at Blairman's and Sudley (one cabinet each)

9A. Snuffbox
by George Bullock and Rundell, Bridge & Rundell

Larchwood with gilt lining.
2.8 (height) × 9.9 cm. (diameter).
Inscribed inside the base with the arms of the Duke of Atholl, and in the lid:

This
BOX
was made from a Larch Tree
102 FEET HIGH
12 FEET IN CIRCUMFERENCE
OF 79 YEARS GROWTH
and contained 252 feet of Timber
it was cut at BLAIR Augt 21ˢᵗ 1817
and
sent to his Majesty's
Dock yard
at
Woolwich

This is the grandest of three surviving larchwood snuffboxes at Blair Castle. The others are presumably those invoiced by Bullock and Co. against the date 17th March 1818: '2 Larch wood snuff boxes . . . 5/- - 10 -'. No other snuffbox is recorded in the bill, and it is possible that the present example was a gift from Bullock to the Duke. Its design and manufacture are recorded in two letters written by Bullock to his patron, the first of which, dated 8th December 1817, from London, epitomises the character of their interest in British woods, with its odour of faintly contrived patriotism:

'I have turnd several snuf Boxes one of the handsomest of which I have sent to Rundell & Bridge to put a Gold lining in it they have promised that

it shall be finished in about a Week or ten days, on the lid inside I propose to have engraved a description of the Tree as shewn on the Card given to me by your Grace any *further* account I shall be happy to add that your Grace may be pleased to favour me with. I flatter myself that this Box independent of the peculiar intrest it must have with all those connected with its growth cannot fail to be hereafter thought a Great curiosity as being made from a Wood first used in the *Kingdom* for the purposes of its Navy.'[1]

Bullock wrote again from '4 Tenterden street Hanover Square/London 11ᵗʰ Janʸ 1818':

' "Rundell and Bridge" sent home the larch snuff Box yesterday . . . I immediately forwarded it, to the Duchess, who thought it had better not be sent to Scotland, as your Grace would be in town so soon; it will therefore be reserved with the others until I have the Honour of seeing your Grace in London.'[2]

This correspondence suggests that Bullock had

an established working relationship with Rundell, Bridge and Rundell. Edmund Rundell, the nephew of Philip Rundell and himself a partner in the firm, is recorded as a patron of Bullock's by two designs for marquetry in the *Wilkinson Tracings*, unbound no. 233, which is inscribed 'for Mr Rundell', and unbound number 252, which is inscribed 'Ed^m Rundell Esqr/Oak Cabinet's Novr 30 1816.'

NOTES
1) Blair Castle Charter Room, 68(7)319
2) As above, 68(8)4.

Provenance: made in 1817-18 for the 4th Duke of Atholl; by descent to the present owner.

Lent by His Grace the Duke of Atholl, Blair Castle.

Exhibited at Sudley

10. *Pair of cabinets*

Oak and ebony veneers with ebonised detailing.
Brass and ormolu inlays and embellishments.
Mona Marble slabs.
99 × 136 × 58 cm.

The design for the inlaid thyrsus panel to the canted sides appears in the *Wilkinson Tracings* (unbound number 221; here fig. 27). A comparably entwined thyrsus with a different central motif is on another cabinet (*see* no. 41). These cabinets display several of the decorative elements employed by Bullock on his grandest furniture. The pattern running horizontally above each foot is one of the most frequent borders on his finest furniture and was apparently in use as early as 1809-10, for it is incorporated in two doors remaining at Storrs Hall which were presumably supplied to John Bolton by the Bullock-Gandy partnership (*see* no. 88). It appears, for example, on nos. 16, 23, 41 and 49. Similar corner mounts can be seen again on the doors of nos. 9, 23, 41 and 43, whilst the brass grilles feature on nos. 39, 40 and 41. The combination of veneers on these cabinets closely resembles the effect of marble and harmonises perfectly with the Mona *verde antico* tops. The inlaid feet, a grander version of those on no. 43, are executed in *première* and *contre-partie* marquetry, on the first and second cabinets respectively, echoing the style of cabinet work at the time of André-Charles Boulle.

A similar use of canted or 'octagon' corners can

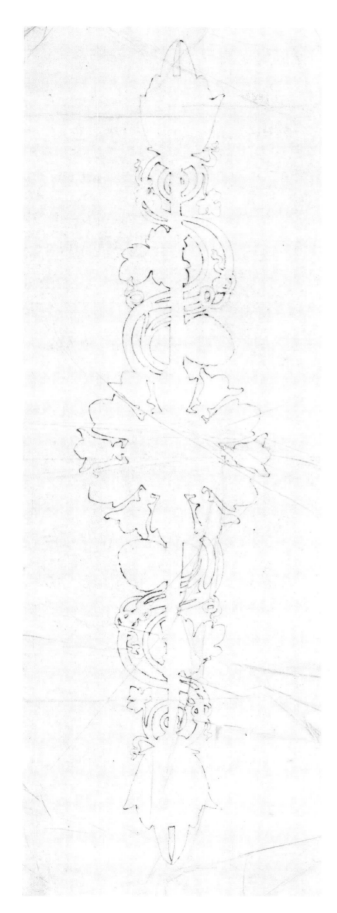

Fig. 27. Design for the marquetry on the corners of a cabinet (no. 10), Wilkinson Tracings, *unbound number 221. (City Museums and Art Gallery, Birmingham.)*

be seen on a cabinet which was originally part of Napoleon's furniture on St Helena.[1]

This exhibit, as well as no. 11, forms part of a magnificent suite made for the Duke of Palmella, several times Portuguese ambassador in London. Palmella was involved in William Beckford's circle and was, by all accounts, a prominent figure in London society.

NOTE
1) E.L. Jackson, *St Helena*, London, 1903, illustration opposite p.224.

Provenance: Don Pedro de Souza e Holstein, 1st Duke of Palmella; by descent to the Visconde de Torrão; sold from Rua do Sacramento a Laga, 24, Lisbon, by Silva's – on the premises 27th-29th April 1987, lot 483; sold Christie's, 25th June 1987, lot 181.

National Museums and Galleries on Merseyside (Walker Art Gallery) – bought with the assistance of the National Art Collections Fund (Eugene Cremetti Fund).

Exhibited at Blairman's and Sudley (one cabinet each)

11. *Pair of candelabra*

Oak veneers and ebonised detailing with applied gilt-gesso embellishments. Cut-glass and silvered metal.
206 cm (height).

A variety of imposing candelabra were included in the Bullock Sale, 1819,[1] and described in the catalogue. Other examples appear in the *Wilkinson Tracings* (pp.110-119), in particular a tracing (on p.118) that shows an inverted lotus with stylised flowers which can be compared to the section joining the shaft and base on no. 11. Another tracing (on p.117; here fig. 28) shows a similar arrangement of candle arms with glass pendants around the plateau. The present examples demonstrate an interesting use of a palmette at the base of the shafts where, more conventionally, one might expect acanthus. This same feature can be seen on the lamp stand illustrated in the plate entitled 'Grecian Furniture' in Ackermann's *Repository*, May 1816 (*see* no. 56). Candelabra of this form, deriving ultimately (via Piranesi) from classical models, were popular vehicles for lighting in the early 19th century. A pair is illustrated in a watercolour by Wild of the Ante-Chamber to the Throne Room at Carlton House.[2] A further example was published (anonymously) in Ackermann's *Repository*,[3] whilst others were designed by Charles Percier and some were made by Pierre-Philippe Thomire.[4]

NOTES
1) Christie's, 3rd-5th May 1819, e.g. 2nd day, lots 30 and 35, and 3rd day, lots 36 and 89.
2) David Watkin, *The Royal Interiors of Regency England*, 1984, p.109.

3) Pauline Agius and Stephen Jones, *Ackermann's Regency Furniture and Interiors*, 1984, p.73, ill. no. 44
4) *La Luminaire*, Paris, n.d., plates XIX and XXVIII.

Provenance: Don Pedro de Souza e Holstein, 1st Duke of Palmella; by descent to the Visconde de Torrão; sold from Rua do Sacramento a Laga 24, Lisbon, by Silva's – on the premises 27th-29th April 1987, lot 478 or 492; sold Christie's, 25th June 1987, lot 178. (Another identical pair was included in the same sale, lot 177.)

Lent by the Board of Trustees of the Victoria & Albert Museum.

Exhibited at Blairman's

12. Two chairs

Oak, painted and parcel gilt. Gilt brass.
101 × 47 × 53.5 cm.

The backs of these chairs bear the crest of the Webster family: 'dragon's head, couped regardant quarterly per fess embattled (vert and or) flames issuing from mouth'. The design for these chairs,

probably by Richard Bridgens, appears in the *Wilkinson Tracings* (p.7) and in *Furniture with candelabra*[1]. It was also illustrated in Ackermann's *Repository* in September 1817 where it was said to be 'for a suite of rooms in the Gothic style' (*see* no. 56).

NOTE
1) Richard Bridgens, *Furniture with candelabra*, 1838 edition, plate 43.

Provenance: Sir Godfey Vassal Webster, Battle Abbey; sold by the Trustees of the Battle Abbey Settled Estates, Christie's, 23rd October 1980, lot 91.

Lent by the Board of Trustees of the Victoria & Albert Museum and the City Museum and Art Gallery, Birmingham (one chair each).

Exhibited at Blairman's (V. & A. chair) and Sudley (Birmingham chair)

Above: *Fig. 28. Design for a candelabrum,* Wilkinson Tracings, *p.117. (City Museums and Art Gallery, Birmingham.)*

Left: *No. 11. Pair of candelabra.*

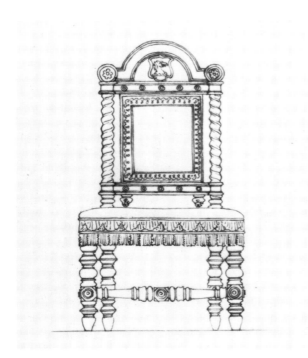

Fig. 29. *Design for a chair (no. 12),* Wilkinson Tracings, *p.7. (City Museums and Art Gallery, Birmingham.)*

Below: Fig. 30. *'The State Chair' from Battle Abbey, from* A Handbook to Battle and its Abbey, *1860. (National Art Library, Victoria & Albert Museum.)*

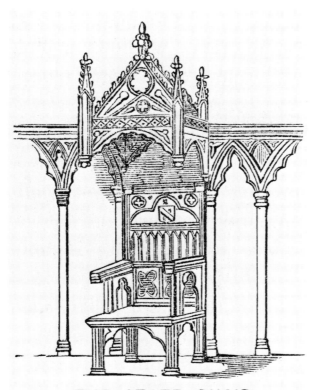

THE STATE CHAIR.

13. State chair

Oak.
178 × 76 × 58.5 cm.

This chair was designed to stand on a dais under an elaborate canopy in the Great Hall at Battle Abbey (*see* fig. 30) and by tradition is made from the timbers of the Mediaeval Hall which Sir Godfrey Webster demolished and replaced with his New Great Hall. It shared the Hall with an enormous painting by F.W. Wilkin of the discovery of Harold's body on the battlefield at Hastings. The antiquarian character of the chair is very much in keeping with the work carried out by Bullock at Cholmondeley and by Bullock and Bridgens at Abbotsford. No designs for it exist, but it forms such a crucial part of the whole Bullock and Bridgens scheme for the Great Hall at Battle that its design may reasonably be attributed to them and most probably to Bridgens himself.

Provenance: Sir Godfrey Vassal Webster, Battle Abbey; the Trustees of the Battle Abbey Settled Estates; Christie's, 23rd October 1980, lot 93 (unsold).

Lent by the Board of Trustees of the Victoria & Albert Museum.

Exhibited at Sudley

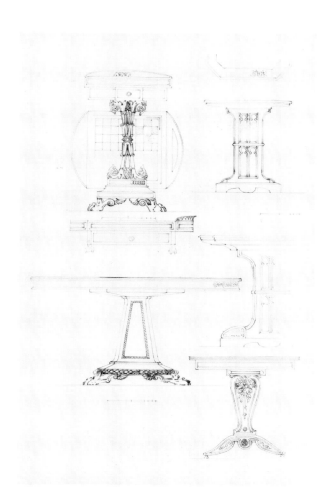

14. Library table

Oak, inlaid with ebony.
77 × 183 × 120.8 cm.

This table, probably designed by Richard Bridgens, was supplied for Battle Abbey c.1817[1]. A close variant of the table exists in a private collection in London, and two versions are illustrated in the *Wilkinson Tracings* (p.31; here fig. 31). At Scone Palace, Perthshire, the Earl of Mansfield has a table with the same base as this exhibit, and a top in burr elm, inlaid with brass and ebony.[2] A neo-classical version of these tables was sold by Christie's on 29th June 1978 (lot 46). *See also* no. 35.

NOTES
1) Martin Levy, 'George Bullock: Some Sources for Identifying his Furniture', *Apollo*, June 1987, Fig. 9.
2) Illustrated in Anthony Coleridge, 'The Work of George Bullock, cabinet-maker, in Scotland: 2', *The Connoisseur*, May 1965, No. 11.

Provenance: Sir Godfrey Vassal Webster, Battle Abbey; sold by the Trustees of the Battle Abbey Settled Estates, Christie's, 23rd October 1980, lot 96.

Lent by the Board of Trustees of the Victoria & Albert Museum.

Exhibited at Sudley

Above: *Fig. 31. Designs for tables*, Wilkinson Tracings, *p.31. (City Museums and Art Gallery, Birmingham.)*

Below: *No. 14. Library table.*

15. Dwarf cabinet

Yew, gilt brass. Plaster.
101.6 × 76.2 × 43.2 cm.

This cabinet was largely designed by J.B.S. Morritt, a close friend of Sir Walter Scott and a noted classical scholar, and was certainly made in Bullock's workshop from yew grown in Morritt's estate at Rokeby in Yorkshire. The plaster cast of Shakespeare's monument at Stratford was taken by Bullock himself (*see* no. 67). In a letter to Morritt

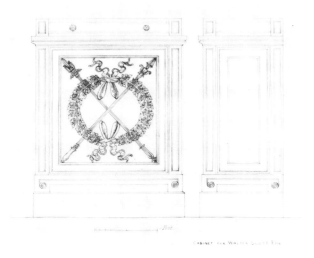

Fig. 32. Design for a cabinet (no. 15), inscribed 'Cabinet for Walter Scott Esq.', Wilkinson Tracings, p.85. (City Museums and Art Gallery, Birmingham.)

16. Stand

Yew, mahogany, ormolu, marble.
92.3 cm (height); top: 64.8 × 64.8 cm.

The *Wilkinson Tracings* (p.107) include a design for a stand made specifically for the silver urn presented by Byron to Sir Walter Scott. The elaborate

dated 22nd November 1816 Scott describes the sensation caused in Edinburgh by the unpacking of the bust and cabinet.[1]

The design for this cabinet appears in the *Wilkinson Tracings* (p.85; here fig. 32). It was originally intended to stand in the niche at the end of the library at Abbotsford. It is presumed that the thyrsii were turned upside down to commemorate Scott's death.

NOTE
1) Clive Wainwright, 'Walter Scott and the furnishing of Abbotsford', *The Connoisseur*, January 1977, Nos. 12 and 14.

Provenance: Sir Walter Scott, Abbotsford; by descent.

Lent by Mrs. Patricia Maxwell-Scott.

Exhibited at Blairman's

classical urn contains ancient bones found in Greece by Byron, and it is appropriately inscribed by both Byron and Scott. A Scott letter of November 1816 records the arrival of the stand and the urn at Abbotsford and mentions that the stand was made by Bullock.[1] The urn survived at Abbotsford, but the stand left the house earlier this century. The design for this stand was identified in the *Wilkinson Tracings* in 1977[2], and the stand itself was discovered in 1981 when it was purchased for Abbotsford by the Faculty of Advocates of Scotland with the help of the National Art Collections Fund.[3] Whether or not it is the one that was originally at Abbotsford has not yet been firmly established.

NOTES
1) Gervase Jackson-Stops (ed.), *The Treasure Houses of Britain*, 1985, p.592.
2) Clive Wainwright, 'Walter Scott and the furnishing of Abbotsford', *The Connoisseur*, January 1977, No. 14.
3) *National Art Collections Fund Annual Report*, 1981, No. 2902.

Provenance: London art market 1981.

Lent by Mrs Patricia Maxwell-Scott.

Exhibited at Blairman's

17. *Four chairs*

Oak.
88.9 × 55.9 × 66 cm.

Four oak dining chairs from the set of twelve made for Abbotsford. The design is in the Victoria & Albert Museum.[1] The correspondence between Sir Walter Scott and Daniel Terry in June 1818 just after Bullock's death makes it clear that these chairs were designed by William Atkinson, but that Richard Bridgens was also involved; the surviving design is probably a finished drawing in Bridgens's hand. The chairs were made in the summer of 1818 in the Bullock workshop after Bullock's death, under the supervision of Atkinson and Bridgens. Their simple and yet sophisticated design and solid, straightforward construction sets them apart from any other Gothic Revival chairs of their date and establishes Atkinson as a furniture designer of importance.

NOTE
1) Clive Wainwright, 'Walter Scott and the furnishing of Abbotsford', *The Connoisseur*, January 1977, Nos. 5 and 6.

Provenance: Sir Walter Scott, Abbotsford; by descent.

Lent by Mrs Patricia Maxwell-Scott.

Exhibited at Blairman's and Sudley (two chairs each)

18. *Sofa*

Mahogany, ebony inlay, ebonised detailing and lacquered metal mounts.
87.6 × 202.4 × 94 cm.

The sofa bears a label stating that it was brought back by Sir Hudson Lowe from St Helena where it had been used by Napoleon. It was part of the furnishings commissioned in 1815, at the instruction of the Prince Regent, for Napoleon's use on St Helena. An announcement, 'House and Furniture for Buonaparte', in *The London Packet; and Lloyds Evening Post* (23rd-25th October 1815) mentions 'two Grecian sofas' for the drawing room.

In the *Lowe Papers*, folio 214, 'Drawing Room for St Helena Nov. 1816' (*see* fig. 34), shows two sofas like this one; folio 212, 'Breakfast Room for St Helena Nov 1815 No 4' (*see* fig. 43), shows another example; and there are a further three shown on other sheets, which may have been slightly less elaborate.

An identical sofa to this exhibit can be seen at Bois-Préau, Malmaison, near Paris, where it forms part of a display representing Napoleon's exile on St Helena. Plate XII of Richard Brown's *Rudiments of Drawing Cabinet and Upholstery Furniture*, 1822, illustrates a sofa of the same design (*see* fig. 33). At least three similar sofas are at Tabley House, which was the Cheshire property of Sir John Leicester (1762-1827). An elaborate, brass inlaid and ormolu mounted sofa with the same front supports to the arms as this, formerly belonging to the 1st Duke of Palmella, was sold by Christie's (25th June 1987, lot 174, illustrated).

Provenance: Napoleon I, St Helena; Sir Hudson Lowe; sold by his

Below: *Fig. 33. Design for a sofa, from Richard Brown,* Rudiments of Drawing Cabinet and Upholstery

Furniture, *London, 1822, Plate XII. (Thomas Heneage.)* Above: *No. 18. Sofa.*

PLATE XII.

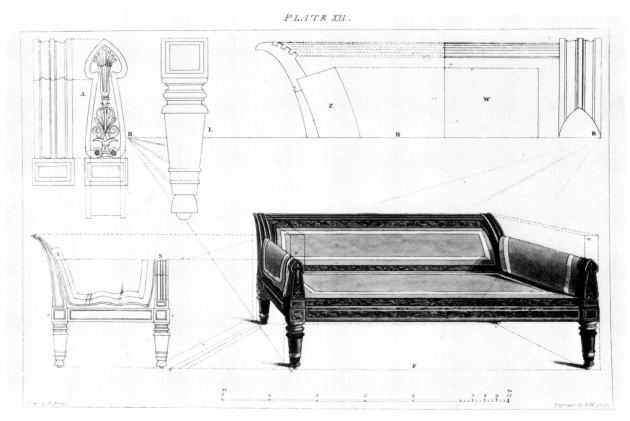

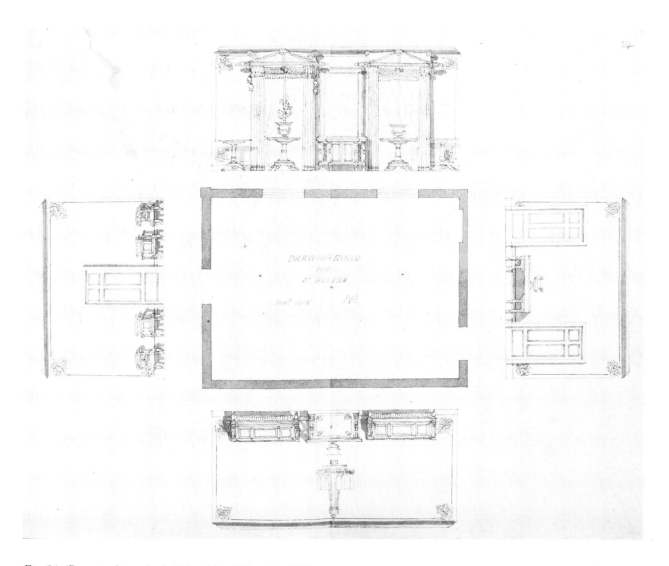

Fig. 34. 'Drawing Room for St Helena' dated November 1815, plan and elevations. (British Library, Add. Mss. 20, 222, Lowe Papers, folio 214.)

executors c.1855; private collection; 'Rathbone' c.1896; Lt. General Kent.

Lent from a private collection.

Exhibited at Blairman's

19. Table

Oak and oak veneer, ebony inlay and ebonised detailing. Brass feet, mounts and inlay.
76.2 × 91.4 cm.

This table must have been part of the furnishings supplied for Napoleon's use on St Helena. Like the sofa (no. 18), it bears a label describing its history and stating that it was brought back to England by Sir Hudson Lowe.

A closely related octagonal table (with a badly split top) was sold by a 'Midwestern Museum' at

Christie's, New York, 26th June 1982, lot 92 (illustrated). Another example, possibly in rosewood, was sold by Bonham's, London, 2nd October 1986, lot 102 (illustrated). This group of tables are all

raised on four short sabre legs issuing from a concave-sided plateau – embellished with inlaid lines and roundels. All the tables carry their tops on thick turned columns, which taper towards the top. A circular table with a similar base was sold by Christie's at the Tew Park sale, 27th-29th May 1987, lot 33 (illustrated). A table at Scone Palace, Perthshire, has a similar, though more elaborate, base.[1]

NOTE
1) Anthony Coleridge, 'The Work of George Bullock, cabinet-maker, in Scotland: 2', *The Connoisseur*, May 1965, No. 9.

Provenance: Napoleon I, St Helena; Sir Hudson Lowe; Sir W. Gordon, 1824; later in the possession of Lord Lee.

Lent from a private collection.

Exhibited at Blairman's

20. Pair of armchairs

Mahogany with ebonised detailing. Brass castors. 87.6 × 63.5 × 55.8 cm.

These chairs bear labels stating that they were used by Napoleon in the Library at Longwood. They formed part of the furnishings provided by the British government, and a pair of chairs of this model can be seen in the elevation for the library in New Longwood House that appears in the *Lowe Papers* (folio 220). However another pair of the same model appears on the elevations for the breakfast room (folio 212; here fig. 43), the drawing room (folio 214; here fig. 34) and the dining room (folio 216; here fig. 8).

Provenance: Napoleon I, St Helena; probably acquired by the 5th Earl of Rosebery (Prime Minister and author of *Napoleon: The Last Phase*, A.L. Humphreys, 1900); by descent.

Lent from the collection of the Earl of Rosebery at Dalmeny House, Edinburgh.

Exhibited at Blairman's and Sudley (one chair each)

Opposite: *No. 20. Armchair.*   Below: *No. 21. Armchair.*

21. Armchair

Ebonised beech, parcel gilt. Brass.
83.8 × 63.5 × 58.4 cm.

Like the pair of chairs now at Dalmeny (no. 20), this chair bears a label confirming that it was once in the possession of Napoleon. It subsequently belonged to Lady Bingham, wife of Major General Sir George Bingham who sailed to St Helena with Napoleon on the *Northumberland* in 1815. Little ebonised beech furniture by Bullock has been discovered so far, however there is another fine chair, with inlaid brass and ormolu embellishments at Bois-Préau, Malmaison[1] (*see* fig. 9). It was also formerly part of Napoleon's furnishings on St Helena. A variant of this exhibit and no. 20 appears in the *Wilkinson Tracings* (p.5; here fig. 50), where it has the same laurel wreath to the back as the chair in fig. 9.

There is a chair identical to the one at Bois Préau

that remains at Longwood House, St Helena – now the residence of the French Consul. A chair of this design is also shown in the 'Marchand' engraving (*see* fig. 7), Five chairs of closely related form, also in ebonised beech, were sold by Sotheby's New York, 1st October 1983, lot 422 (illustrated).

NOTE
1) This chair, originally part of a larger set, corresponds with those shown in designs among the *Lowe Papers* (*see* figs. 8 and 30).

Provenance: Napoleon I, St Helena; Major General Sir George Bingham; Emma, Lady Bingham; by descent from her nephew, Lt. Col. G.P. Mansel to the present owners.

Lent by Major and Mrs John Mansel.

Exhibited at Blairman's

22. Sofa table

Oak and oak veneer, ebonised detailing. Brass.
69.8 × 152.4 (width when open) × 68.6 cm.

The design for the decoration inlaid into the legs of this table appears in the *Wilkinson Tracings* (unbound number 234); it is inscribed 'For Mrs Ferguson's table April 1817'. The border around the top of the table also appears in the *Wilkinson Tracings* (unbound number 212; here fig. 42) and has been identified on several other pieces of documented Bullock furniture (*see* no. 35). The overall form of this sofa table closely resembles one also invoiced 1817 to M.R. Boulton for Tew Park.[1] The Tew table is raised on arched legs with the same inlaid pattern. Both tables are supported by four 'turned standard columns' (as described on several sofa tables in the catalogue of the Bullock Sale, 1819.) Another version of this arrangement of columns can be seen on the rosewood table sold by Christie's, 29th June 1978, lot 46, illustrated. A further example, in mahogany (with fixed top inlaid in satinwood) with the same patterns to the top and legs as the present table is in an English private collection. An oak sofa table of similar form to no. 22 exists in a private collection.[2]

The particular shape of the supports for the flaps and also the type of turned stretchers with horizontal fluting to the centre can be seen on other Bullock sofa tables, including no. 48.

NOTES
1) Tew Park sale, Christie's, 27th-29th May 1987, lot 34, illustrated.
2) Sold by Christie's, 19th November 1987, lot 46, illustrated.

Provenance: Mrs Robert Ferguson, c.1817; by descent to the present owners.

Lent from a private collection.

Exhibited at Blairman's

23. Pair of cabinets

Ebonised rosewood and ebony veneer with brass
inlay and ormolu mounts; green Mona Marble
slabs and scagliola panels.
92.4 × 109.2 × 63.5 cm and
92.7 × 109.5 × 63.5 cm.
The scagliola panels are inscribed:
1681/Laurentius/Bonuccelli Fe: and *1681/Laurentius
Bonuccelli/Fecit*

This pair of cabinets is documented by a design in
the *Wilkinson Tracings* (unbound number 237) for
the boulle marquetry pattern on the doors, which
appears in *première-* and *contre-partie* on the first and

*Fig. 35. Design for the marquetry on the doors
of a cabinet (no. 23), inscribed 'for* Lord Abercorn's
Cabinet G. Bullock, May 1817', Wilkinson Tracings,
*unbound number 237. (City Museums and Art Gallery,
Birmingham.)*

second cabinets respectively. The design is inscribed 'for/Lord Abercorn's/Cabinet [sic] G Bullock, May 1817' and also bears the unidentified initials WH found in reverse on several other *Tracings*. However, this design (*see* fig. 35) is unique in bearing Bullock's name.

The cabinets are shown in a watercolour, dating from 1848, of the drawing room (or saloon) at Bentley Priory where they stand either side of a grand Regency cabinet and a full-length portrait, apparently that of the 1st Marquess (1756-1818) by Sir Thomas Lawrence, which remains at Barons Court.[1] This was presumably the house, and indeed the position, for which the cabinets were originally made: Bentley Priory, which had been altered by Soane in the period 1788-98, was again enlarged by Robert Smirke between 1810 and 1818 (the only house where Lord Abercorn was engaged in architectural improvements at the relevant date.)[2]. This presumption is endorsed by an entry in the monthly account book for the Priory and London, in the account for November 1817:

'Bullock draping Aber deens & Knights
Busts £28 Tables 103 £161.19'[3] (*see* nos. 70 and 71).

No Bullock tables have been traced from this commission; nor has any other Bullock item been found in the Abercorn accounts, so it is possible that the 'tables' referred to are in fact the present pieces: £103 compares very plausibly with the charge for the Blair Atholl cabinets (*see* no. 9). The cabinets probably remained at Bentley Priory until at least 1869 when the 1st Duke of Abercorn bought Hampden House in Mayfair, and they can be identified in an inventory of the latter house

taken in 1875.[4]

Although Lord Abercorn apparently employed Bullock only at Bentley Priory, he should be seen in the context of the circle of Scottish clients that Bullock so successfully cultivated. At Duddingston House, Sir William Chambers's masterpiece near Edinburgh, Lord Abercorn was a neighbour of Sir Walter Scott, and may well have been introduced by him to Bullock, who was working at Abbotsford in the same period (*see* nos. 15-17). Scott was a friend of the Marquess and a regular correspondent of Lady Abercorn; he stayed at the Priory on at least one occasion, and remarked more than once on the improvements taking place there.[5]

The present cabinets were evidently made in order to show off the two Italian scagliola slabs by Lorenzo Bonuccelli, depicting subjects from Ovid's *Metamorphoses:* The Rape of Europa and Mercury and Argus.

Bonuccelli also signed the scagliola table top showing four hands of cards, a late 17th-century watch, and a 17th-century musical score from Callaly Castle – sold by Christie's, on the premises, 22nd-24th September 1986, lot 117 – and he may have been responsible for a group of similar table tops inlaid with playing cards, which includes two set into late 17th-century table frames at Wilton.

The paramount importance of the Abercorn slabs, however, lies in their pictorial landscape scenes and brilliant colour, achieved fifty years before the activities of Don Enrico Hugford, who has hitherto been credited with developing the Italian scagliola technique to make such naturalism possible.[6] Bullock's interest in rare materials

and virtuoso techniques, attested by the 'curious mosaic, inlaid and marble tables' he displayed for sale as early as 1805, suggests that he might have procured these slabs himself; but they are otherwise most likely to have been brought back from the Grand Tour, perhaps that of the 8th Earl of Abercorn (1712-89), the Marquess's uncle.

These cabinets bear an obvious relationship to the group associated with the pair from Blair Castle, especially to the almost exactly contemporary one in the Fitzwilliam Museum (fig. 25; *see* no. 9). But with only detailed variations in the formal design, Bullock has achieved totally different effects by his masterly use of contrasting materials: on the Fitzwilliam piece the qualities of the larchwood and Glen Tilt marble are brought out by a relatively sparing use of brass and ebony, while the all-over black and gold scheme of the present pieces makes a superb setting for the jewel-like scagliola panels. The effect is enhanced by the 'counterpoint' Bullock has introduced between the two cabinets, using *première*- and *contre-partie* inlay alternately on the columns as well as on the doors.

The design for the marquetry on the doors, already referred to (*see* fig. 35), also appears in another version in the *Wilkinson Tracings* (p.154), 'doubled-up' to show the whole of the boulle pattern for one panel; the *Tracings* also include a slightly variant design for the inlaid pattern on the columns (unbound number 205). The inlay patterns on the frieze and the moulding above appear on much of the Palmella suite and on numerous other pieces (*see* nos. 10 and 36). On the present cabinets the frieze pattern runs out from the centre in both directions, preserving their perfect symmetry.

NOTES
1) The watercolour, now at Barons Court, is inscribed in the bottom left corner, 'Drawing Room – the Priory'; the date is possibly concealed under the mount, which is in turn labelled 'The Saloon, Bentley Priory, Stanmore, 1848.'
2) Howard Colvin, *Dictionary of British Architects 1600-1840*, London, 1978, pp.769, 744. J.M. Gandy, Bullock's partner in 1809-10, made several drawings of Bentley Priory (including interior views of the hall), all of which probably date from c.1798-1800 when he was working for Soane, and are not related to Bullock's commission in 1817 (*see* Pierre de la Ruffinière du Prey, *Catalogues of Architectural Drawings: Sir John Soane*, Victoria & Albert Museum, London, 1985, no. 212).
Barons Court, built by George Steuart, 1779-81, had also been enlarged by Soane, 1791-95 (Colvin, *see* note 2 above, pp.781, 769; *Country Life*, 12th, 19th and 26th July 1979, pp.86-89, 162-165, 232-235); while Duddingston House, built by Chambers in 1763 for the 8th Earl, was not materially altered by the 1st Marquess (David Walker, 'Duddingston House, Edinburgh', *Country Life*, 24th September 1959, pp.358-361).
3) Public Record Office of Northern Ireland, Abercorn Papers, D623/C/17/11 (unpaginated). The monthly accounts for the period 31st October- 29th November 1817, also list, among 'Extra Bills', 'Bullocks Bill 161.19' (Abercorn Papers, D623/C/17/24), but the bill itself does not apparently survive.
4) Abercorn Papers D623/D/11/5, 'Inventory of . . . Hampden House, Green Street, Park Lane. The Property of His Grace the Duke of Abercorn. August 1875 . . .' p.80. The house had previously been inventoried with the contents purchased in 1869 (Abercorn Papers, D623/D/11/3).
5) H.J.C. Grierson (ed.), *The Letters of Sir Walter Scott*, 1937, Vol. XII,

pp.99-102 (to Mrs. Scott, from the Priory, 30th March 1807); Vol. II (1932), p.378 (to Lady Abercorn, 30th September 1810); Vol. IV (1933), p.308 (to Lady Abercorn, 29th November [1816]). Scott's father (also Walter) had been agent to the 8th Earl on the Duddingston estates; his brother Tom, who inherited this position under the 1st Marquess, grossly mismanaged the latter's affairs and was extricated from the resulting crisis by Scott himself.
6) *See* John Fleming, 'The Hugfords of Florence (Part 1),' *The Connoisseur*, October 1955, pp.106-110; Hugh Honour, 'Scagliola for Georgian Homes,' *Country Life*, 22nd June 1967, pp.1627-1630. It has been long-established, however, that pictorial scagliola was being produced in South Germany from the early 17th century (Erwin Neumann, 'Materialien zur Geschichte der Scagliola', *Jahrbuch der Kunsthistorischen Sammlungen in Wien* 55 (1959), pp.75-158, especially pp.127-144).

Provenance: Made for John James, 9th Earl and 1st Marquess of Abercorn, 1817, probably for Bentley Priory, Stanmore, Middlesex, where the cabinets remained in 1848; Hampden House, Park lane, 1875; thence by descent to the present owner.

Lent by His Grace the Duke of Abercorn, Barons Court, Co. Tyrone.

Exhibited at Sudley

24. *Inkstand*

Ebonised mahogany with ebony and inlaid ivory. Ormolu and glass.
9.5 × 41 × 22 cm.

This is described in a bill which now forms part of

Fig. 36. Designs for two inkstands, Wilkinson Tracings, *p.123. (City Museums and Art Gallery, Birmingham.)*

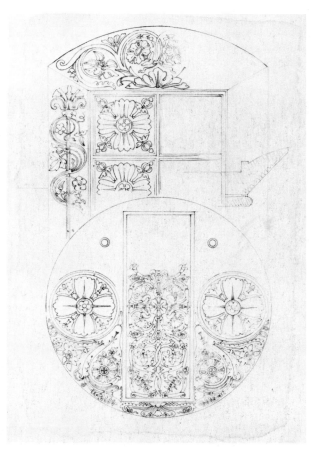

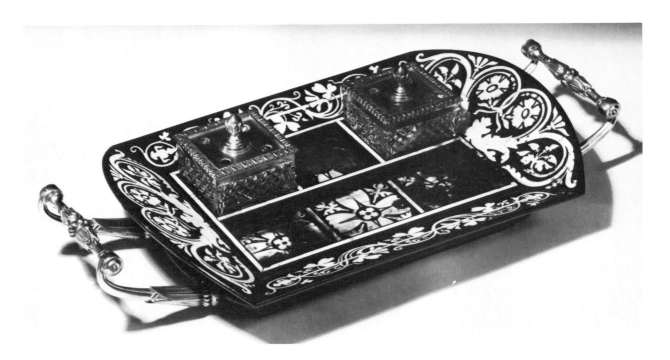

the Tew Archive as 'An inkstand richly inlaid of Ivory and Ebony with Brass handles £12'. It was invoiced by Bullock to M.R. Boulton in 1817.

There are no fewer than four designs relating to this inkstand in the *Wilkinson Tracings* (p.123 and unbound numbers 241, 242 and 249; *see* figs. 36-39), of which three are full-scale patterns for the inlay. The detail of the end (unbound number 249) is inscribed 'for Inkstand Mr Boulton' and to the centre with the letters HW which occur else-where in the tracings (sometimes reversed). Were these perhaps the initials of a draughtsman in the workshop? The design for the sides (unbound number 241) is inscribed 'for Ink Stand 1817'. There were several lots in the catalogue of the Bullock Sale, 1819, described as 'tray-shaped inkstand' with various different finishes; their overall form probably resembled the present example.

A rosewood and brass *contre-partie* inkstand of very similar form and decoration to this one was sold on the London art market in July 1987. It was designed without the carrying handles and lacked the glass bottles.

Provenance: Matthew Robinson Boulton, Tew Park; sold Christie's Tew Park sale, 27th-29th May 1987, lot 13.

National Museums and Galleries on Merseyside (Walker Art Gallery).

Exhibited at Sudley

*Fig. 37 (*left*) and Fig. 38 (*below*). Designs for details of inkstand (no. 24),* Wilkinson Tracings, *unbound numbers 242b and 249 respectively. (City Museums and Art Gallery, Birmingham.)*

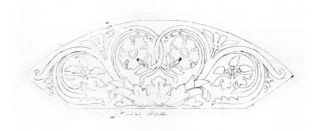

25. Sofa

Oak and holly.
85.2 × 198 × 82 cm.

Two identical sofas were invoiced by Bullock to M.R. Boulton at Tew Park in 1817. One was for the Library and the other for the Drawing Room; both are described in a bill in the Tew Archive. That for the Library was '1 Oak Sofa richly inlaid with Holly french stuf'd & covered with Green twillid Calico welted with yellow Velvet with Cushions &c. £32.10s.' The one in the Drawing Room is described as '1 Oak Sofa french stuffed and covered with Pink imbos[d] milled Calico welted with Brown Velvet with Cushions &c. £32.10s.'

As was customary at this period, both sofas were supplied with loose covers and these are fully itemised in the bill. For the Library sofa there was:

1 Loose case for Sofa of Brown Calico

16. Y. Brown Calico	2/6	2 ----
37. Black Silk Galloon	-/5	- 15 5
Thread Cutting & making		1 4 -

1 Jeranium Damask Do. for Do.

16 Y. Chintz	5/9	4 12-
16 " White Calico	1/6	1 4 -
37 " Galloon	/5	- 15 5
Thread. Cutting & making 1 12 -'		

For the Drawing Room sofa there was:

1. Loose Case for Do. of Brown Calico as Library	3.19.5
1. Do. of Damask Chintz as Do.	8. 3.5.

It is not possible to deduce which room the exhibited sofa came from, but both examples were included in the Christie's Tew Park sale, 27th-29th May 1987.

A watercolour of the Morning Room at Tew Park, dated 1849, is preserved in the Tew Archive (and was illustrated in the Tew Park sale catalogue, p.22). It shows one of the two sofas as well as other Bullock furniture, including one of the two pairs of fire screens (*see* no. 26).

There is a design for a sofa of the Tew Park model in the *Wilkinson Tracings* (p.67). Unlike the details for the inkstand (no. 24) and the small cabinet (on p.82 of the *Tracings*), the design for the sofa is not inscribed with Boulton's name. A sofa of similar form is illustrated on p.59 of the *Tracings*, and other close variants appear in elevations of rooms such as Battle Abbey on p.75; another appears on p.73.

Provenance: Matthew Robinson Boulton, Tew Park; sold at Christie's Tew Park sale, 27th-29th May, 1987, lot 11. (The other, identical sofa was included in the same sale, lot 32.)

Lent from a private collection.

Exhibited at Sudley

26. *Pair of firescreens*

Oak and holly veneers with gilded beech. Brass.
160.8 cm.

Two pairs of firescreens were invoiced by Bullock to M.R. Boulton in 1817.[1] Those for the Library were itemised as 'Two Oak fire Screens inlaid with Holly & fluted in Green Sarsnet £16', and those for the Drawing Room as '2 Oak Fire Screens inlaid with Holly with Mounts fluted in Pink Silk £16'. One pair with green silk, described as being from the Library, was sold at the Tew Park sale.[2] However, the appearance of the same green silk on one of this pair of firescreens makes it impossible to be certain which pair is which. These two have bases veneered in oak with the inlaid pattern in holly; the bases of the other pair were executed in *contre-partie*.

NOTES
1) Tew Archive, bill.
2) Tew Park sale, Christie's, 27th-29th May 1987, lot 10.

Provenance: Matthew Robinson Boulton, Tew Park, 1817; thence by descent to the present owner.

Lent from a private collection.

Exhibited at Sudley

27. *Four chairs*

Oak inlaid with holly.
83.8 × 48.3 × 50.2 cm.

The design for these chairs appears in the *Wilkinson Tracings* (p.5; here fig. 50). They are designed with a similarly deep rake to the back as those sold by Christie's from the Dining Room at Tew Park,[1] and are part of a set of sixteen chairs formerly in the same house. It is not possible positively to

Opposite: *No. 26. Pair of firescreens.*

identify these chairs in Bullock's account to M.R. Boulton, which records no other long suites apart from two sets of six oak chairs (apparently not inlaid), supplied for the Library and Drawing Room at a cost of £18.18. 0 per six.[2] However, the extensive correspondence[3] reveals that furniture was frequently swapped around, and it is possible that these chairs came to Tew during one of these changes. A further set of ten chairs of virtually the same design as these, but not from Tew Park, exist in a private collection.[4]

Bullock's use of dark, formalised inlays into pale wood on these chairs, and frequently elsewhere on his furniture, seems to anticipate the decoration on *bois clair* furniture so fashionable in France during the 1820s.

NOTES
1) Tew Park sale, Christie's, 27th-29th May 1987, lot 53.
2) Tew Archive, bill.
3) Tew Archive, correspondence.
4) Sold by Christie's, 19th November 1987, lot 90.

Provenance: Tew Park, probably Matthew Robinson Boulton; thence by descent to the present owner.

Lent from a private collection.

Exhibited at Blairman's and Sudley (two chairs each)

28. Commode-stool

Oak and holly. The white ceramic pot by Wedgwood (embossed mark) is original.
55 × 56 × 47 cm.

This stool is probably one of the seven 'Night stools' invoiced by Bullock to M.R. Boulton in 1817 at a cost of £4.10s. each.[1] Christie's sale at Tew Park[2] included two similar stools (lots 282 and 283), although this example was the only one with a pollarded oak, veneered top.

Stools of this design are illustrated on four separate sheets in the *Lowe Papers* showing 'Officers Bed room(s) for St Helena' (folios 226, 230, 234 and 240). A fifth, grander inlaid version is depicted in the 'Best Bedroom' (folio 224; here fig. 40). Another stool from Tew Park, with a veneered top as in this exhibit, was sold at Christie's, 8th October 1987, lot 46 (illustrated).

NOTES
1) Tew Archive, bill.
2) Clive Wainwright, 'Fame for the faceless man of the cabinet', *The Independent*, 30th May 1987.

Provenance: Matthew Robinson Boulton, Tew Park; sold Christie's, Tew Park sale, 27th-29th May 1987, lot 281.

National Museums and Galleries on Merseyside (Walker Art Gallery).

Exhibited at Sudley

29. Wardrobe

Oak and holly.
192 × 119.5 × 56 cm.

This wardrobe was probably one of the five in oak with holly mouldings invoiced by Bullock to M.R. Boulton in 1817 at a cost of £21 each.[1] Lots 270 and 271 at the Tew Park sale[2] were similar but

severely damaged examples of the same design. As with the commode-stool (no. 28), several wardrobes of this design (with the addition of finials) are illustrated in the *Lowe Papers* (*see* fig. 40).

Folio 234 in the *Lowe Papers* shows an 'Officer's Bedroom' and reveals other examples of bedroom furniture echoing pieces supplied to Tew Park, such as the pot-cupboard (lots 254 and 255)[3], the dressing table (lots 290-292), the toilet-mirror (lots 287-289) and the clothes-horses (lot 260).

NOTES
1) Tew Archive, bill.
2) Tew Park sale, Christie's, 27th-29th May 1987.
3) Lot 255 is now in the collection of the City Museums and Art Gallery, Birmingham.

Provenance: Matthew Robinson Boulton, Tew Park; sold Tew Park sale, Christie's, 27th-29th May 1987, lot 269.

Lent by the City Museums and Art Gallery, Birmingham.

Exhibited at Sudley

30. Chamber ware

Moulded earthenware with ochre glaze and orange decoration. Manufacturer unknown.

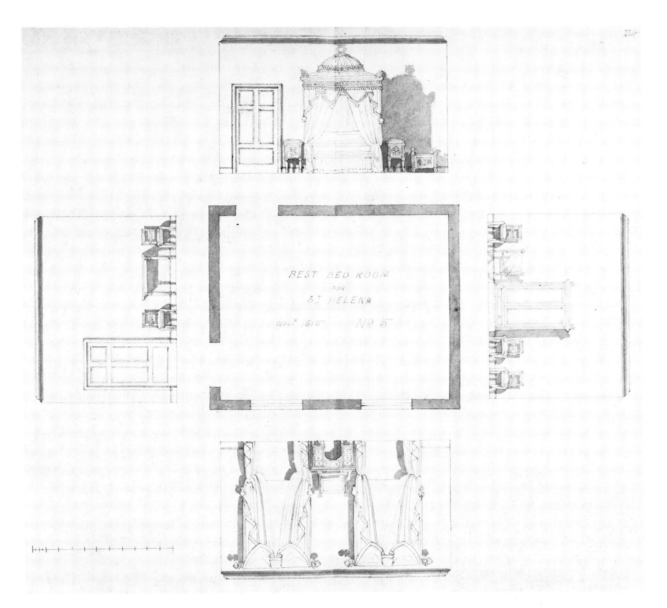

Fig. 40. 'Best Bed Room for St. Helena' dated November 1815. Plan and elevations. (British Library, Add. Mss. 20,222, Lowe Papers folio 224.)

Among the chamber ware that survives are the jug, two-handled bowl, soap dish and pair of toothbrush holders illustrated here. These may well be part of the several 'Chamber service(s) complete bordered' invoiced by Bullock to M.R. Boulton in 1817 at a cost of 3 guineas each, although other sets are also recorded in the same bill.[1] According to an inscription in an album in the Tew Archive, these ceramics were originally designed to be sent to Napoleon for use at Longwood, St Helena, but were not sent out because the decoration was thought too redolent of the victor's laurels.[2]

It is known that, in addition to making furniture for Napoleon, Bullock was also charged with the responsibility of supplying many other items for his household, including various ceramic services. *The London Packet; And Lloyd's Evening Post* in an article entitled 'House and Furniture for Buonaparte', 23rd-25th October 1815, reported, 'The table services have been provided by Mr. Bullock, from the most eminent manufacturers in the kingdom, and consist of the fairest, though not the most extravagent, specimens of our own proficiency in the various walks of mechanism and art.' *The Times* (24th October 1815), in an identically titled article, reported, ' . . . the breakfast service is of Wedgwood's most beautiful pale blue composition, with a white cameo relief, modelled by Flaxman . . . the dinner service is white and gold, the centre of each plate, dish etc containing an elegantly executed landscape of British scenery.' The description of this last service sounds like the work of the Derby factory. In addition to the above, there are parts of a tea service by Spode at Bois-Préau, Malmaison, which is said to have been used

by Napoleon on St Helena. From this evidence, it is clear that many different factories were engaged in supplying ceramics to Napoleon.

The unusually strong forms and bold decoration of the chamber ware suggest that they may have been designed by Bullock: they bear little resemblance to contemporary commercial productions. The jug and bowl illustrated in folio 234 of the *Lowe Papers* are a strong indication that Bullock participated in decisions concerning what form such pieces should take.

NOTES
1) Tew Archive, bill.
2) *See* the Tew Park sale catalogue, Christie's, 27th-29th May 1987, p.244.

Provenance: Matthew Robinson Boulton, Tew Park; sold Christie's Tew Park sale, 27th-29th May 1987, lots 690-697 (part).

Some pieces from National Museums and Galleries on Merseyside (Walker Art Gallery); others lent from various private collections.

Exhibited at Blairman's and Sudley (a selection at each)

31. *Two fenders*

Lacquered brass and steel.
25.5 (height excluding rests) × 150 × 43.2 cm.
19.8 (height excluding rests) × 134 × 48 cm.

The design of these fenders is attributed to Bullock on the grounds of stylistic parallels between the relief ornament and his familiar decorative motifs. In particular, the central flowerhead should be compared to that on the handle of the jug that forms part of the chamber service from Tew Park (*see* no. 30). Although no metal fire furniture was included in the 1817 Tew bill, these are not the only pieces from the house to bear the imprint of Bullock's design. Three basket grates in the Tew Park sale (lots 4, 27 and 48) were attributed to Bullock on the basis of an unsigned drawing in the Tew Archive, and this attribution is strengthened by some strikingly similar grates in another

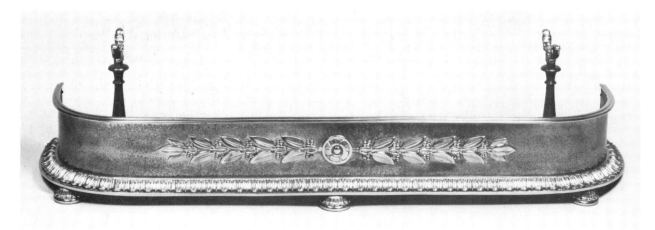

house with documented Bullock connections. The existence of a 'Brass Room' in his London workshop, together with a number of wooden moulds for brass work (*see* p. 50) demonstrates that Bullock was equipped to execute his metalwork designs, but it is possible that some of the heavier work was contracted out to a brass founder.

A few fenders were among items in the Bullock Sale, 1819; two were described as 'metal bronzed'.[2]

NOTES
1) *See* the Tew Park sale catalogue, Christie's, 27th-29th May 1987, pp.38-39 (lot 27 and the drawing illustrated).
2) Bullock Sale, Christie's, 3rd-5th May 1819, 1st day, lots 76 and 120.

Provenance: Probably Matthew Robinson Boulton; Tew Park sale, Christie's, 27th-29th May 1987, lots 5 and 973. One fender is in the collection of the National Museums and Galleries on Merseyside, Walker Art Gallery (bought with the assistance of the Merseyside Decorative and Fine Arts Society, South Liverpool Branch); the other has been lent from a private collection.

Exhibited at Blairman's and Sudley (one each)

32. Two boxes

Oak, ebony and various marbles.
10.2 × 55.8 × 49.5 cm (each).

These two boxes were perhaps made to contain workshop samples to help patrons select marble slabs for their furniture. In the catalogue of the Bullock Sale, 1819, lot 43 was described as 'A small square flat cabinet of variegated fine oak, inlaid and mounted with ebony, containing 3 trays in divisions, with 32 fine specimens of British marbles, lock and key'; lot 79 was 'A small square flat cabinet, inlaid with ebony, containing 9 beautiful specimens of Mona marbles, lock and key.' The boxes contain various specimens of British and some foreign marbles.

Provenance: Bullock Sale, Christie's, 3rd-5th May 1819, 1st day, lots 43 and 79, bought by 'Sir W.C.' and 'Sir W. Cumming', £5.5.0 each; by descent; London art market, 1985.

Lent from a private collection.

Exhibited at Blairman's and Sudley (one box each)

33. Table

Oak veneer with ebony inlays and ebonised detailing.
69.8 × 111.8 (diameter).

This table was among the large number of objects purchased by the Earl of Wemyss at the Bullock Sale, 1819. It was described in the catalogue as: 'A circular table of very scarce and finely veined oak, with running border of flowers and foliage, of ebony on massive triangular panelled stand, bronzed claw feet and castors, 3ft 8in diameter.'

The pattern for the inlaid border on the table appears in the *Wilkinson Tracings* (unbound number 208; here fig. 41). It was also used around the top

Fig. 41. Design for marquetry on table (no. 33), Wilkinson Tracings, *unbound number 208. (City Museums and Art Gallery, Birmingham.)*

of a table from Tew Park, which is of oak inlaid with holly.[1] Another oak and holly table (in an English private collection) has this pattern, with the addition of an inlaid 'beaded border' and an elaborate marquetry three-sided base raised on curled-under feet. Two mirror images of the border design can be seen in the *Wilkinson Tracings* (unbound numbers 206 and 232; 232 is inscribed 'FOR LADY SPENCER'S table' and dated 1818.)

The source for the form of this table is probably Plate 39 of Thomas Hope's *Household Furniture,* 1807, which shows a table from Duchess Street, now in the Victoria & Albert Museum.

NOTE
1) Christie's, Tew Park sale, 27th-29th May 1987, lot 33.

Provenance: Bullock Sale, Christie's, 3rd-5th May 1819, 1st day, lot 83, bought by 'E. of Whims' [Earl of Wemyss], £25.4.0d. By descent to the present owners.

Lent by the Earl of Wemyss and March and Lord Neidpath.

Exhibited at Blairman's

34. *Chimneypiece*

Mona Marble and ormolu.
101.6 × 99 cm.

This was described in the catalogue of the Bullock Sale, 1819, as 'A chimneypiece of Mona verd antique marble, of elegant design with pannelled pilasters and richly mounted Grecian capitals, and mouldings of or-moulu: opening, 3 feet 10 by 3 feet 6'; it was bought by 'Townley', presumably Peregrine Towneley.[1] The dimensions approximate to the width between the pilasters and the height from floor to architrave; so it is possible that the inner fillets of real(?) marble were procured and inserted after the sale. The chimneypiece now stands in the dining room at Towneley Hall, where Jeffry Wyatt was working on alterations between 1812 and c.1820.[2]

This chimneypiece closely resembles Bullock's design for a 'Chimneypiece of Mona Marble', published in Ackermann's *Repository*, January 1816

(*see* no. 56); both have identical ormolu capitals to the pilasters.

NOTES
1) 'Townley' was also the purchaser of lot 65 on the 3rd day of the sale, 'A Devonshire marble slab, damaged, 3ft. 8 by 2ft.' at 14s.
2) The compiler is grateful to Susan Bourne for providing this information.

Provenance: Bullock Sale, Christie's, 3rd-5th May 1819, 1st day, lot 108, bought by 'Townley,' £32.11s; Towneley Hall.

Reproduced by kind permission of Towneley Hall Art Gallery and Museums, Burnley Borough Council.

35. *Sofa table*

Rosewood with brass inlay and ormolu mounts.
70.6 × 172.5 × 91.3 cm.

This piece was described in the catalogue of the Bullock Sale, 1819, as 'A sofa table of rosewood, with octagonal ends and broad arabesque border of elegant design, inlaid with brass, supported on solid rosewood standards: also richly inlaid with devices in brass and mounted with or-moulu, 5ft. 8 by 3ft. wide.' Sir William Cumming, who bought it, was by far the largest purchaser at the sale, acquiring 78 of the 360 lots (a few of his purchases can be identified in the catalogue of the sale of Gordonstoun in 1948[1]). The deeply-chamfered 'octagonal' corners (which appear again on the

Fig. 42. Design for marquetry on sofa table (no. 35), Wilkinson Tracings, *unbound number 212. (City Museums and Art Gallery, Birmingham.)*

Palmella cabinets, *see* no. 10) were also a feature of several other tables described in the Bullock Sale. The design (template size) for the inlaid border pattern on the top of this table survives among the *Wilkinson Tracings* (unbound number 212; here fig. 42). It also appears in the frieze of an undocumented cabinet formerly in Queen Mary's possession,[2] and, in rosewood on brass, in the frieze of a fully-provenanced cabinet in a private collection.[3] The brass inlay pattern on the outside of the pedestal

ends, with engraved detail of the highest quality, is repeated in *contre-partie* on their inside faces, and echoed in a pedestal table (no. 50). The corbel-like ornaments at the feet find parallels on the malachite-topped table (no. 36), which is also identified from the 1819 sale, and on the unprovenanced dwarf bookcase (no. 42), where they are indeed used as corbels. Comparison between the present table and the library table from Battle Abbey (no. 14) shows how the same basic design could be superficially adjusted to suit the neoclassical or the Gothic taste.

NOTES
1) Anderson and England, Elgin, and Central Marts Ltd., Elgin,

24th August 1948.
2) Marlborough House sale, Christie's, 1st-2nd October 1959, lot 45.
3) An almost identical design appears in the *Wilkinson Tracings*, p.87 (front and side shown at bottom of page).

Provenance: Bullock Sale, Christie's, 3rd-5th May 1819, 2nd day, lot 34, bought by Sir W[illiam] C[umming], £31.10s.; by descent to the present owner.

Lent from a private collection.

Exhibited at Sudley

36. *Table*

Rosewood, ebony and tortoiseshell veneers.
Inlaid brass and ormolu mounts. Malachite top.
76 × 140 × 58 cm.

This table matches precisely the description of the one bought by 'Bentley' at the Bullock Sale, 1819: 'AN OBLONG TABLE of sumptuous Buhl manufacture, the top composed of an oval slab of VERY RARE and PRECIOUS MALACHITE, 4ft 2½″ × 1ft 5½″ in a border of ebony and tortoiseshell, inlaid with brass supported on rosewood standards, also splendidly inlaid with brass in rich arabesques and mounted with massive or-moulu, on castors.' At £85, this was the most expensive lot in the three-day sale. It is interesting to note that in the catalogue description the emphasis and dimensions are given to the malachite, reflecting contemporary interest in rare and precious stones.[1]

The brass inlaid border to the top, which is one of the simpler examples emanating from Bullock's workshop, is found on many pieces (including nos. 23, 48 and 51). The same border appears on several lots, originally made for the 1st Duke of Palmella (1781-1850), that were sold at Christie's, 25th June 1987. These include the footstool (lot 171), the sofa (lot 174), the display stand (lot 179) and the pier-glasses (lot 180), which are all illustrated in the sale catalogue. In addition the design has been seen incorporated into the decoration of several pieces of grand furniture probably supplied for the house where they remain. These include a magnificent low cabinet with ormolu heads at the top of the pilasters for which an almost identical design appears in the *Wilkinson Tracings* (p.87). The same pattern appears in ebony on an oak ground around the top of a sofa-table at Boughton, Northamptonshire.[2]

NOTES
1) Martin Levy, 'George Bullock: Some Sources for Identifying his Furniture', *Apollo*, June 1987, Fig. 4.
2) This table may well relate to either of two payments made to Bullock by the 4th Duke of Buccleuch through his account at Coutts, 23rd June 1813 and 16th November 1814 (information kindly provided by John Cornforth).

Provenance: Probably the Bullock Sale, Christie's, 3rd-5th May 1819, 2nd day, lot 63, bought by Bentley for £85; London art market, 1980.

Lent from a private collection.

Exhibited at Blairman's

37. *Tripod table*

Laburnum and rosewood veneers, oak with ebonised detailing. Brass inlay and feet. 72.5 × 75.5 cm (diameter).

This is a grander, though less elaborate, version of the table supplied to Blair Castle (no. 8). A pair of tables of the same design can be seen among the *Lowe Papers*, inscribed 'Drawing Room for St Helena, Nov. 1815' (folio 214; here fig. 34). The truncated sabre legs issuing from a concave-sided plateau on this tripod table are characteristic of the Bullock workshop. Slightly larger tables employed a similar arrangement with four legs (*see* no. 19). On still larger tables a variant of this construction is employed, with five vertical turned supports and S-scroll legs. This can be seen on the oak and ebony inlaid breakfast table that was supplied for Napoleon's use on St Helena (and is now in the Russell-Cotes Art Gallery, Bournemouth). The roundels at the top of the legs are a recurring feature on Bullock's furniture. As in this case, they often serve to emphasise a change of direction or a corner.

Provenance: London art market, 1985.

Lent from a private collection.

Exhibited at Blairman's

38. *Cloakstand*

Mahogany and beech, with ebonised detailing. 200.7 cm.

A design for a stand of this form, on a sheet inscribed 'Back Hall No 22 St Helena', exists among the *Lowe Papers* (folio 222). There is a similar stand, but with a single row of pegs, in the *Wilkinson Tracings* (p.13) and also in Ackermann's *Repository* (July 1822 – Cloakstand and Flowerstand; *see* no. 56). The text in the *Repository* comments that the cloakstand ' . . . may perhaps be rendered more convenient by having another row of pegs at the top.'

A stand with two rows of pegs was supplied to M.R. Boulton in 1817 for the hall at Tew Park. It was described in the bill as 'An Oak Hat Stand with tray for umbrellas' and cost £6.10.-.[1]

NOTE
1) Tew Archive, bill.

Provenance: London art market, 1986.

Lent by James Stirling Esq.

Exhibited at Blairman's

39. *Bookcase*

Goncalo Alves veneer with ebonised detailing. Brass grilles and ormolu mounts.
177.8 × 76.3 × 37.5 cm.

Two bookcases of this form are illustrated in the *Lowe Papers* on a sheet inscribed 'Breakfast Room for St Helena Nov. 1815 No 4' (folio 212; here fig. 43). The drawing shows bookcases that were intended to have inlaid brass patterns to the lower door panels.

In 1920, the pair of bookcases actually supplied

for Napoleon were advertised for sale in *The Connoisseur*[1]. As shown in the advertisement, they had glazed doors top and bottom and the lower doors opened to reveal two rows of seven small drawers. The pediment mounts were the same as on this exhibit. The advertisement does not reveal how they were veneered but does say that the columns, with small ormolu mounts to the centre, were of ebony. Their present location is unknown.

The pediments to these cabinets probably derive from Plate 14, No. 3 of Thomas Hope's *Household Furniture*, 1807, which illustrates an identically surmounted dressing glass.

Plate XVIII in Richard Brown's *Rudiments of Drawing Cabinet and Upholstery Furniture*, 1822, illustrates a 'Lady's Book-case, with Cabinet', which is

another close variant of this exhibit. It is shown with inlaid brass patterns to the upper doors and the details have a more rounded look than those in the above examples.

Lot 98 on the third day of Christie's Bullock Sale, 1819, was a bookcase of very similar description to the versions mentioned above: 'A beautiful small rosewood Lady's bookcase and cabinet, with upper folding doors, the pannels of Buhl work, with a drawer supported by four turned rosewood columns, mounted with ebony, the lower part with brass folding doors, enclosing 14 cedar wood drawers, with satinwood fronts filletted with ebony, and with ebony knob handles, 5'10" high.' It is interesting to note that this is described as a 'lady's bookcase and cabinet', which is close to Richard Brown's title, and, in addition, that the height is the same as that of the present exhibit.

An identical bookcase to this, now in an American private collection, is illustrated in *Fanfare*

Fig. 43. *'Breakfast Room for St Helena', dated November 1815. Plan and elevations. (British Library, Add. Mss. 20,222, Lowe Papers, folio 212.)*

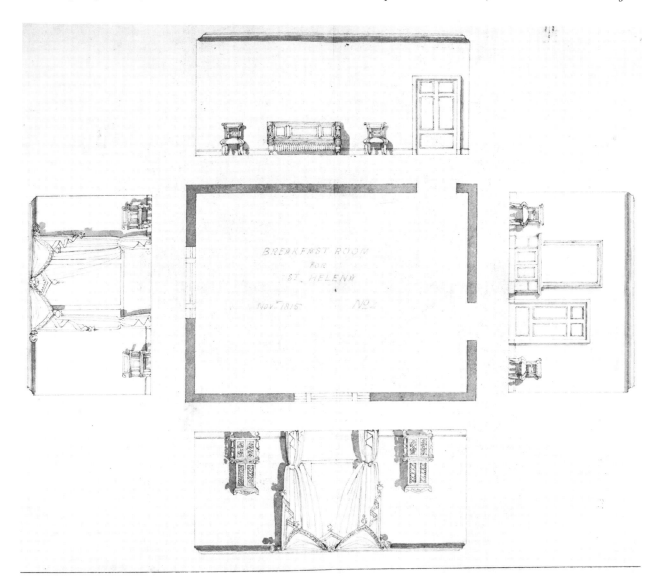

for Europe – The British Art Market, 1973 (p.192). Another small cabinet of similar form, without the upper part and fitted with small drawers, is now in a private collection in London.

NOTE
1) *The Connoisseur*, September 1920, p.LIX. We are grateful to Timothy Clifford for drawing this to our attention.

Provenance: London art market, 1985.

Lent from a private collection.

Exhibited at Blairman's

40. Cabinet

Mahogany and rosewood veneers with parquetry of various woods. Brass inlay and grilles.
98.8 × 126.4 × 50.2 cm.

The overall form and decoration of this cabinet is perhaps most comparable with an untraced cabinet, which makes similar use of parquetry drawer fronts, that is illustrated in fig. 24. The latter was,

according to Brian Reade, branded *G. Bullock* on the front edge of each drawer.[1] It should also be compared to nos. 6 and 41. All four cabinets are supported on unusually deep plinths and break forward either side of a raised centre section containing a drawer.

NOTE
1) Brian Reade, *Regency Antiques*, 1953.

Provenance: Bought from H.W. Keil (Cheltenham) Ltd, 1962.

Lent by Cheltenham Art Gallery & Museums.

Exhibited at Sudley

41. Cabinet

Rosewood veneer with ebony and ebonised detailing. Brass inlay and grilles; ormolu mounts. Mona Marble slabs.
97.8 × 135.9 × 49.5 cm.

Below: *No. 40. Cabinet.*

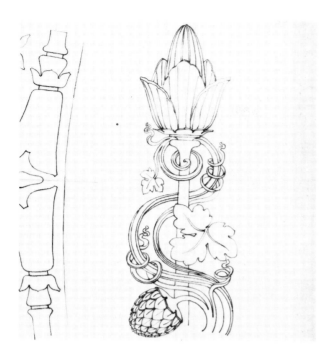

This cabinet is the grandest example in the group including nos. 6 and 40. The inlaid thyrsus on the central doors appears in the *Wilkinson Tracings* (p.135; here fig. 44) and inlay of the same pattern is shown on a cabinet in the *Tracings* (p.92; here fig. 46). The four ormolu mounts applied to the corners of each door exist on many other cabinets (including nos 9, 10 and 43), and are also illustrated on several pieces in the *Tracings*. The double-heart-shaped grilles are often found on Bullock furniture and can be seen, for example, on nos. 10, 39 and 40, and in designs in the *Tracings* (e.g. pp.84 and 101).

Provenance: London art market, 1980.

Lent by the Board of Trustees of the Victoria & Albert Museum.

Exhibited at Blairman's

Left: *Fig. 44. Design for marquetry thyrsus on door of cabinet (no. 41)*, Wilkinson Tracings, *p.135. (City Museums and Art Gallery, Birmingham.)*

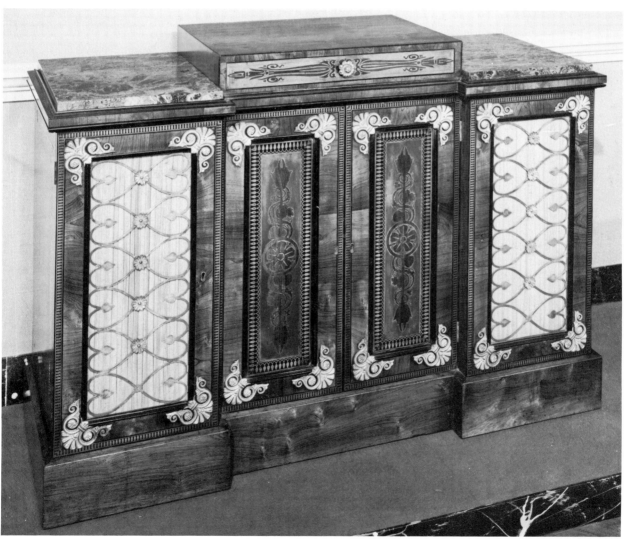

42. Bookcase

Rosewood veneer. Brass inlay and ormolu
mounts. Black and yellow veined marble slab.
(The marble replaced.)
86.5 135 × 40.8 cm.

The design for this bookcase appears in the *Wilkinson Tracings* (p.91; here fig. 45), where it is shown

Fig. 45. Design for a bookcase with glazed superstructure. Front and side elevations, Wilkinson Tracings, p.91. (City Museums and Art Gallery, Birmingham.)

with the addition of a glazed super-structure.[1]
The unusual feature of raising the plinth of the
bookcase on a separate base is one that can be
seen on other pieces illustrated in the *Tracings* (e.g.
pp.82 and 93), and is among the notable idiosyn-
crasies identifiable in furniture from the Bullock
workshop. It can also be seen on no. 15.

NOTES
1) Martin Levy, 'George Bullock: Some Sources for Identifying his
Furniture', *Apollo*, June 1987, Fig. 2.

Provenance: Christie's, 1st December 1977, lot 138.

Lent by The City Museums and Art Gallery, Birmingham.

Exhibited at Sudley

43. Pair of cabinets

Rosewood veneer with ebonised detailing. Brass
inlay and grilles and ormolu mounts. Mona
Marble slabs.
80.6 × 83.4 × 38.2 cm. and
80.6 × 87.6 × 38.4 cm.
(excluding marble tops).

A cabinet of this design, with differences of detail,
appears in the *Wilkinson Tracings* (p.92; here fig.
46). The unusual form of feet on these cabinets
can be seen again on another pair illustrated in
Plate XXII of Richard Brown's *Rudiments of Drawing
Cabinet and Upholstery Furniture*, 1822, and, in a more
elaborate version, on the Palmella cabinets (*see* no.
10). A possible source for the design of the feet

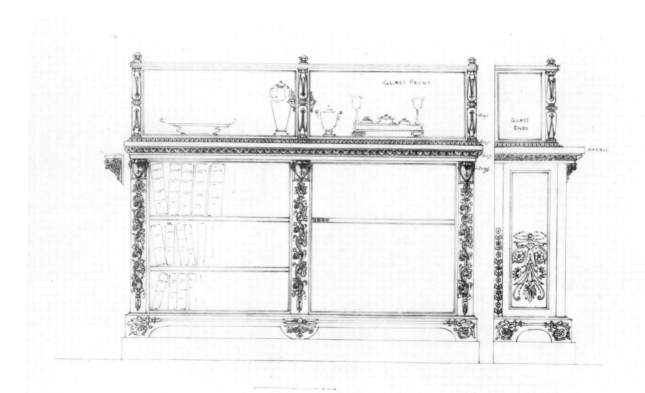

Fig. 46. Design for a cabinet, Wilkinson Tracings, p.92. (City Museums and Art Gallery, Birmingham.)

might be Plate 53, No. 4 in Thomas Hope's *Household Furniture*, 1807. As Brian Reade observes, feet of this style were 'in vogue from about 1815 to about 1825 and were much used by George Bullock.'[1]

The slight variation in the width of these two cabinets suggests that they were originally commissioned for a particular location.

NOTE
1) Brian Reade, *Regency Furniture*, 1953, Fig. 43 and p.97.

Provenance: London art market, 1950s.

Lent from a private collection.

Exhibited at Blairman's

44. Cabinet

Maple and oak veneers with ebony inlay and ebonised detailing. *Verde antico* marble slab. (The marble replaced.)
94 × 122 × 44.5 cm.

The three marquetry patterns, to the frieze, doors and plinth, are all familiar, both from the *Wilkinson Tracings* and from other pieces of furniture. One version of the frieze pattern in the *Tracings* (unbound number 251) is dated 18th March 1816. The same pattern can be seen in brass on ebony on the pair of cabinets from Blair Castle (no. 9). The door pattern is described in the *Tracings* (unbound number 240; here fig. 47) as 'For Mrs Barrons [Barrows?] Oak Book Commode'. Underneath this is written 'Pub^d Augt 1816', suggesting that this design may have been made available to other cabinet-makers. It was certainly popular and can be seen on several other cabinets. This exhibit has the pattern in ebony on a pale ground; a small cabinet (Paris art market, 1985) had the same pattern in *contre-partie*. An example in ebony on a brass ground decorates each door of a grand cabinet in the Fitzwilliam Museum, Cambridge (*see* fig. 25), whilst the *contre-partie* version can be seen on an exceptional cabinet now in an American private collection.[1] It is interesting to note the different effects achieved by the varied use of the same motif. The shaped plinth, dropping in a semi-circle to the centre, is a recurring feature in Bullock's work and can be recalled on countless

Below: *Fig. 47. Design for marquetry on cabinet (no. 44), Wilkinson Tracings, unbound number 240. (City Museums and Art Gallery, Birmingham.)*

pieces as well as in the *Wilkinson Tracings*; the same applies to the bold decoration of the plinth (*see* nos. 9 and 23).

A maple and ebony collector's cabinet in the Victoria & Albert Museum[2] is closely allied to this exhibit. It has three doors with a raised section to the centre and is decorated with the same three inlay designs in *contre-partie*.

NOTES
1) Illustrated in Helena Hayward (ed.), *World Furniture*, 1979, Fig.768.
2) Illustrated in Frances Collard, *Regency Furniture*, 1985, plate 18.

Provenance: London art market, 1985.

Lent by James Stirling Esq.

Exhibited at Blairman's

45. *Pair of crane neck tables*

Rosewood(?) veneers, ebonised and parcel gilt detailing. Painted and parcel gilt cast-metal legs. Brass inlay and ormolu mounts.
78.8 × 73.8 cm (diameter).

A detailed design for the crane necks appears in the *Wilkinson Tracings* (p.201); it shows screw-plates top and bottom demonstrating how these legs were to be fixed. There is a table of similar form to no. 45 in the *Tracings* (p.109) and a sidetable with the same supports (p.92).

A table of comparable form to the present example was included in the Bullock Sale, 1819 (3rd

day, lot 52): 'A tripod, composed of 3 cast-metal cranes necks and center standard richly gilt with Porphyry Mona top, 2 ft. 2 diameter, and on triangular ebonised plinths, inlaid with brass, on gilt lions paw feet and castors.'

Two card tables with closely related bases to these are known. One was formerly in the collection of the late Thomas Upcher of Sheringham Hall, Norfolk, and the second was sold by Christie's, 21st November 1985, lot 83 (illustrated). The striking use of crane neck supports (the appellation is taken from the Christie's sale description above) appears to reveal a clear debt to contemporary French furniture; a factor apparent in much of Bullock's oeuvre. The use of metal legs and a wooden top (unusual in English furniture) has parallels in French Empire tables.

The crane necks themselves are surely derived from the swans incorporated in, for example, designs by Charles Percier, furniture made by Jacob Frères and metal-work by both M.-G. Biennais and J.-B.-C. Odiot. Similar motifs, slightly differently treated, appear in Thomas Hope's *Household Furniture*, 1807.[1]

NOTE
1) For example, the vases in plates 34 and 35.

Provenance: London art market, 1950s.

Present location unknown.

46. Sofa table

Oak veneer, ebony and oak inlay and ebonised detailing.
72.5 × 150 × 66 cm.

The concave-sided, curving base with turned-under feet and applied roundels is similar to a sofa table supplied for Blair Atholl.[1] The vegetal marquetry pattern at each corner of the base appears in the *Wilkinson Tracings* (unbound number 218). The table is veneered with vigorously figured oak, which may well be the type of veneering

frequently described as 'variegated' in the catalogue of the Bullock Sale, 1819. The table top, raised on a massive column, has two drawers to the frieze.

NOTE
1) Anthony Coleridge, 'The Work of George Bullock, cabinet-maker, in Scotland: 1', *The Connoisseur*, April 1965, No.7.

Lent by James Stirling Esq.

Provenance: London art market, 1986.

Exhibited at Blairman's

47. *Games table*

Oak with ebony and satinwood inlays and ebonised detailing. Brass castors.
74.4 × 65.5 × 42.8 cm.

A very similar table to this one, but in mahogany, was on the London art market in 1980. Two other slightly larger versions are known, of which one was supplied by Bullock to M.R. Boulton in 1817 for Tew Park, described as 'An Oak Chess & Back-gammon table inlaid with Holly and white mould-ings. Brass railing round the edge £22.[1] This table, now in a private collection, has a top measuring 73.6 × 52.1 cm. The second, larger example, which remains in the house for which it was al-most certainly made, is not raised on castors and has an inlaid pattern around the top of the pull-out slide executed in ebony inlaid into oak. This pattern, for which there is a design in the *Wilkinson Tracings* (unbound number 219), also appears, in holly, on the table from Tew Park. The overall form of all these tables should be compared to the bog oak and marble-topped table at Blair Castle.[2]

NOTES
1) Tew Archive, bill.
2) Anthony Coleridge, 'The Work of George Bullock, cabinet-maker, in Scotland: 1' *The Connoisseur*, April 1965, No.3.

Lent by James Stirling Esq.

Provenance: London art market, 1985.

Exhibited at Blairman's

48. *Sofa table*

Oak veneer, ebony inlay and ebonised detailing. Brass inlay.
74.9 × 173.4 (width when open) × 67.9 cm.[1]

The end-support of this table should be compared with one that appears in the *Wilkinson Tracings* (p.30; here fig. 48). Plate IX of Richard Brown's *Rudiments of Drawing Cabinet and Upholstery Furniture*, 1822, shows another table with similar, vase-shaped ends and also the same type of stretcher.[2] The inlaid brass border is a familiar one on furniture

from Bullock's workshop (*see* no. 36), as are the 'octagon corners' which are recorded as a detail on several sofa tables in the catalogue of the Bul-lock Sale, 1819.

NOTES
1) Simon Jervis, review of Burlington House Fair, *The Burlington Magazine*, September 1985, p.657.
2) Martin Levy, 'George Bullock: Some Sources for Identifying His Furniture', *Apollo*, June 1987, Fig. 10.

Provenance: London art market, 1985.

Lent from a private collection.

Exhibited at Blairman's

49. *Table*

Laburnum veneers with ebonised beech. Brass inlay and ormolu.
76.8 × 51.5 × 38.8 cm.

Various tables and stands exist with similar square bases supporting ebonised beech columns. A stand with identical base and column, the top support-ing a Meissen dish, was sold by Christie's from Cullen House, Scotland (22nd-24th September

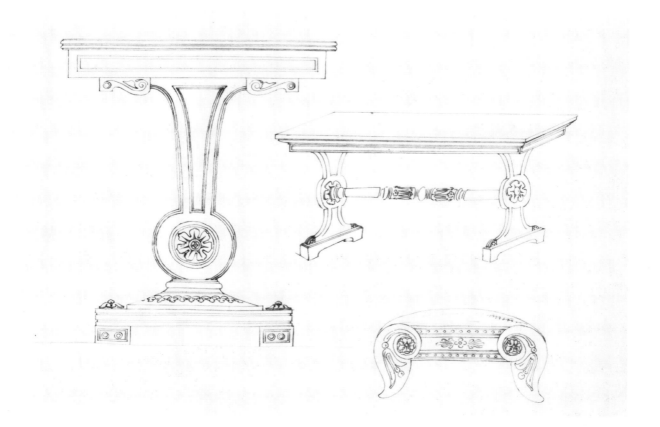

Above: *Fig. 48. Designs for table and footstool,* Wilkinson Tracings, *p.30. (City Museums and Art Gallery, Birmingham.)*

1975, lot 875, illustrated) – possibly the present example. Another table (no. 7) with the same trumpet-shaped column supported on a rather more elaborate (but similarly conceived) base was supplied by Bullock to the Duke of Atholl in 1814 for Blair Castle. The grandest table in this group, mixing elements from this table and no. 7, was sold by Sotheby's (12th July 1963, lot 99, illustrated) – it had brass inlay to the column as well as two inlaid patterns to the frieze surrounding the rectangular marble top.

Provenance: Bonham's London, 27th November 1975, lot 86.

Lent by Mr. and Mrs. Timothy Clifford.

Exhibited at Blairman's

50. Table

Ebony veneer, brass inlay, ormolu; top of various marbles.
86 cm (diameter).

This table has not yet been associated with any

Right: *No. 49. Table.*

111

Italy; it contains no native British stone. It is possible that Bullock imported such tops and sold them in his marble works, but there is as yet no evidence of this.

51. Stand

Rosewood veneers, ebony and ebonised detailing. Brass inlay and ormolu. Malachite top with black marble to the centre.
104.1 × 83.8 × 83.8 cm.

Neither the history of this stand[1] nor how it came to Sudbury is documented.[2] The overall form corresponds to a stand in the *Wilkinson Tracings* (p.106; here fig. 49). The thyrsus (in this case, entwined with trailing hops and with a mask of Bacchus at its centre) was a much-favoured motif on Bullock's furniture. Various adaptations of it

Above: *No. 50. Table.* Below: *Detail from base.*

known Bullock commission. Though several variants of the hop-entwined thyrsus occur in the *Wilkinson Tracings*, none of these are identical to that on the base of this table. The combination of ebony and brass used here is rare among the surviving pieces by Bullock, but demonstrates most effectively how influenced he was by the 'Boulle Revival' then underway in the French Empire style. The elaborate marble top is largely of classical Roman marbles and must have been made in

112

can be seen in this catalogue, notably on nos. 10 and 41; its use is noted in the decoration of many pieces described in the catalogue of the Bullock Sale, 1819. Several of the *Tracings* (e.g. unbound number 221, here fig. 27, and p.135, here fig. 44) show designs for inlaid patterns based on the thyrsus. Bacchic motifs were considered appropriate adornment for dining-room furniture, but it is not clear that this was the intention with the present piece.

The overall form of this exhibit should be compared to the Abbotsford stand (no. 16). Related examples appear in the *Tracings* (pp.104, 105 and 107). Sometimes they have square-section legs, and on other designs they are shown raised on fluted or plain columns.[3]

NOTES
1) We are grateful to John Morley for drawing this piece to our attention.
2) This stand is said to have been made to support a malachite and ormolu candelabrum brought back in 1802 by Admiral Sir John Borlase-Warren as a gift from St Petersburg which he visited as Ambassador Extraordinary to congratulate Tsar Alexander on his accession.
3) A jardinière supported on a similarly conceived stand is illustrated in Helena Hayward (ed.), *World Furniture*, London, 1979, Fig. 763.

Above: *Fig. 49. Designs for a stand*, Wilkinson Tracings, *p.106. (City Museums and Art Gallery, Birmingham.)*

Provenance: by repute, Admiral Sir John Borlase-Warren; ? by descent; acquired by National Trust with Sudbury, 1967.

Lent by The National Trust (from Sudbury, Derbyshire).

Exhibited at Sudley

52. Four chairs

Mahogany.
83.8 × 53.3 × 43.2 cm.

The design for these chairs appears in the *Wilkinson Tracings* (p.5; here fig. 50).[1] A rather less taut version of this design is illustrated in Plate VII of Richard Brown's *Rudiments of Drawing Cabinet and Upholstery Furniture*, 1822. Plate 14 of Richard Bridgens's *Furniture with candelabra* (1838 edition) illustrates a debased version but one that nonetheless discloses a common origin, particularly in the triangular embellishment of the back. The columns and horizontal sections of the backs of the chairs in this exhibit bear comparison with Plate 24, No. 3 in Thomas Hope's *Household Furniture*, 1807. A chair of similar conception, but lacking the triangular section to the back, was sold at Christie's (8th May 1985, lot 103, illustrated). It bore a label stating that it had belonged to Napoleon on St Helena and was thus probably part of the furnishings ordered in 1815 at the instruction of the Prince Regent.[2] Another mahogany example of the same form as the St Helena chair exists in a British private collection; the geometric decoration to the back is in inlaid ebony and has applied roundels where the lines scroll round the back in the examples exhibited here.

NOTES
1) Martin Levy, 'George Bullock: Some Sources for Identifying His Furniture', *Apollo*, June 1987, Figs. 5 and 6.
2) An identical chair remains at Longwood House, St Helena – now the residence of the French Consul.

Provenance: London art market, 1984.

Lent by James Stirling, Esq.

Exhibited at Blairman's and at Sudley (two chairs each)

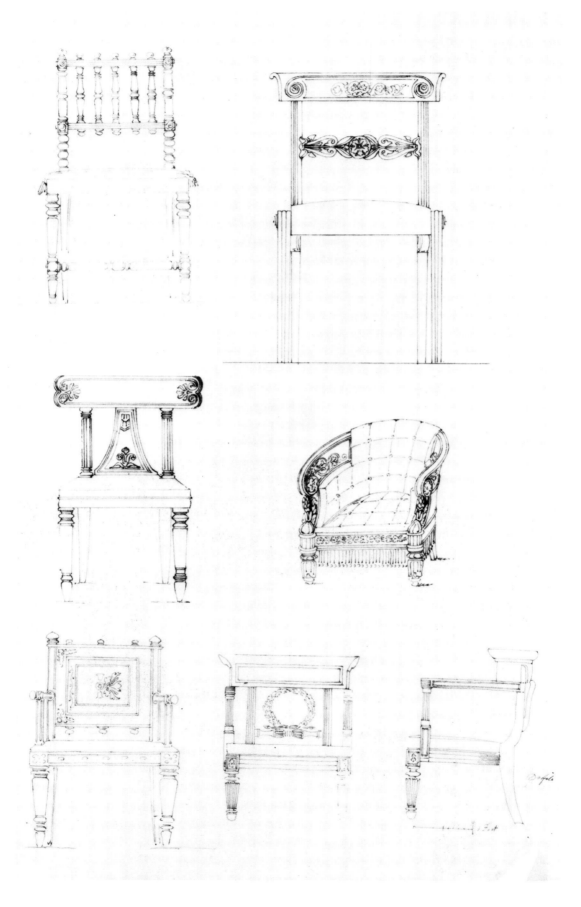

114

Opposite: *Fig. 50. Designs for chairs*, Wilkinson Tracings, *p.5. (City Museums and Art Gallery, Birmingham.)* See also *nos. 20, 21 and 27.*

Above: *Fig. 51. Design for a table, from Richard Bridgens, Furniture with candelabra, 1838 edition, Plate 38.* Below: *No. 53. Writing Table.*

53. *Writing table*

Walnut with walnut veneers and inlays of ebony and various light woods. Original tooled leather writing surface.
72.4 × 127 × 66.7 cm.

A design corresponding to this table was published by Richard Bridgens in *Furniture with candelabra* (plate 38, 1838 edition; here fig. 51). It seems unlikely that a commercial cabinet-maker executing this table after a published design would have conceived such splendid and elaborate decoration to the top and so an earlier date appears reasonable, particularly bearing in mind the fact that Bridgens had created sophisticated historicist designs as early as 1817 (*see* no. 12). The bold strapwork decoration to the top with mask heads and *trompe l'oeil* nails is clearly inspired by Renaissance sources and may well derive directly from the work of Johann Jakob Ebelmann (active 1598-1609).[1]

Another table, executed in oak, now in the Victoria & Albert Museum, was supplied for Mamhead, Devonshire in about 1838. It is very close in form to this exhibit and clearly based on the same Bridgens design.[2]

Right: *Fig. 52. 'Great Library Table' at Aston Hall, from Richard Bridgens,* Furniture with candelabra, *1838 edition, Plate 35.*
Below: *No. 54. Writing Table.*

NOTES
1) *See* Simon Jervis, *Printed Furniture Design Before 1650*, Furniture History Society, 1974, pp.36-38, and particularly plates 204-215.
2) Frances Collard, *Regency Furniture*, 1985, p.186.

Provenance: London art market, 1986.

Lent from a private collection.

Exhibited at Blairman's

54. *Writing table*

Walnut, with walnut veneers and ebony inlay.
76 × 149.5 × 104.5 cm.

A table of this form was first designed by Richard

Bridgens for James Watt of Aston Hall, Warwickshire. The drawing, which survives in the Watt Family Archive, is signed and dated 1823.[1] The design was published by Richard Bridgens in *Furniture with candelabra* (plate 35, 1838 edition; here fig. 52), described as 'GREAT LIBRARY TABLE at Aston Hall'. Several versions of this table, in a variety of sizes and woods, have appeared on the art market in recent years. One such, in oak, was acquired by the City Museum and Art Gallery, Birmingham, for display at Aston Hall.[2]

NOTES
1) Virginia Glenn, *Furniture History Society Journal*, 1979, plate 102B.
2) Glenn, as above, plate 103B.

Provenance: London art market, 1983.

Lent by Manchester City Art Galleries.

Exhibited at Sudley

55. *Deer candelabrum*

Pen and ink with black wash and watercolour.
51.2 × 19.9 cm.
Inscribed at the top 'Candelabra at Littlecot [sic] House. Lieut Gen Popham'. Signed and dated: 'GAM Feb 22 1819'. A scale is drawn along the bottom of the drawing and a height of eleven feet marked vertically against the left side of the candelabrum.

The drawing depicts a version of one of the most successful examples of 'sculptural furniture' executed by Bullock. If the inscription can be taken at face value, the word 'Candelabra' suggests that there were at least two examples at Littlecote, the Wiltshire home of the Popham family from 1589 to 1922. With its collection of armour, Littlecote seems to have been a house in which Bullock would have been at home.

Two versions of the candelabrum appear in the *Wilkinson Tracings*: one at the foot of a grand staircase, possibly 4, Tenterden Street (p.1; here fig. 3), and a slightly less finished design (p.13).[1] A further variant was published as Plate IV of Richard Bridgens's *Furniture with candelabra*, 1826,[2] where the description claims that it was 'Designed and etched by R. Bridgens'.

Lot 30 on the second day of the Bullock Sale, 1819, was 'A noble and lofty candelabrum, the centre shaft covered with foliage bronzed, and terminated by a cluster of 3 deers heads . . .'[3] Neither this nor the Littlecote candelabra has been traced.[4]

Until the recent discovery of the Bullock Stock in Trade Sale, it was not known that there might be in existence as many as 290 coloured designs by Bullock. The initials 'GAM' remain a mystery but the date, 'Feb 22 1819', may be significant as it falls within the period between Bullock's death and the major clearance sales of May 1819. It is conceivable that during this period 'GAM' inscribed the drawing to record what it represented.

If this is the case, it would probably have been included among lots 36-42 on the third day of the Stock in Trade Sale. No other 'Bullock' drawings of this type have been recorded.

NOTES
1) Martin Levy, 'George Bullock: Some Sources for Identifying his Furniture', *Apollo*, June 1987, Fig. 1.
2) The same design is Plate 20 in the 1838 edition.
3) Levy, as note 1 above, p.427.
4) A pair of candelabra in the collection of the Museum and Art Gallery, Scunthorpe, are close variants of this model, but lack the deer's heads.

Provenance: New York art market, 1987.

Lent from a private collection.

Exhibited at Blairman's

56. *Plates from Ackermann's Repository*

Hand-coloured aquatints.

Each page of Ackermann's *The Repository of Arts* measures approximately 23.4 × 14.8 cm., although the size of the printed image varies from issue to issue.

The Repository of Arts, Literature, Commerce, Manufactures, Fashions and Politics was a monthly periodical published between 1809 and 1828. Each issue carried a design for an example of 'Fashionable Furniture' or an interior, taken from a variety of sources. There are eight plates to which Bullock's name is attached:

'Chimney Piece of Mona Marble' January 1816 (81)[1], 'Drawing Room Window Curtain' February 1816 (82), 'Grecian Furniture' May 1816 (85), 'Dining Room' August 1816 (88), 'An English Bed' November 1816 (91), 'Drawing Room Window Curtains' December 1816 (92), 'Drawing Room Window Curtain' April 1817 (93), 'Fashionable Chairs' September 1817 (95). In addition to these, 'Drawing Room Table, Chairs and Footstools' June 1824 (140), are described in Ackermann's text as in the ' . . . character and style [of] the late Mr G. Bullock.'

There are a further five plates not attributed in

Opposite: *'Grecian Furniture', May 1816.*
Below: *'Drawing Room Window Curtain', February 1816.*

DRAWING ROOM WINDOW CURTAIN

119

CHIMNEY PIECE OF MONA MARBLE.

Above: *'Chimney Piece of Mona Marble', January 1816.*   Below: *'Chimney Piece of Mona Marble', November 1821.*

CHIMNEY PIECE OF MONA MARBLE.

the text to a particular designer, but which are likely to have been associated with Bullock. They are:

'French Sofa Bed' March 1816 (83) – this design also appears in the *Wilkinson Tracings* (p.41).

'A Mona Marble Chimney Piece' October 1816 (90) – the form of this chimneypiece, as well as the material from which it is made can be compared to the plate for January 1816.

'Chimney Piece of Mona Marble' June 1817 (94) – executed in Mona Marble, this chimneypiece is almost identical to one in the *Wilkinson Tracings* (p.29) which forms part of a scheme for the Dining Room at Battle Abbey. The design is reminiscent of examples found at Abbotsford, particularly in the employment of a shallow Gothic arch. It is interesting to note, in passing, that there is a chimneypiece of very similar design in the Great Knight's Hall designed by K.F. Schinkel at Stolzenfels, near Koblenz. Might Schinkel, who was in England in 1826, have been aware of the plates published a few years earlier by his compatriot Rudolph Ackermann?

'Chimney Piece of Mona Marble' November 1821 (119) – again executed in Mona Marble, this example appears to be a variant of the January 1816 design.

'Cloak Stand & Flower Stand' July 1822 (124) –

both the cloak and flower stands appear together in one of the *Wilkinson Tracings* (p.97). A variant of the flower stand was published in Richard Bridgens's *Furniture with candelabra* (Plate 25, 1838 edition).

Finally, the plate for December 1822, 'An Egyptian Chimney-Front' (129), might be considered because of the use of Mona Marble, although there is little else to connect it with Bullock's style and so it cannot be attributed to him with the same certainty as those above.

It seems likely that Bullock provided Ackermann with a selection of designs which he was free to use as he pleased. There seems to be no other explanation for the inconsistency with which Bullock's name is attached to the plates, and this view is strengthened by the fact that Bullock's work was still being used after his death.

These plates are particularly interesting both as a reflection of part of the mature range of Bullock's output and as an important record of what some of his interiors might have looked like.

NOTE
1) The numbers in brackets refer to the plates in *Ackermann's Regency Furniture & Interiors*, Crowood Press, 1984.

National Museums and Galleries on Merseyside (Walker Art Gallery); and private collection.

Exhibited at Blairman's and Sudley

'Fashionable Chairs', September 1817.

Above: *'Dining Room', August 1816.*   Below: *'Drawing Room Window Curtain', April 1817.*

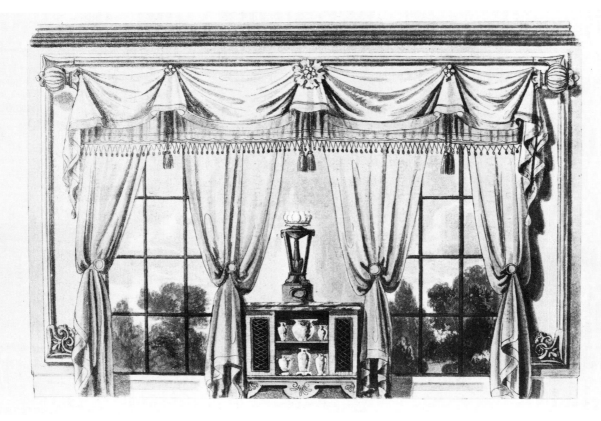

'An English Bed', November 1816.

Above: *'Chimney Piece of Mona Marble', June 1817.*   Below: *'A Mona Marble Chimney Piece', October 1816.*

Above: *'French Sofa Bed', March 1816.*

Below: *Drawing Room Window Curtains', December 1816.*

'Cloak and Flower Stand', July 1822.

George Bullock: Sculptor

TIMOTHY STEVENS

In August 1811 the Liverpool Academy, in the presence of its President, George Bullock, gave a dinner to mark the birthday of its patron, the Prince Regent. A guest might well have agreed with the opening lines of the report on the event in the *Liverpool Mercury* of 16th August:

'The improvement of Society cannot be measured by a more correct scale than by the progress of the Arts. That honourable and virtuous employment of the human faculties, which harmonizes the manners, and incites the generous rivalry of emulative abilities, marks, by its extent, the height to which true civilization has attained, and how far the energies of mind have entered into the pursuits of society.'

Certainly in Liverpool the 'progress' made by the Arts in the years immediately before 1811 had been spectacular, and the rich mix of London and local artists in the 1st and 2nd Academy Exhibitions of 1810 and 1811 was a testimony of the growing artistic influence of Liverpool. A perceptive guest, however, might have considered that the 'progress' owed more to the flair and drive of the Academy's founder President than to changes in society. After the death of Henry Blundell, its first patron, Bullock had, for instance, secured the Prince Regent as Patron of the Liverpool Academy.

When the President had proposed the health of William Roscoe and Roscoe had replied, Bullock 'in a neat and appropriate speech expressed his sense of the honour done him – his satisfaction at seeing his exertions attended with so much success, and his determination to persevere in that course of conduct, which had entitled him to the approbation of the society.' Further toasts were given followed by 'original songs, among many which [sic] were sung by Mr Bennet, of the Liverpool Theatre, and many other Gentlemen connected with the Academy.' Had a guest on this very convivial evening toured the 2nd Annual Exhibition of the Academy, he would have been able to view busts by its President of Lord Tamworth, William Roscoe, Master Betty – the Young Roscius and W. Stevenson displayed alongside busts by the outstanding sculptor of the metropolis, Francis Chantrey, of John Horne Tooke, Sir

Francis Burdett, J.R. Smith and Benjamin West. In the sculpture section there were also models by John Gibson, who was soon to establish for himself a reputation as a neo-classical sculptor in Rome. Although Bullock's representations may have lacked the technical virtuosity and subtlety of characterisation that were such a feature of Chantrey's busts, the few that exist display a striking individuality. It is this quality that sets him apart from the average neo-classical bust-maker.

Henry Fuseli, who was a friend of William Roscoe, wrote rather acidly to him on 20th August 1811, after reading the report in the *Liverpool Mercury*:

'We ('Nos Poma en corps') have been presented with the Liverpool Mercury, & the Convivial Transactions of Your Academy under the Auspices of Mr President Bullock:

τον δ'ουτ'αρ Σκαπτηρα θεοι θεσαν, ουτ Άροτηρα,
ουδ αλλο τι Σοφον, πασης δ'ημαρτανε τεχνης.

[The gods made that man neither a digger nor a ploughman, nor skilled in any other way; he has failed in every art.

Addio.] '[1]

Fuseli's low opinion of the Liverpool President was perhaps in one sense justified. Bullock, who had probably had no formal training or apprenticeship, could well have appeared to lack the concentration and drive of artists such as Fuseli himself or Chantrey. Bullock's genius lay in a rich combination of skills and in an ability to respond to unusual opportunities. The reappearance of busts at the Liverpool Academy that had already been exhibited at the Royal Academy suggests that he was uncertain whether or not he wanted to establish for himself a reputation as a bust maker. Indeed, most of the subjects for his busts were friends such as William Roscoe (*see* no. 61) or Henry Blundell (*see* no. 59) or people he had met through friends such as Sir James Edward Smith, the correspondent of Roscoe (*see* no. 62). Other sitters were celebrities such as John Philip Kemble (*see* no. 76), Mrs Siddons (*see* nos. 73-75) or Master Betty – the Young Roscius (*see* no. 81), whose busts would have been likely to draw large numbers of visitors to the Liverpool showroom. What Bullock does not seem to have wanted to do was establish a solid, conventional business on the lines of S. and J. Franceys, who were leading masons and fireplace manufacturers in Liverpool. The handful of monuments in the *Wilkinson Tracings* and the three monuments so far traced do not suggest that he had much inclination to make church memorials a substantial part of his business. Perhaps, as with his busts, he restricted himself to commissions from friends or friends of friends.

Too few busts have so far surfaced for a proper assessment to be made of Bullock's approach to his sitters or of his attitude to bust-making to be formed. Nevertheless the use of a life-cast as the basis for the busts of Dr William Hey in 1816 (*see* no. 69) tempts the speculation that Bullock had a particular fascination, like so many of his contemporaries, with the study of physiognomy. His brother William also had an interest in the practical problems of recording the shape of a head and had invented a machine called a 'physiognotrace' for the production of silhouettes at his Liverpool Museum.

The presence of the then very controversial Dr Spurzheim, one of the founders of the theory of phrenology, at a breakfast given by Bullock in Tenterden Street in 1815 to examine the cast of the bust of Shakespeare (*see* no. 67) further indicates this interest which would perhaps explain Bullock's fascination with famous men and women, particularly those who worked in the theatre. At this breakfast, the head of another guest, Sir Walter Scott, then at the height of his fame as a writer, was compared with that of the long-dead bard (*see* no. 95).

In his study, *The Physiognomical System of Drs Gall and Spurzheim founded on an Anatomical and Physiological Exhibition of the Nervous System in General, and of the Brain in particular, and indicating the Dispositions and Manifestations of the Mind*, 1815 (p.551), Dr Spurzheim complained:

'It is well known, that modern artists have entirely neglected the configuration of the head. I have often observed, that they give the shape of their own head to their figures, or they desire the individual they can most easily procure to sit for a model, attending in their choice to little else than age, sex, etc. As, however, each talent and each peculiar character is inseparable from a peculiar form of the head, this must now become an essential study for artists, as well in order to imitate nature exactly, in the painting of portraits, as to compose ideal forms which are not in contradiction with natural configuration.'

The life cast of Dr Hey (*see* no. 69), taken in 1816, might imply an attempt by Bullock to follow Dr Spurzheim's principles.

Bullock's other sculptural activities appear to have been modest. Besides the new architectural details modelled for Speke Hall, only the accomplished wax of Henry Blundell of 1801 (no. 58) and the rather dumpy classical female figures holding candlesticks of 1804 (no. 63) have been traced. (The marked difference in quality suggests that the latter may be workshop productions.) In complete contrast, both in terms of size and ambition, is the planned monument of Lord Nelson of 1807 (no. 87), which was designed to be cast in artificial stone. Whether this was a uniquely ambitious project or not is unknown. The topographer and antiquarian John Britton rightly regarded it at the time as an attempt to create an 'English style'. Perhaps this model of 1807 was the catalyst that led Bullock to exploit British woods and to create a 'national' furniture style which consciously blends British elements and classical design.

Inevitably, a lack of sufficient material prevents the proper formulation of an assessment of Bullock's achievement as a sculptor. For him, sculpture was only part of his total artistic activity which he continued to practise until at least 1817, when he 'improved' two busts for Lord Abercorn (nos. 70 and 71).

Like his brother William, he was a man of many parts – architect and interior designer (one is tempted to attribute to him Henry Blundell's Pantheon at Ince Blundell) as well as antiquarian, artistic organiser and cabinet-maker. His ability to think as a sculptor must have helped to give his furniture its powerful, three-dimensional quality. While his achievements in sculpture may not have been as considerable as in the field of furniture, here, as in everything he touched, he challenged the accepted conventions.

NOTE
1) Liverpool Public Library, Roscoe Papers, 920 ROS, 1711. Fuseli is quoting a corrupt version of the fragmentary Homeric poem, the *Margites*, which more reliably reads:

τὸν δ'οὔτ' ἀρ'σκαπτῆρα θεοὶ θέσαν οὔτ' ἀροτῆρα
οὔτ' ἄλλως τι σοφόν. πάσης δ' ἡμάρτανε τέχνης.

The chief anomaly (ἄλλο τι. which does not scan, for ἄλλως τι) is found in the manuscripts of Clement of Alexandria's *Stromateis*, one of the intermediate sources for this passage. Fuseli may have had access to this version through Roscoe's library, which included numerous early editions of the works of Homer; and since Fuseli had previously quoted the same passage in another letter to Roscoe (Roscoe Papers, 920 ROS, 1703, 22nd February 1806), it may have been a private literary joke. (The compiler is grateful to Lucy Wood for this information.)

In the following section, catalogue nos. 57 to 72 are sculptural works that have been traced; nos. 73 to 95 cover recorded but as yet untraced work.

57. A Sculptor with a Bust of Mr Blundell

by Joseph Allen (1770-1839)

Oil on canvas.
127 × 100.5 cm.

Although Bullock was not named in the title for this painting when it was first exibited in 1808 at the Royal Academy (number 29), it is reasonable to assume that the sculptor is Bullock because the bust being modelled is identical to no. 59.[1]

Allen's career has several similarities with that of George Bullock. He was born in Birmingham and began his artistic career modestly, producing designs for japanned trays. After training at the Royal Academy Schools, which he entered on 23rd November 1787, he built up a clientele mainly in the north-west of England, working principally in Preston, Liverpool, Manchester and Wrexham.

He was a founder member of the Liverpool Academy (1810) and exhibited there until 1812, from Manchester and from George Bullock's Bold Street premises. John Bolton (*see* no. 88) and William Hey (*see* no. 69) both sat for him. Unlike Bullock, Allen failed to establish himself in London and retired to Erdington, near Birmingham.

In addition to this portrait, there was a bust of 'The Late George Bullock Esq' (now untraced) shown by Samuel Joseph (1791-1850) at the Royal Academy in 1819 (number 1219). There was also a portrait of 'Mrs. Bullock and children' by Joseph's cousin, George Francis Joseph (1764-1846) shown at the Royal Academy in 1817 (number 349).

NOTE
1) M.G. Bennett, *Merseyside: Painters, People and Places*, Walker Art Gallery, 1978, pp.19-20 (text), p.65 (plates).

Provenance: John Lane, sold Sotheby's 1st July 1925; Burgess Standley, USA, from whom purchased 1973.

National Museums and Galleries on Merseyside (Walker Art Gallery).

Exhibited at Blairman's

58. Portrait relief of Henry Blundell

Wax.
25.5 × 19 cm.
Signed and dated: *G Bullock 1801* (on scroll) and *G. Bullock 1801* (on glass behind tableau).

The identification of the sitter as the collector Henry Blundell of Ince (1724-1810) is based on Bullock's bust of him (no. 59) and the slightly later portrait of Henry Blundell by Mather Brown[1] (for biography of Henry Blundell, *see* no. 59).

At present this coloured wax is the only known example of Bullock's work in this medium and the earliest securely dated work by him. It supports the conclusion that Mrs Bullock, a wax modeller who is recorded as exhibiting in Birmingham in 1794, was his mother and that his initial training was as a modeller of small items in wax and rice paste (*see* nos. 73, 74, 76, 77).

Although within the tradition of Samuel Percy and other wax modellers, the competence of this piece, still in its original frame, would suggest that perhaps Bullock worked as a wax portraitist at his brother's museum in much the same way that William Alporte (died 1831) worked there as a resident silhouettist at a later date.

NOTE
1) Illustrated in Dorinda Evans, *Mather Brown*, 1982, Fig. 142.

Provenance: Edric van Vredenburgh, from whom purchased 1981 by Leeds City Art Gallery.

Lent by Leeds City Art Gallery.

Exhibited at Sudley

59. Bust of Henry Blundell

Marble.
70 cm.
Signed: *G. Bullock Sculpt.*

The collector Henry Blundell (1724-1810) was presented with the house Ince Blundell near Liverpool by his father in 1761. But it was only after his father's death in 1773 that he embarked actively on the formation of a picture collection and acquired antique marbles on a substantial scale. Unlike most of his contemporaries, he bought the work of living British artists, particularly those with connections in the north-west, Richard Wilson from North Wales, John Deare the sculptor and George Stubbs, both born in Liverpool, and Edward Penny from Cheshire. How far he was a major force in local artistic matters is now not clear. What is known is that he was President of the Society for Promoting the Arts in Liverpool, 1783-87, and Patron in 1810 of the newly-founded Liverpool Academy for which he provided £1,600. George Bullock clearly felt a considerable debt of gratitude to Blundell: he had himself painted by Joseph Allen (*see* no. 57) working on the model of the Blundell bust, which he had probably made three or four years before (*see* no. 60). A letter from the painter Henry Fuseli to Bullock of 21st August 1804 shows that at least once Bullock acted as Blundell's agent:

'Sir.
According to Your directions Mr. Blundels picture was by the Care of Mr. Haughton Sent off, addressed to You, for Liverpool, Last tuesday week. I hope the pains I have taken in giving it the Last finish will meet with approbation. I remain Sir your obliged humble Servt.

H. Fuseli'[1]

Unless the description on Scriven's engraving (*see below*), 'from a marble bust executed by G. Bullock A.D. MDCCCIV' is incorrect, it is likely that this is the marble which was shown at the Royal Academy in 1804.

The plaster bust (no. 60) presumably records Bullock's original model. The only significant differences in the marble are the absence of the frills, to the cravat (which may have proved too difficult to carve) and slight changes at the base of the bust. Essentially it is a bust by a modeller rather than a carver. The rather individual and unconventional slanting sides from the shoulders recall contemporary ceramic busts such as the bust of Nelson of about 1806 by the Herculaneum Pottery (Liverpool Museum).

Blundell's Bank Book records payments to George Bullock in 1804 of £10 (4th May), £30 (9th May), £10 (23rd May), £21 (26th May), £21

Opposite page: *No. 59. Bust of Henry Blundell.*

(28th May), £8 (5th June) and £172.18.0 (19th June).[2] Whether any of these were connected with payment for this bust is not known.

It was exhibited in 1804 at the Royal Academy (number 934) and in 1810 at the Liverpool Academy (number 192).

In 1809 the bust was engraved by E. Scriven as a frontispiece to *Engravings and Etchings of the Principal Statues, Busts, Bass-reliefs, Sculptural Monuments, Cinerary Urns, Vases, etc, in the collection of Henry Blundell Esq. at Ince,* 1809.

NOTES
1) Quoted from the *Cely-Tresilian Scrapbooks of Autographs* by kind permission of the Society of Antiquaries.
2) Blundell's Bank Book is in a private collection.

Provenance: the sitter; by descent to Sir Joseph Weld who presented it in 1959 to the Walker Art Gallery, Liverpool.

National Museums and Galleries on Merseyside (Walker Art Gallery)

Exhibited at Sudley

60. Bust of Henry Blundell

Plaster.
71 cm.

A plaster cast of the model for no. 59. Bullock's statement of 14th December 1807 to Stephen Tempest (*see* no. 63A) of Broughton Hall listed a charge of £5. 5s for this bust against the date 22nd

131

April 1807. Bullock also supplied a 'Large Truss Bracket' for it at £1.11.6. Two boxes for these pieces together with 'Booking and Cartage' came to a further 16s 2d. These items reappear on Bullock's statement of 9th December 1813, which also records a payment by Tempest of £30 on 17th December 1807.[1]

NOTE
1) Tempest Papers, private collection. The compiler is indebted to the present owner for tracing the account.

Provenance: By descent to the present owner.

Reproduced by kind permission of the owner.

61. Bust of William Roscoe

Plaster.
76.5 cm.

William Roscoe (1753-1831), the son of a Liverpool market gardener and publican, was the outstanding figure in Liverpool in his day. In 1796 he gave up a highly lucrative legal career to cultivate the arts and sciences, modelling himself on the great Florentine merchant princes of the Renaissance. He was a poet, patron, art historian, botanist, agriculturalist, the author of *The Life and Pontificate of Leo X*, 1805, and collector, as well as a leading anti-slavery campaigner and politician.

Roscoe's support for Bullock appears to have started when the sculptor arrived in Liverpool, and his introduction of Bullock to his circle makes Thomas Johnes of Hafod's description of Bullock as Roscoe's 'protegé'[1] seem very apt. Later in 1810 Roscoe acted as Treasurer of the newly founded Liverpool Academy of which Bullock was President.

In addition to this bust and the ebony cabinets (*see* no. 6), Bullock also assisted with the decor at the celebration banquet given to mark Roscoe's election as M.P. for Liverpool in 1806. The *Liverpool Chronicle* of 26th November 1806 described the room in glowing terms:

'The room, being the most spacious that could be procured in the town, was fitted up for the occasion in a style of appropriate taste and elegance, under the direction of Mr. John Slater, and was illuminated in the most brilliant manner by Mr. George Bullock. At the upper end, in a large centre window, which was covered with a rich damask crimson curtain, stood an elegant bronze female figure, large as life, holding in her right hand a patent lamp. At the opposite end of the room, a beautiful appropriate transparency, exhibiting

A BUST OF MR. ROSCOE.
Under which was the following inscription,
AN HONEST MAN IS THE NOBLEST WORK OF GOD
And at the base in large characters,
MERIT, INDEPENDENCE, HONOUR'

The identification of the present bust with the one exhibited by Bullock in 1804 is made on stylistic grounds and on the basis of the age of the sitter. Another cast is in the possession of the Governors of the Liverpool Boys' Institute School.

The bust was exhibited at the Royal Academy in 1804 (number 849), almost certainly at the Liverpool Academy in 1810 (number 193), and again at the Liverpool Academy in 1811 (number 167).

NOTE
1) Liverpool Public Library, Roscoe Papers, 920 ROS. 2223, letter from T. Johnes to Roscoe, 15th March 1808.

Provenance: Liverpool Royal Institution; presented in 1969 by the University of Liverpool to the Walker Art Gallery.

National Museums and Galleries on Merseyside (Walker Art Gallery).

Exhibited at Sudley

62. Bust of Sir James Edward Smith

Plaster.
69.8 cm.

Sir James Edward Smith (1759-1828), the famous botanist and founder of the Linnean Society, was a friend and correspondent of Roscoe. His numerous publications include *A Tour to Hafod in Cardiganshire, the seat of Thomas Johnes Esq. M.P.*, 1810.

Bullock was first mentioned in the Roscoe/Smith correspondence in 1803. On the 28th August 1803 Roscoe wrote:

'I have already sent the Books to Mr. Bullock as you desired but I understand the package intended for you will not leave Liverpool till tomorrow.'[1]

The books went astray, as Smith wrote to Roscoe on the 23rd September 1803:

'I am much mortified at not having received your books, my writing desk, etc. from Mr. Bullock. Might I beg you to enquire when and how he sent them? Mr. Stevenson, too, has received nothing.'[2]

The bust first features in the friends' correspondence in Roscoe's letter of New Year's greeting of the 1st January 1804:

'When the whole range of our Houses are finished Mr. Bullock has promised to present us with your bust to decorate our central building.[3] We would however be content with a plaister cast as I long since carried off the original model to place in my gallery at Allerton.'[4]

Smith wrote approvingly of the bust on the 7th February 1804 from Norwich:

'Pray when you see Mr. Bullock tell him my bust is highly approved especially by my own family, who neved [sic] liked any portrait of me before.'[5]

Opposite: *No. 61. Bust of William Roscoe.*

Roscoe responded on 11th February 1804:

'I am glad to hear your bust is well liked – the original model which Mr. Bullock gave me & which I value much more than the cast, has long since taken up its stature in my Gallery. He has promised us a cast for our central conservatory, where I hope soon to see it placed.'[6]

Smith responded on the 15th February 1804:

'So you have honoured my bust with a place in your gallery! I am glad you have the original, but I thought Bullock meant to exhibit it this year.

I really think you ought to have much more illustrious busts in your conservatory though it would be affectation in me not to be pleased with so high an honour. I hope your's will be placed with it, which while it will double my real satisfaction & gratification, will do away all censure as to your having the bust of a living character in your public building.'[7]

The original model (now untraced) which Roscoe took to Allerton Hall was later proudly displayed by him with other busts of his heroes and friends in his sitting room at Lodge Lane, Liverpool.[8] It had been exhibited at the Royal Academy in 1804 (number 855) and the Liverpool Academy in 1810 (number 196).

The early provenance of this black painted (bronzed?) cast is unknown. It is possible that it is

the Botanic Garden version. The steep sides of the body of the bust can be paralleled in the bust of Henry Blundell (no. 59). There is a drawing of the bust by Mrs Dawson Turner in the Victoria & Albert Museum, together with an etching by her derived from the latter. Another cast was formerly owned by the Linnean Society.

NOTES
1) Liverpool Public Library, Roscoe Papers 920 Ros 4448.
2) *The Linnaean Society Smithian Correspondence*, Vol. VII, kindly brought to the compiler's attention by Professor James Moody.
3) The 'central building' is that of the newly created Liverpool Botanic Gardens with which Roscoe was closely involved.
4) Liverpool Public Library, Roscoe Papers 920 Ros 4450.
5) Liverpool Public Library, Roscoe Papers 920 Ros 4451.
6) *The Linnaean Society Smithian Correspondence*, Vol. VII.
7) Liverpool Public Library, Roscoe Papers 920 Ros 4452.
8) *See* Henry Roscoe, *Life of William Roscoe*, 1833, p.378, for a description of the sitting room. A watercolour copy of a picture of this room by Samuel Austin, showing the busts described by Henry Roscoe, is in the Walker Art Gallery (inv. no. 2520).

Provenance: Liverpool Royal Institution; presented by the University of Liverpool 1969 to the Walker Art Gallery.

National Museums and Art Galleries on Merseyside.

Exhibited at Sudley

63. *A Pair of candlesticks*

Plaster, glass and gilt metal.
61 cm.
Inscribed: *G. Bullock Pub. Jan 1804.*

These gilt plaster figures, standing on black painted bases holding gilt metal candlesticks with cut-glass drip pans hung with drops, first published by Ralph Edwards,[1] are the only certain decorative pieces by Bullock known to the compiler. How much of Bullock's stock in Liverpool was of his own design and manufacture, as opposed to wares bought from other makers for retail, is not known.

Purchases of small amounts of clay from the Herculaneum Pottery and the occasional payment for firing items suggests that the scale of his own manufacturing enterprise was modest at this date although it was to increase later. In 1807 there are payments for 4¾ cwts of clay, 'beddit pans' and four payments for firing. The latter include a tablet, two leaves and figures. Payments in 1808, as well as covering the purchase of clay, include: 23rd April 'for firing Claws 8/9d'; 7th September 'for firing Figures 13/8d'; 10th September 'for firing 10 Claws 7/6d'; 14th October 'for firing Figs 8/9d'. An advertisement placed in the *Liverpool Chronicle* by Bullock on 27th June 1804 underlines the importance of stock obtained from other suppliers:

'G. BULLOCK
SENSIBLE of the many flattering marks of approbation which he has received from the Encouragers of the Fine Arts in Liverpool, begs leave to return them his grateful acknowledgments: with a view of making himself more worthy of

their favours, he has taken pains to improve his acquaintance with the present state of the Arts in the Metropolis; and has selected from the various articles of taste in Bronze, now so prevalent in the fashionable circles, a few of the choicest Specimens; and in order to display them to advantage, intends to remove from the Museum to the Large Room at Mr. Stoakes's, next door to the Athenaeum, the opening of which, for the inspection of his Friends, will be duly announced.

G.B. takes the liberty to observe, that the experience he has had, together with the considerable increase of his Manufactory, will enable him to exhibit a very large assortment, much below the former prices, which in point of execution will be found inferior to none in the kingdom.'

Ornamental items such as these presumably figured in the 'extensive and valuable Collection of Bronze and Bronzed Figures, Tripods, Candelabra, Vases, Busts, and Brackets' offered in the sale of his stock that took place in Liverpool in March 1806.[3] The figures seem to be painted black under the present gilding, which appears to be of considerable age.

NOTES
1) Ralph Edwards, 'George Bullock as Sculptor and Modeller', *The Connoisseur*, July 1968, pp.172-173.
2) Liverpool Public Libary, Herculaneum Pottery Records 380 MD 48 Ledger 1806-1817, p.161.
3) Advertisement in the *Liverpool Chronicle*, 26th February 1806, p.2, col. 5.

Provenance: Private collection; Christie's, 21st November 1985; London art market; Birmingham City Museum and Art Gallery, 1986.

Lent by Birmingham City Museums and Art Gallery.

Exhibited at Sudley and Blairman's (one candlestick each)

63A. *Monument to Robert Blundell*

St. Helen's, Sefton, Merseyside

Marble.
91 cm (height).
Main inscription:

> THIS
> MONUMENT
> was erected to
> the Memory of
> ROBERT BLUNDELL Esqr
> of Liverpool.
> who died in his 53ᵈ Year
> As a Tribute
> of Grateful Remembrance
> by
> STEPHEN TEMPEST Esqr
> of
> BROUGHTON HALL
> in the
> COUNTY OF YORK
> Augᵗ 9ᵗʰ 1807

Robert Blundell (1753-1807) was the son of Robert Blundell (1700-1773) of Ince Blundell and his second wife Margaret, daughter of Hugh Anderton. It was probably Robert's half brother Henry Blundell who recommended Bullock to his son-in-law Stephen Tempest. Bullock's statement to Tempest, dated 14th December 1807, lists a charge of £28. 10s. at 16th October 1807 for 'Monument to R. Blundell Esq. putting up Dᵒ cutting letter &c.' The same item re-appears on a later statement of 9th December 1813, together with the charge of 25th August 1808 for '2 Men two days each putting up Monument', £1, and 7s. for other expenses.[1]

The bronzed (green painted) drapery held by a gilt leaf pin setting off a very simple plaque surrounded by a wreath of gilt laurel leaves demonstrating Bullock's talent for giving elegance even to a modest commission.

Commissions such as this monument for the Blundell Family Chapel underline Henry Blundell's importance in launching Bullock's early career.

NOTE
1) Tempest Papers, private collection; the compiler is extremely grateful to the present owner who found these accounts for him.

64. *Monument to The Reverend Glover Moore, M.A.*

St Cuthbert's, Halsall, Lancashire

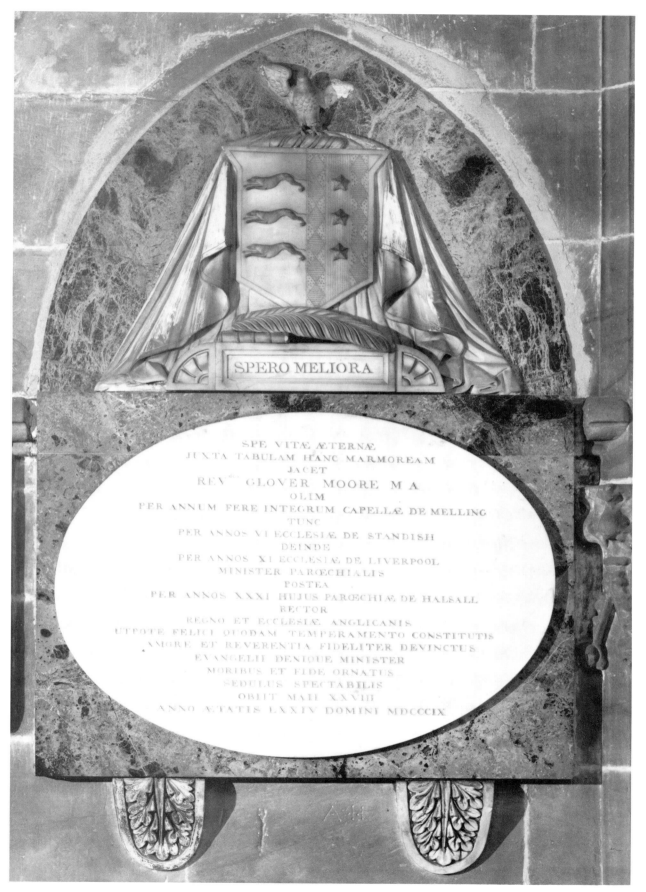

SPERO MELIORA

SPE VITÆ ÆTERNÆ
JUXTA TABULAM HANC MARMOREAM
JACET
REV^{dus} GLOVER MOORE M A
OLIM
PER ANNUM FERE INTEGRUM CAPELLÆ DE MELLING
TUNC
PER ANNOS VI ECCLESIÆ DE STANDISH
DEINDE
PER ANNOS XI ECCLESIÆ DE LIVERPOOL
MINISTER PARŒCHIALIS
POSTEA
PER ANNOS XXXI HUJUS PARŒCHIÆ DE HALSALL
RECTOR
REGNO ET ECCLESIÆ ANGLICANIS
UTPOTE FELICI QUODAM TEMPERAMENTO CONSTITUTIS
AMORE ET REVERENTIA FIDELITER DEVINCTUS
EVANGELII DENIQUE MINISTER
MORIBUS ET FIDE ORNATUS
SEDULUS SPECTABILIS
OBIIT MAII XXVIII
ANNO ÆTATIS LXXIV DOMINI MDCCCIX

Marble and Mona Marble.
108.7 cm (height).

Signed and inscribed: G BULLOCK FECIT, on the thickness of the oval, and SPERO MELIORA (I hope for better things) under the Coat of Arms. Translation of the main inscription:[1]

> In the hope of eternal life
> close to this marble tablet
> lies
> The Reverend Glover Moore MA
> parish priest
> formerly
> for almost a whole year of the chapel of Melling
> then
> for six years of the Church of Standish
> next
> for eleven years of the Church of Liverpool
> thereafter
> for thirty-one years rector of this parish of Halsall
> To the Kingdom and the Church of England
> in the harmonious alliance they enjoy
> he was faithfully devoted in love and respect
> Finally he was a zealous [and] admirable minister of the gospel
> distinguished by his morals and religious faith
> He died May 28th 1809
> in his 74th year

Glover Moore (1736-1809), the son of Nicholas Moore of Barton, near Halsall, Lancashire, matriculated at Brasenose College, Oxford, in 1756. He married a daughter of the celebrated Liverpool surgeon Antrobus (the arms on the monument are Moore impaling Antrobus). After being a curate at St Nicholas, the parish church of Liverpool, where he was recorded as a seat holder in 1783, he was Rector of Halsall from 1778 until his death.

There are drawings in the *Wilkinson Tracings* that relate to the cresting and right-hand acanthus leaf corbel, and are inscribed 'Revd Glover Moore'. The *Tracings* also include ten other designs for

Fig. 53. Design for a monument, Wilkinson Tracings, p.191. (City Museums and Art Gallery, Birmingham.)

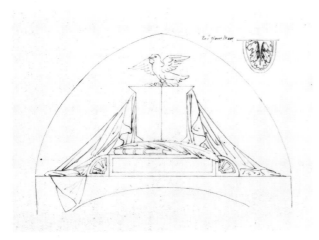

138

monuments, but so far only two other monuments (*see* nos. 63A and 66) are known to the compiler.

NOTE
1) Translation kindly given by Howard Moseley.

65. Bust of Mrs. Jolliffe

Marble.
66 cm.
Signed: *G Bullock sculpt*

Elizabeth Rose, the illegitimate daughter of Robert Shirley, 7th Earl Ferrers, married Hylton Jolliffe of Merstham, Surrey, in 1804. Hylton Jolliffe was M.P. for Petersfield almost without a break between 1796 and 1834. His wife died on 13th January 1809, aged 24; 'the remains of this very amiable young lady were interred on the 25th in family-vault at Bredon.'[1] As the bust was first exhibited over a year after the sitter's death, it may be based on a death mask. Few contemporary sculptors could rival the verve of the two ringlets of hair falling over her forehead.

The bust was exhibited at the Liverpool Academy in 1810 (number 198).

In the same collection as this bust is one identified as William George Hylton Jolliffe, later 1st Baron Hylton (1800-95), which has been attributed to George Bullock, although the compiler knows of no documentary evidence for this.

An octagonal table of zebra wood in the Bullock Sale, 1819 was bought by a person called 'Jolliffe'.[2]

NOTES
1) *Gentlemen's Magazine*, January 1809, p.94.
2) Christie's, 3rd-5th May 1819, 2nd day, lot 51.

Provenance: By descent to the present owner.

Reproduced by kind permission of the owner.

66. Monument to Anna Maria Bold
St Luke's, Farnworth, Lancashire.

Marble and Mona Marble.
76.2 cm.

Signed and inscribed on thickness of lower tablet: G. BULLOCK, FECIT. MONA MARBLE WORKS, LONDON.

Anna Maria, eldest surviving daughter of Peter Bold, inherited from her father in 1762 Bold Hall and its estate, which had been held by her family since at least the 13th century. She left the estate to Peter Patten of Bank, the son of her sister Dorothea and husband Thomas Patten, who assumed

Opposite: *No. 65. Bust of Mrs Jolliffe.*

Sacred to the Memory of
Mrs ANNA MARIA BOLD,
Daughter of the late.
PETER BOLD Esqr
of
Bold Hall,
*Many years Representative in Parliament
for the County Palatine of Lancaster,*
She died Novr 25th 1813,
Aged 81.

This Monumental Tablet can faintly describe her Virtues,
its narrow limits preclude their enumeration;
Pious without Bigotry; benevolent without ostentation;
cheerful without levity; Serious but not austere.
Her means were extensive, her bounty was commensurate
with her means; and never were talents committed
to a more faithfull Steward.
Affectionate towards her friends; mild to her dependants;
that truly Christian virtue, Charity, in its most
extensive signification, adorned her life.
Indisposition prevented an active display of her amiable
character; but it may be truly said
She was employed in doing good.
After a long life passed in the discharge of her duties
social and relative she was summoned to her reward in another
and a better world; the grief of her surviving friends
is much alleviated, by the consoling hope,
that she has been found faithfull
and is invited to enter into the Joy of her LORD.

THIS MONUMENT WAS ERECTED
IN GRATEFUL REMEMBRANCE
OF A BELOVED SISTER,
BY MARY HUNT,
AND EVERILDA BOLD.

the additional name of Bold. The Bold chapel at Farnworth is especially rich in early 19th-century monuments, including work by Pietro Tenenarni, Francis Chantrey and S. Franceys of Liverpool.

67. *Bust of William Shakespeare*

Plaster.
83.8 cm.
Inscribed:

> MOULDED BY Geo. BULLOCK
> FROM THE ORIGENAL [SIC]
> IN THE CHURCH
> AT
> STRATFORD
> DECR 1814

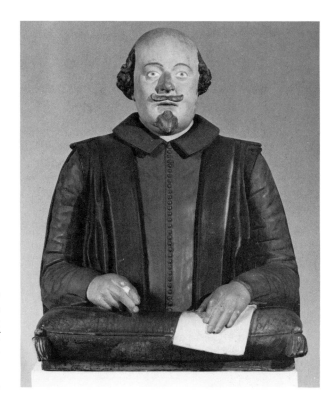

John Britton (1771-1857), the antiquarian, had, like many of his contemporaries, an obsessive interest in Shakespeare's physiognomy, and there is a vivid account of his commissioning of this cast in his autobiography.[1] It was later the subject of an animated conversation at a breakfast in Bullock's house in Tenterden Street in 1815:

'In the year 1814, I incited Mr. George Bullock to make a cast of the *Monumental Bust* of the Poet, and afterwards obtained reduced copies of the head for the gratification of many Shaksperians. From the same Bust, I also caused a very beautiful and truthful picture to be painted by my late valued friend, Thomas Phillips, Esq., R.A. and had an equally faithful copy in mezzotint, engraved from that picture . . . To promote respect for, and confidence in the original Bust and its graphic representations, I wrote an Essay to present to each purchaser of the print, and therein endeavoured to justify my firm conviction that the Stratford Effigy was the most authentic and genuine Portrait of the Bard.

Some curious and interesting circumstances are connected with these proceedings. Mr. Bullock's visit to Stratford was made under the most favourable auspices. Through the influence of my old friend, Mr. Robt. Bell Wheler, the historian of Stratford, (a most devoted Shaksperian,) Mr. Bullock readily obtained permission from the Vicar, (the Rev. Dr. Davenport,) and the parochial authorities, to take a mould of the Bust; and many and interesting were the comments of the Artist on that precious memento of the Immortal Bard. He was much alarmed on taking down the "Effigy" to find it to be in a decayed and dangerous state, and declared that it would be risking its destruction to remove it again.

Intimate with Walter Scott, Benjamin West, P.R.A., and Dr. Spurzheim, Mr. Bullock invited those gentlemen and myself to breakfast with him in Tenterden Street, shortly after his return from Stratford; on which occasion the host took a cast from the head of Scott. During the repast, much

was said about Shakspere and the Bust; for the latter had never before been subjected to the examination of such a conclave of critics. In the different relations of personal portraiture, physiognomy, and craniology, it was deeply scrutinized and commented on both by the painter and the physician; and respecting the mental powers of the Bard, whose singular head and features the cast represented, the Scotch Poet was not merely eloquent but enthusiastic.'(*See also* no. 95.)

Bullock himself wrote enthusiastically to Britton in December 1814 from Stratford about the project:

'You will be no less surprised to find me at *this time* employed in moulding the Shakspere, than pleased to hear that in excellence, as a model, it even surpasses the description you gave me of it. I am so delighted with it, that I have actually caught the spirit of inspiration; and, notwithstanding the difficulty of the undertaking, (which is very great) and the unfavourable time of the year, I am going on vigorously, and I hope to accomplish my task to our mutual satisfaction. I arrived in Stratford on Monday evening, and immediately sent your letter to Mr. Wheler, who kindly gave me instructions how to proceed in obtaining permission to mould it, and I had every preparation made, and assisted in erecting a sort of scaffolding, before I was fully aware of the difficult task I was going to perform. In short, instead of one day's work, I have found four or five; as I mean to mould the whole figure. It is a fine work of art, and *I perceive on the face evident signs of its being taken from a cast*, which at once stamps the validity of its being a real likeness. For my own part, though staying here so much longer than I expected will be inconvenient to my London affairs, yet, so much gratified am I with the bust, and so thoroughly convinced of its being a good likeness, that I would cheerfully make any sacrifices to obtain a faithful cast, which I have no fear of doing.' (December 1814).[2]

How many casts were made from Bullock's mould is unclear, but in addition to the one given by Bullock to Sir Walter Scott for Abbotsford, there are casts in the Soane Museum (acquired before 1835) and at Shakespeare's Birthplace, Stratford-upon-Avon. Another was owned by James Watt of Aston Hall, Birmingham.[3] (See also no. 68.) It is possible that Bullock made a new mould from his first cast as R.B. Wheler records,

'To multiply the casts from Mr. Bullock's first and consequently valuable mould, will be now impossible: for after that which he had in London, and one which I possess (the latter only half way down the body of the bust) were made, the original mould was broken up, and thrown into the Avon.'[4]

An engraving by W. Wood (after a painting by Thomas Phillips of Bullock's cast) appeared in *Annals of the Fine Arts* (published by Britton in 1816), I, pp.95-98.

NOTES
1) John Britton, *Autobiography*, 1850, pp.6-9.
2) As note 1.
3) Sold Christie's, 16th April 1849, lot 53, £4.4s.0d. Illustrated in *Furniture with candelabra and interior decoration designed by R. Bridgens*, 1838, p.50.
4) R.B. Wheler, letter to *Gentleman's Magazine*, Vol. 85, January 1815.

Provenance: Liverpool Royal Institution until 1960s. Acquired in 1967 by the Walker Art Gallery

National Museums and Galleries on Merseyside (Walker Art Gallery).

Exhibited at Sudley

68. Bust of William Shakespeare

Plaster.
73.7 cm.

As well as making a complete cast of the bust on Shakespeare's Memorial in Stratford-on-Avon (*see* no. 67), George Bullock made another of the head and shoulders only. Whether it was this version or the complete cast that William Scouler (died 1854) used for the reduced bust he later made for Britton is not known.[1] This cast, the only one traced by the compiler, was given by Bullock to Robert Bell Wheler (1785-1857), an antiquary and author of *History and Antiquities of Stratford-on-Avon*.

NOTE
1) John Britton, *Autobiography*, 1850, pp.6-9.

Provenance: Robert Bell Wheler; presented by Miss Ann Wheler to Shakespeare's Birthplace, Stratford-on-Avon.

68A. Casts of architectural detail from Melrose Abbey

On 12th November 1816, Sir Walter Scott wrote to Daniel Terry about a visit from Bullock, who was advising Scott on additions planned for Abbotsford: 'Mr Bullock will show you the plan, which I think is very ingenious. He has promised to give it his consideration with respect to the interiors . . .'[1] After listing the various projected new rooms, Scott added that there was also planned 'a study for myself, which we design to fit up with ornaments from Melrose Abbey. Bullock made several casts with his own hands – masks and so forth, delightful for cornices etc'. Perhaps other casts of these heads were among the '32 plaister casts, from ancient carved scriptural and other subjects' sold at the Bullock Stock in Trade Sale (Christie's, 3rd day, 15th May 1819) as lot 26 to 'Phillips' for £2.10. Some of the Melrose casts used in the study are still *in situ* in the cornice of the Armoury. Others used in the Dining Room have been destroyed.

NOTE
1) H.J.C. Grierson (ed.), *The Letters of Sir Walter Scott, Vol. IV 1815-17*, 1933, pp.289-290. The compiler is extremely grateful to Dr James Corson for his help with this entry. For Dr Corson's views on the dating of the letter, *see* his Notes and Indext to Sir Herbert Grierson (ed.), *The Letters of Sir Walter Scott*, 1979, p.124.

69. Bust of William Hey

Marble and Mona Marble socle.
70 cm.
Signed and dated: G. BULLOCK FECIT 1816.

William Hey (1736-1819), F.R.S., one of the leading figures of his day in Leeds, was senior surgeon at Leeds General Infirmary, 1773-1812, and twice Mayor of that town, 1787-89 and 1810-12. Among his friends were Joseph Priestley, scientist and dissenter, and Benjamin Gott (1762-1840), the outstanding Leeds woollen manufacturer and a founder member of the Leeds Philosophical and Literary Society, of which Hey was President in 1783.

John Pearson gives a vivid account of the commissioning and execution of this alert bust, which shows the sitter informally dressed and wearing a soft cap.

'Mr. Hey possessed the esteem and friendship of many of the principal persons in Leeds; but no one, probably, held his talents in higher estimation than Mr. Gott. This gentleman was not less distinguished for the amenity of his manners, his correct taste in polite literature, his acquirements and skill in arts and science, than for his public spirit, and a noble munificence which was conspicuous on all those occasions which called for the exercise of benevolence and liberality. Mr. Gott was desirous of possessing a bust of Mr. Hey,

but had some fears that he might not obtain the object of his wishes if he allowed his friend time for deliberation. The late Mr. Bullock, an artist of eminence, was introduced by Mr. Gott, who said, in an easy and familiar manner, to Mr. Hey, "I shall be obliged to you if you will permit the gentleman who is with me to take a cast of you; come, sit down, it shall be done now; it will require a few minutes only." No time being allowed to Mr. Hey for consideration, the cast was taken, and a bust was afterwards executed in beautiful marble, which had a place in the Exhibition at Somerset House in 1816, and is now in Mr. Gott's mansion, at Armley, near Leeds.

143

The most competent judges allow that this bust offers a fine specimen of the art of the sculptor, is a striking likeness of the original, and well expresses the manly sense and profound powers of thinking by which he was distinguished. Several busts were afterwards made by Mr. Bullock in plaster of Paris, at the particular request of various friends of Mr. Hey.'[1]

One of these plasters, probably one of the many formerly owned by Leeds Philosophical and Literary Society,[2] is in the Leeds Museum.

Why Benjamin Gott chose Bullock is now unknown. Gott may have met him through William Ewart of Liverpool, a business associate, whose daughter Margaret (1795-1845) married William, 3rd son of Benjamin Gott, in 1821. The bust was exhibited at the Royal Academy in 1816 (number 943).

No other bust from Bullock's London period has been traced (but *see* nos. 70-71).

NOTES
1) John Pearson, *The Life of William Hey, Esq., F.R.S.*, 1822, pp.64-65.
2) R.V. Taylor, *Supplement to the Biographia Leodiensis*, 1868.

Provenance: Benjamin Gott; University of Leeds (Brotherton Library).

Lent by the University of Leeds (Brotherton Library).

Exhibited at Sudley

70. *Bust of George Hamilton Gordon 4th Earl of Aberdeen*

by Joseph Nollekens and George Bullock

Marble.
73.6 cm.
Signed and dated: *Nollekens F[t] 1813.*

Lord Aberdeen (1784-1860), a leading politician of his day and Prime Minister at the time of the outbreak of the Crimean War, married in 1805 Lady Catherine Elizabeth Hamilton, third daughter of John, 1st Marquess of Abercorn. Aberdeen was a distinguished scholar and enthusiastic supporter of Greek independence.

Joseph Nollekens (1737-1823) exhibited a bust of Lord Aberdeen at the Royal Academy in 1814 (number 801). As no other version is known, it is likely that this marble is the exhibited piece. A payment to Bullock by Lord Abercorn for 'draping Aber deens & Knights Busts'[1] is recorded in the monthly account book (Bentley Priory and London 1811-1817) for November 1817. Bullock, by providing larger and grander shoulders, has given to the 18th-century proportions of the Nollekens bust the swagger and scale of the busts of the age of Chantrey. It is not recorded whether Nollekens was consulted about this extraordinary alteration. Interestingly, another Nollekens bust, that of Sir

Peter Burrell, 1st Lord Gwydyr (1754-1820), now in Edenham Church, Lincolnshire, has been transformed in a similar way, but there is no documentation to link this remodelling with Bullock.[2]

NOTE
1) Public Record Office of Northern Ireland, Abercorn Papers, D623/C/17/11 Monthly Account Book (Bentley Priory and London) 1811-17. The prices given, £28 for the busts and £103 for 'tables' (*see* no. 23), do not add up to the £161.19 given as the total in Bullock's bill in the final column. The same total is given in the accounts for '1817 October 31st-November 29th' (D.623/C/17/24). Either the bill included other items not detailed or the clerk simply could not add up.
2) Information kindly provided by John Kenworthy-Brown.

Provenance: by descent to the present owner.

Reproduced by kind permission of His Grace the Duke of Abercorn.

71. *Bust of Richard Payne Knight*

by John Bacon the Younger and George Bullock.

Marble and bronze.
57.2 cm (height).
Signed and dated: *J. Bacon F[t] May 1814.*

John Bacon the Younger (1777-1859) exhibited a

bust of the celebrated connoisseur Richard Payne Knight (1750-1824), at the Royal Academy in 1811 (number 954) and 1812 (number 931). The 1812 exhibit is probably the marble without bronze drapery that is now in the British Museum. It seems reasonable that the bronze addition on the present example can be equated with the payment from the Marquess of Abercorn to Bullock for 'draping Aber deens & Knights Busts' in the monthly account book.[1]

Until a provenance for the bust can be established, however, the attribution to Bullock of the enrichment of the bust with bronze drapery must be treated with caution. The 'Knight' noted in the accounts may not be Richard Payne Knight, although it seems likely as Abercorn and Knight were friends and no other bust of Knight is recorded.

NOTE
1) Public Record Office of Northern Ireland, Abercorn Papers D623/C/17/11; monthly account book (Bentley Priory and London) 1811-17, entry for November 1817.

Provenance: Christopher Gibbs Limited, 1971; Cyril Humphris, from whom bought by the National Portrait Gallery, 1972.

Lent by the Trustees of the National Portrait Gallery.

Exhibited at Blairman's

72. *Pair of vases*

Marble.
27 × 18.5 cm.

While there is no documentation for this pair of black marble Campana-shaped vases, the low-cut relief decoration of flowers and leaves can be closely paralleled in a number of designs for brass inlay that appear in the *Wilkinson Tracings*. Furthermore, their presence in a house for which Bullock supplied furniture makes their attribution to him likely.

The well-placed vase of restrained design is very much a feature of the interiors recorded in the *Wilkinson Tracings* and in Ackermann's *Repository of the Arts*. It is likely that documented pieces similar to these will emerge in due course.

Provenance: By descent to the present owner.

Lent from a private collection.

Exhibited at Blairman's

73. *Portrait of Mrs. Siddons*

Sarah Siddons appeared as Queen Catherine in a production of *Henry VIII* that took place in Birmingham in August 1800. Bullock, never slow to take advantage of public interest, announced in *Aris's Birmingham Gazette* on 22nd September (p.3, col. 4):

'Mrs. Siddons having done G. BULLOCK the

145

Honour of sitting for her Portrait, and as the Public may have an Opportunity of Judging of the Model, it is now placed in the Exhibition belonging to Mr. William Bullock, in Portugal House, New Street, where it will remain a short Time previous to its being sent to London.'

The use of the word 'Portrait' (rather than bust) suggests that this may have been a wax similar to that of Henry Blundell (*see* no. 58).

Untraced

74. Mrs. Siddons as Queen Catherine

Rice paste.

Exhibited at William Bullock's Liverpool Museum[1] and then at his London Museum (*see* no. 73).

NOTE
1) *A Companion to the Liverpool Museum at the House of William Bullock*, 1808, p.104.

Provenance: William Bullock; sold among the contents of his Egyptian Hall on 29th April 1819 as lot 38 to 'Matthews' for £6.

Untraced

75. Colossal bust of Mrs. Siddons in the character of Melpomene

Sarah Siddons appeared in Liverpool in the summer of 1807 and wrote to a friend from Liverpool on 15th July 1807, 'The houses are tolerably good. I cannot expect to be followed like the great genius Master Betty you know; but I hope to put about £1,000 into my pocket this year.'[1]

The bust was exhibited at the Royal Academy in 1808 (number 916).

NOTE
1) Letter quoted in Thomas Campbell, *Life of Mrs. Siddons*, 1834, p.319.

Untraced

76. Portrait of William Kemble in the character of Cato

Rice paste.

This piece, exhibited at William Bullock's Liverpool Museum,[1] and then his London Museum, is perhaps identical to the 'rice paste' bust of the actor in the same role shown without mention of an artist at William Bullock's Museum at Portugal House, New Street, Birmingham,[2] in 1800. In the 12th edition of the *Companion* Kemble's role changes to Coriolanus,[3] but only a bust of the actor as Cato was listed at William Bullock's 1819 sale.[4]

NOTES
1) *A Companion to the Liverpool Museum at the House of William Bullock*, sixth edition, 1808, p.14.
2) *Aris's Birmingham Gazette*, 11th August 1800, p.2, col.3.
3) *A Companion to Mr. Bullock's London Museum and Pantherion*, twelfth edition, 1812, p.18.
4) *Facsimile London Museum Sale Catalogue*, 1st day, 29th April 1819, lot 37.

Provenance: William Bullock, sold as lot 37 among the contents of his Egyptian Hall on 29th April 1819 to 'Matthews' for £6.

Untraced.

77. Equestrian model of Edward the Black Prince

Rice paste.

This is presumably the model that was advertised by William Bullock in *Billinge's Liverpool Advertiser*, on 21st June 1802:

'MUSEUM

W. BULLOCK respectfully informs the Public, that he has just added to his Collection a most Beautiful Equestrian MODEL of EDWARD the BLACK PRINCE, in complete Armour, executed in a manner that has claimed the admiration of every one that has seen it.'

The piece went on from Liverpool to London; the later museum handbooks name George Bullock as the modeller.[1]

In the *Wilkinson Tracings* (p.198), there is a drawing showing a helmet, breastplate and gauntlet, all embossed with a lion head, with the inscription 'The Armour of Edward the Black Prince in the Tower'. These belong to the celebrated 'Lion Armour', still in the collection of the Royal Armouries at the Tower of London, and now believed to be Italian or French of about 1550.[2]

Among the 'Casts from Armour in the Tower of London, etc.' sold by Christie's on the third day of the Bullock Stock in Trade Sale, 1819, was 'A suit of armour of Edward the Black Prince, cast from the original in the Tower' (lot 20, bought by 'Atkinson' for £2.11s). Also sold on the same day were moulds for this suit (lot 23, bought by 'Atkinson' for £2.2s) and part suits of casts (lots 21 and 22, bought by 'Cubitt' for £1.14s and £1.13s respectively). The sale also included moulds for the armour of Guy, Earl of Warwick (lot 24, bought by 'Atkinson' £2.12.6d).[3]

It is likely that should the model in question be found, the Black Prince will be in 16th-century armour rather than the 12th-century suit he wears on his tomb in Canterbury Cathedral.

NOTES
1) *A Companion to the Liverpool Museum of William Bullock*, 1808, p.12; *A Companion to the London Museum of William Bullock*, 1813, p.15.
2) The compiler is grateful to Ian Eaves, Keeper of Armour, at the Royal Armouries, for this information. For a full discussion of the earlier history of the 'Lion Armour', *see* Claude Blair, 'Notes on the history of the Tower of London Armouries, 1821-55, *The Journal of the Arms and Armour Society*, Vol II, 1956-58, pp.233-253.

3) For this armour *see* Ian Eaves and Thom Richardson, 'The Warwick Shaffron', *The Journal of the Arms and Armour Society*, Vol. XII, 1987, pp. 217-222.

Untraced

78. *Bust of W. Stevenson*

Probably the W. Stevenson of 97 Pall Mall, then the Royal Hotel, which Bullock gave as his London base in the 1804 Royal Academy catalogue.

The bust was exhibited at the Royal Academy in 1804 (number 838) and the Liverpool Academy in 1811 (number 170).

Untraced

79. *Bust of a Gentleman*

Exhibited at the Royal Academy in 1804 (number 850).

Untraced

80. *Bust of a Gentleman*

Exhibited at the Royal Academy in 1804 (number 851).

Untraced

81. *Bust of Master Betty, the Young Roscius*

William Henry West Betty (1791-1874), the actor, appeared in Liverpool in 1805. An admirer of both Master Betty and the sculptor contributed the following laudatory lines on the bust to the *Liverpool Chronicle* of 9th January 1805:

'Whence hast thou caught thy bold Promethian art?
There needs no stolen spark, Life to impart:
Could BACON's *brazen Head*, with thine appear,
Thine need not speak; we see YOUNG ROSCIUS
  here.
"Time is," how rich his youthful blossoms blow!
"Time was," his equal Ages ne'er could shew;
"Time's past," such beauties could *Pygmalion* give?
THY BUST, without a miracle shall live:
Yet *whilst he lives*, (alas! that he must die!)
We view thy Sculpture with less anxious eye,
But, when the dart of fate's unerring doom,
His mortal part shall summon to the tomb,
Long, as on Eagle's wings, his fame shall soar,
As *years revolve*, we prize thy work *the more*.
Despite of *Time*, all who THY BUST behold,
Shall own YOUNG ROSCIUS *never can be old*.'[1]

The bust was shown at 'The Rooms of Bullock and Stoakes', together with the busts of John Bolton (no. 88) and Joseph Birch (no. 82), all of which Bullock announced on 13th March 1805 were shortly to be sent to the Royal Academy,[2] and the bust of Master Betty was exhibited there in 1805 (number 800). On 5th June Bullock informed subscribers to the bust that 'copies are now ready for inspection and delivery at the Bronze Furniture and Figure Ware-Room, next door to the Athenaeum, Church-street.'[3]

Not to be outdone, William Bullock advertised in the *Liverpool Chronicle* also on 13th March 1805:

'BUST OF THE YOUNG ROSCIUS
The inhabitants of Liverpool and its vicinity, are respectfully informed, that a Bust of MASTER BETTY in ACHMET, taken since his late illness by Mr. Gahagan, Sculptor, will in a few days be published, under the patronage of the DUKE OF CLARENCE.

Subscriptions of 3 guineas each, are received by W.H. BETTY, Esq. No. 12, Bedford-street, Bedford-square; Mr. Jaques, 14, High Holborn; Mr. Gahagan, 5, Bentick-street, Soho, London; and Mr. W. Bullock, at the Museum, Liverpool, where the Bust may be seen.'[4]

On 19th June 1805 in the *Liverpool Chronicle* William Bullock announced that at his showrooms 'a bust of Master Betty, finely executed in statuary marble, is now open for public inspection.'[5]

In 1811 the Bullock bust was exhibited at the Liverpool Academy (number 169).

NOTES
1) *Liverpool Chronicle*, 9th January 1805, p.3, col. 2.
2) *Liverpool Chronicle*, 13th March 1805, p.1, col. 1.
3) *Liverpool Chronicle*, 5th June 1805, p.1., col. 1.
4) *Liverpool Chronicle*, 13th March 1805, p.2, col. 3.
5) *Liverpool Chronicle*, 19th June 1805, p.2, col. 3.

Untraced

82. *Bust of Jos. Birch*

This perhaps represented Joseph Birch (1755-1833) of Red Hazles, Prescot, near Liverpool, a Liverpool merchant, ship-owner and East India Company stockholder. A Whig in politics, he unsuccessfully contested Liverpool in 1802 and in 1806 vacillated between standing for Liverpool or Nottingham, finally becoming M.P. for the latter.

The bust was exhibited at the Royal Academy in 1805 (number 781).

Untraced

83. *Bust of John Blackburne, M.P.*

John Blackburne (1754-1833), M.P. for Lancashire

1784-1830, usually supported the Tory administrations in Parliament, particularly those of Pitt. John Nash designed a façade for his family seat, Hale Hall, near Liverpool.

The bust was exhibited at the Royal Academy in 1805 (number 813) and the Liverpool Academy in 1810 (number 194).

Untraced

84. Bust of Dr. Wilkinson, L.L.D., F.A.S.[1]

The sitter is probably John Wilkinson, M.D., F.R.S. (died by 1819), who was elected a member of the Society of Antiquaries in 1795. It is less likely to be the John Wilkinson (died by 1811) of Hardendale, Westmorland, who was elected 1807.

The bust was exhibited at the Royal Academy in 1806 (number 840) and at the Liverpool Academy in 1810 (number 197).

NOTE
1) F.A.S. is an early, alternative rendering of F.S.A. Dr Wilkinson is given as F.A.S. only in the Liverpool Academy catalogue.

Untraced.

85. Bust of H.R.H. The Duke of Gloucester

William Frederick, second Duke of Gloucester (1776-1834), while Commander of the forces in the district, lived from September 1803 until at least 1806 at San Domingo, Liverpool. He succeeded to the Dukedom in 1805. The Duke, like William Roscoe with whom he corresponded, was a keen supporter of the rights of negroes.

The bust and its publication were advertised by Bullock in the *Liverpool Chronicle*, 15th January 1806:

'GRECIAN ROOMS

His Royal Highness the DUKE of GLOUCESTER having been graciously pleased to command a Bust of himself, to be modelled by Mr. George Bullock, the Nobility and Gentry are most respectfully informed, that his Royal Highness has given permission for the same to be published.

Subscriptions will be received at the banking house of Messrs. Gregsons, Clay, and Co. and at the Grecian Rooms, next door to the Athenaeum, Church-street.

Price of the Bust Six Guineas each.

Such Ladies and Gentlemen as wish to secure the possession of a Bust of his Royal Highness, are requested to subscribe their names as soon as convenient, as the number is not to exceed the extent of the subscription, and the copies will be delivered in the strict order of subscribing.'

Bullock announced in the *Liverpool Chronicle* on 26th February 1806 (p.2, col. 5), that the bust was 'now finished' and that it would be 'exhibited in the Grecian Rooms prior to its being removed to the Royal Academy.'

The bust was exhibited at the Royal Academy in 1806 (number 839) and the Liverpool Academy in 1810 (number 191).

Untraced

86. Bust of Sir William Elford, Bart

Sir William Elford (1749-1837) of Bickam, Devon, was M.P. for Plymouth, 1796-1806, and Rye, 1807-1808, and a Pittite by persuasion. He was also an amateur artist and showed frequently at the Royal Academy between 1774 and 1837.

The bust was exhibited at the Royal Academy in 1807 (number 1081).

Untraced

87. Model for Monument to Nelson

On 15th November 1805, within a month of the death of Nelson at Trafalgar, the Mayor of Liverpool presided over a meeting of citizens which resolved to erect a monument to the hero behind the Town Hall.[1] A committee, which included John Bolton (*see* no. 88), Joseph Birch (*see* no. 82) and William Roscoe (*see* no. 61), was formed to manage the project. It quickly raised £9,000 and invited John Flaxman, J.C. Rossi, Richard Westmacott and John Bacon to submit maquettes to it by 1st February 1807 (according to Joseph Farrington).[2] In the event, the committee chose a model by Matthew Cotes Wyatt (1777-1862) which was executed with technical help from Westmacott and finally unveiled in 1813.

Whether Bullock was invited to send in a model to the committee is not known. However, he did so and backed up his contribution with a pamphlet of explanation. The only copy of the latter known to the compiler is signed *Geo: Bullock* and dated 16th March 1807.

Part of this descriptive pamphlet was reprinted in *The Monthly Magazine* for 1st May 1807 (p.397) which added (presumably incorrectly) that Bullock's monument was 'about to be erected at Liverpool.'

While the monument by Wyatt and the model by Bullock have some aspects in common, such as the seated captives and the pyramidal form, they belong to two very different artistic traditions. Wyatt's use of allegory, the apotheosis of a nude Nelson with the loss of an arm discreetly hidden by drapery, was quite contrary to Bullock's approach, although very much in tune with the

A MONUMENT to the MEMORY of LORD NELSON,

classical academic taste of William Roscoe. Bullock's captives are unashamedly contemporary tars in trousers, while Wyatt's idealised nude figures hark back to 17th-century Italian prototypes. The introduction of boarding nets for the railings would have grated on Roscoe's artistic sensibilities, but in this, as in his furniture, Bullock was attempting to create a consciously 'British style', a blend of classical correctness and contemporary references (*see* the text of Bullock's pamphlet reproduced below).

So far as is known, this was Bullock's only attempt at a major monument. The nature of the artificial stone which he proposed to use is not known, nor is any work of his in this medium known to survive.[4] The feebly modelled monument by Wyatt that was eventually chosen, with its tired classicism, makes one regret that Bullock's nationalistic extravaganza was not backed by the selection committee. This sentiment is certainly expressed by one contemporary source, the author of an article in the *Literary and Fashionable Magazine* (May 1807, Vol. 1, No. VII, pp.388-389), who waxed lyrical in praise of the model:

'We have been favoured with the sight of Mr George Bullock's design for this monument, through the medium of the engraver who is to execute the plate, which we do not hesitate to pronounce the most spirited and appropriate in its composition, the most correct and chaste in its allusions, and the most striking in its general effect, of any of the models we have hitherto seen designed to commemorate the exploits of this great commander. It is in fact what the model of a monument for a British admiral ought to be – British . . . If we have succeeded in conveying to our readers an idea of Mr Bullock's grand and

149

masterly design, we believe they will agree with us that it is more appropriate, or, in other words, more truly British than any of the models which we have before had occasion to notice. The artist has confined himself strictly to his subject. Nothing is introduced which does not tend to the illucidation of his story, and the idea of making the heads of the ships fac similes of the men of war, which carried the victorious flag of Lord Nelson in his different engagements, cannot be too much commended. This is giving a monument, what it ought to have, the soberness of historical truth. Nothing can be conceived more ridiculous than the impropriety into which some artists have fallen, of representing the British Admiral standing on the prow of a Roman galley, or adorning his monument with the beaks of triremes, in imitation of the rostral column at Rome. Besides, the heads of our ships of war are frequently most exquisite and tasteful pieces of sculpture. We have seen the head of the Victory, and we can scarcely conceive any object which could form a more beautiful ornament for a piece of colossal statuary. The heads of the other ships in which this great man fought, the Captain, the Vanguard, and the Elephant, are, we dare say, equally highly finished and beautiful, and, together, cannot fail to form a most interesting and impressive group. While such materials as these are at hand, and while their merit and individuality must strike every observer of taste, we are surprised that any artist should be found so enamoured of the antique as to crowd the tomb of a British Admiral with Greek and Roman engines of war.'

This issue of the journal also contained, as its frontispiece, an engraving of Bullock's model.[5]

NOTES

1) Liverpool Public Library, Record Office. *Report of the committee for superintending the erection of the monument to the memory of the late Right Honourable Lord Viscount Nelson in the area of the Liverpool Exchange completed Oct. XXI/MDCCXII.*
2) Kathryn Cave (ed.), *The Diary of Joseph Farington*, 1982, Vol. 7, p.2760; entry for 14th May 1806.
3) Liverpool Public Library, Mayer Papers, 920 MAY, *Letters on Art*, Vol. 2, p.6.
4) This material was also advertised in the *Liverpool Chronicle* on 22nd October 1806, p.1, col.2.
5) The same engraving was reproduced again in Thomas Troughton, *History of Liverpool*, extra illustrated edition, Vol. II, 1810, Plate 27.

Text of Bullock's pamphlet

TO THE

Gentlemen forming the Committee for the Erection of a Naval Monument, in Liverpool, to the Memory of the late Lord Nelson.

GENTLEMEN,

THE same liberal and public spirit, which has, upon innumerable occasions, distinguished the inhabitants of this GREAT COMMERCIAL TOWN, has again displayed itself in a novel point of view. Contemplating, with deep regret, the too well-founded complaint, urged by the artists of Great Britain, of a deficiency of national encouragement, and of the few opportunities afforded by the public for generous competition, – sensible also that the arts can only be fostered and matured into perfection by the patronage of communities, and by national reward, the inhabitants of Liverpool have nobly stepped forward; and by proposing to the efforts of sculpture a subject dear to the heart of every Briton, by disdaining the meanness of private patronage, by calling forth the noble spirit of emulation, by offering that reward, which alone can instigate the aspiring mind of science, – honor and public applause; – they have given an example of liberality and discriminating generosity, which at once merits the gratitude of the arts, and the imitation of the country.

Having presumed, Gentlemen, to enroll my name amongst those of the artists who aspire to the honor of erecting a Monument to the memory and fame of the heroic Lord Nelson, I trust the following remarks, and description of the model, produced for your inspection and consideration, will not be deemed unacceptable or intrusive. Animated and inspired as this hero was, by the most ardent and enthusiastic love of his country, to that country, and its products, only, should a monument to his departed worth be indebted for its composition; – *British trophies alone*, should commemorate *British valor*.

In thus perpetuating the remembrance of a hero, who lives in the hearts of his countrymen, it becomes a necessity of the highest importance to represent the principal achievements of his life, by the most faithful and intelligible analogies, so as to be comprehended by the generality of observers. I have, therefore, studiously abstained from distant and intricate allegories. To unite grandeur of composition to effect worthy of a national work of such magnitude, has been my chief aim; how far I have succeeded in accomplishing my desires, your judgment, Gentlemen, is to decide. In the statue of Lord Nelson, I have endeavoured to express that calm and dignified composure for which he was so pre-eminently distinguished in the hour of danger; – his effigy is, therefore, plain and simple, placed in a firm and decided attitude; the Union Flag and Anchor are introduced as the distinguishing mark of his professional rank, at the same time pointing out the means by which his fame and glory were obtained. The pedestal, on which the hero stands, is encircled with a double coil of British Cable resting on the plinth, and enriched by the representation of his four principal engagements, viz. – St. Vincent, the Nile, Copenhagen, and Trafalgar; four Figures of Victory, whose hands are united by crowns of laurel, suspended over each battle, are the supporters of this column, representing an unbroken chain of splendid victories. The cornice of the column is composed of leaves of British Oak: on the sub-plinth are seated four nautical figures, emblematical of the four great battles fought; these figures do not convey any idea of captivity more than is absolutely necessary to shew defeat: the body of the sub-plinth is enriched with the heads of the four ships in which these brilliant exploits were achieved, at once perpetuating the glory of the British Navy, and the ships by which its glory was confirmed. The heads of the Men of War are to be FAC SIMILES of the respective ships as in action: conveying to posterity the identity of the individual vessels which contributed to fix its fame on an immutable base. The whole is erected on a mural base, guarded by four lions couchant, emblematical of the indigenous and native valor of Great Britain, forming the grand bulwark to the whole, and intimating, that courage is the surest guide to naval glory. On the projecting sides of the mural base, in raised Bronze letters, appears a description of each battle, and of every ship engaged, together with that of its opponent, and on the front the sum total of the vessels taken and destroyed, by which each captain's name becomes enrolled with that of his ship, and is handed down to future ages, together with his beloved and lamented chief. This monument, the grateful effusion of liberality to British valor and departed excellence, rises from an encircled quadrangle, containing 1500 feet of water*, to be supplied by the pipes already fixed, and which can easily be brought to feed the reservoir, appearing to issue from four heads placed in the intermediate spaces of the mural base, representing the four great and principal rivers of England, Ireland, Scotland, and Wales, as contributing to commerce, and promoting that naval exertion, the cultivation of which has so firmly cemented the maritime interest and power of this proud and happy island. The circle is encompassed by a correct imitation of boarding nets, illuminated by ships' lanthorns, the whole forming an enriched Naval Pillar, of an order almost new, strictly conforming to the rules of Corinthian architecture in all its dimensions, and possessing the peculiar recommendation, of being indebted to no *Foreign or adventitious ornament* for its support: no *Heathen Mythology* is here introduced, nor any foreign attribute; as it has been my principal ambition to erect such a nautical monument with *British materials*, as shall at once tell the history of that hero, whom Britons still lament, and convey to posterity the plain, unvarnished tale of *British courage, fortitude, and glory.*

In the erection of a Monument of such national importance, and which should stand, for ages, a memorial of the gallant actions of our departed Hero, the choice of the material, in which it is to be executed, requires the most serious attention; the two principal objects of consideration should be Beauty and Durability. Marble is certainly the most beautiful, but, at the same time, the most perishable, of all other materials used for statues, or works which are exposed to the open air; which, in this climate, acts by its saline particles with such force, as to occasion the decomposition of the surface of the Marble; thus, in comparatively a few years, the sharp and spirited projections, as well as the more delicate touches of the Sculptor's art, will be obliterated, and the whole, in a few years more, become a crumbling ruin. The duration of Marble, exposed to the open air, and near the sea, cannot be estimated at more than from thirty to fifty years.

Bronze is not liable to this objection; but there cannot be a principal whole, or grand effect, produced by it. In fact, the beauty of a large composition is not attainable. The effect of Bronze is never well displayed to advantage, but in equestrian statues, as they alone admit the light between the base and the figure. The appearance, in general, is so gloomy, that in several instances the Bronze has been painted and gilt, of which there are some examples in the Metropolis. The only composition approaching to groupe, in Bronze, is at Somerset House, representing the King, with a figure of Neptune reclining at his feet. The effect is in the highest degree sombre and heavy, which occasions it to be generally overlooked, unless particularly called into notice, although executed by the first of modern artists, the late Mr. BACON. A Bronze groupe, with a stone base, has a parti-coloured appearance, from the extremes of black and white, and is wanting in that harmony which constitutes the real excellence of art.

Artificial Stone next presents itself to our consideration; it unites the beauty of Marble with the durability of Bronze, being a mixture of different substances vitrified, and is, therefore, not subject to the decomposition of the one, or the heaviness of the other, the colour being extremely beautiful, resembling Marble. The Assurance-office, in Lombard-street, may be cited as a proof of these qualities; where it retains its colour, beauty, and effect, uninjured by the weather, in a close and confined situation. In many parts of England may be found specimens of its beauty and durability. It is neither subject to the green incrustation received by good Bronze, which is extremely scarce; to the black, which proceeds from inferior metal; nor to the vegetation of moss, to which Marble is liable. In times of election, or popular tumult, Bronze may be mutilated, and stolen for its value, and, once injured, cannot be repaired; on the contrary, Artificial Stone, if defaced, can be easily restored.

The wish of giving every information on the subject in my power will, I trust, be my apology for the length of these remarks, proceeding from a desire that the liberality so nobly displayed on

*The introduction of so great a body of water, might be particularly useful to this part of the town; as it would conduce to the safety of the surrounding buildings, in case of fire; and thereby, materially influence the rate of insurance on them.

this occasion should be attended with every possible effect the Arts are capable of bestowing.

Should the Model I have the honour of submitting to you, Gentlemen, merit your approbation, and obtain your suffrage, I propose its erection in Artificial Stone; the completion of which I will undertake for the limited sum of eight thousand pounds, the Bronze letters, forming the inscription, not exceeding in number three thousand.

With sentiments of the highest respect,

I have the honor to subscribe myself,
Gentlemen,

Your obedient, humble servant,

Geo. Bullock

88. Bust of John Bolton

Colonel John Bolton (1756-1837) was a Liverpool merchant, who took an enthusiastic part in the local defence movement. In 1803 he raised and equipped 800 men for the First Battalion of the Liverpool Volunteers, 'Bolton's Invincibles'. From 1806 he employed J.M. Gandy, Bullock's partner in 1809-10, to repair and extend the ancient Bolton Hall in Yorkshire, bought by him in 1804.[1] Gandy also remodelled Storrs Hall on Lake Windermere which Bolton had purchased in 1808. Evidence of Bullock's contribution to the latter house survives in a pair of mahogany doors with brass and ebony inlay (see no. 10) and in other fittings very close to Bullock's style. At Storrs Colonel Bolton entertained many distinguished guests including George Canning, Sir Walter Scott and William Wordsworth. Like William Hey and Bullock himself, Bolton and his wife both sat to Joseph Allen (1770-1839).[2]

The bust was exhibited at the Liverpool Academy in 1810 (number 195).

NOTES
1) For a discussion of the alterations, see Clive Wainwright, 'The Romantic Interior in England', *National Art Collections Fund Review*, 1985, p.85.
2) The portrait of John Bolton is now in the Walker Art Gallery, Liverpool. It is catalogued in M.G. Bennett, *Merseyside Painters, People and Places*, Walker Art Gallery, Liverpool, 1978, Vol. 1, p.20-21 and illustrated, in Vol. 2, p.66.

Untraced

89. Bust of the late Mr. Cukitt

This is perhaps John Cukitt, an attorney who had an office in Lord Street, Liverpool, in the early 1800s.

The bust was exhibited at the Liverpool Academy in 1810 (number 199).

Untraced

90. A Bust

Exhibited at the Royal Academy in 1810 (number 767).

Untraced

91. Bust of Lord Tamworth

Robert Sewallis Shirley (1787-1824), styled Lord Tamworth, predeceased his father Robert, 7th Earl Ferrers. Mrs. Jolliffe (see no.65) was his father's illegitimate daughter.

This bust was exhibited at the Liverpool Academy in 1811 (number 165).

Untraced

92. Bust of James Sadler

James Sadler, the aeronaut pioneer, gave a hot-air balloon display in Liverpool in 1785. In October 1812 he attempted to cross the Irish Sea from Dublin but came down near the Island of Anglesey. His son William was also an aeronaut with Liverpool connections.

The bust was exhibited at the Liverpool Academy in 1812 (number 263) and the Royal Academy in 1813 (number 944).

Untraced

93. Bust of Mr. Blundell

It has been assumed in the past that this is either another bust of Henry Blundell of Ince, who died in 1810, or a version of that shown at the Royal Academy in 1804 (see no. 59). However, in the R.A. listing of 1813 no initials are given for the sitter, who is also not described as 'the late'. It may prove that this is a bust of Charles Robert Blundell (1761-1837), the son of Henry. A far more distinguished collector than his father, C.R. Blundell added over 100 paintings to the collection at Ince, including the early Italian and Northern paintings, and was a heavy buyer of Old Master Drawings and prints at the sale of the collection of William Roscoe in Liverpool in 1816.

The bust was exhibited at the Royal Academy in 1813 (number 918).

Untraced

94. Bust of Colonel Fraser

The sitter was presumably Colonel Charles Fraser, Bullock's mysterious financial backer, whose conduct towards Bullock so appalled Daniel Terry: 'George's fate was something accelerated by . . . the fantastic, damnable conduct of the monied partner Col Frazer, an old crackbrained East Indian Jackass.'[1]

The bust was exhibited at the Royal Academy in 1814 (number 784).

NOTE
1) Letter from Daniel Terry to Sir Walter Scott, 15th May 1818, National Library of Scotland, MS 3889, f.94.

Untraced

95. *Life Mask of Sir Walter Scott*

Plaster.

Of the breakfast held in 1815 at Tenterden Street in honour of the cast of William Shakespeare (*see* no. 67), attended by Benjamin West, Walter Scott, Dr. Spurzheim and John Britton, Britton recorded that:

'The language of Mr. Scott, on the poetry of Shakspere, was fluent and copious; but he scarcely noticed the plaster-cast. He could repeat almost every striking passage in the plays and poems of the Bard, and applied many of them to characterize their author. On being asked to look at and give his opinion of the Bust, he chiefly alluded to the lofty, towering forehead, and conical crown; the simple, boyish lips, and their pleasing expression; but he could not reconcile himself to the extraordinary, and, as he remarked, the unnatural space between the nose and the upper lip. This, all agreed, manifested some error in the sculptor, until Bullock looking at Mr. Scott, said that his features had the same peculiarity, even more remarkably than those of Shakspere. Scott doubted this, and even wagered that it was not so; when a pair of compasses was employed to settle the question, and the modern Bard lost his wager by a quarter of an inch. The cast of Scott's head, taken on this occasion, was the first he sat for: Chantrey's fine and speaking Bust was not executed till some years afterwards.'

This life cast, which was at Abbotsford in 1871,[2] was very likely the one made by Bullock on this occasion, although the opinion has been expressed that it may be French.[3] Dr James Corson has kindly pointed out that the casting of Scott's head is discussed in a letter from Johann Kaspar Spurzheim of 12th April 1828.[4] He also drew attention to a cast owned by Henry G. Atkinson in 1840 which may be that at Abbotsford in 1871.[5]

NOTES
1) John Britton, *Autobiography*, 1850, pp.8-9.
2) *The Scott Exhibition, Edinburgh 1871*, catalogue, 1872, pp.167-168.
3) Lawrence Hutton, *Portraits in Plaster*, 1874, pp.188-189.
4) Reproduced in *The Phrenological Journal*, Vol. 8, March 1834, pp.371-374.
5) *The Phrenological Journal*, new series, 1840, Vol. 13, p.180.

Untraced

Chronology

LUCY WOOD

G.B. denotes George Bullock, and W.B., his brother William Bullock. 'George Bullock' indicates someone who may possibly not be identical with the subject of this exhibition.

Catalogue numbers given for the busts exhibited by Bullock at the Liverpool Academy and the Royal Academy refer to the present exhibition.

1778

24th August: A 'George Bullock', son of William and Elizabeth Bullock, baptised at All Saints, West Bromwich.

1782 or 1783

G.B. born, if aged 35 at his death as stated.

1794

26th May: Mrs Bullock advertises the arrival of her waxworks exhibition in Birmingham.

1796

16th May: Mrs Bullock advertises her exhibition at 87 Bull Street, Birmingham; *14th November:* she reopens her exhibition at her own house, 29 Bull Street, and it subsequently tours Midlands towns in 1797 and 1798.

1797

27th March: 'Mrs Bullock & Son' offer modelling and drawing lessons at their 'modelling and statuary warehouse', 29 Bull Street, Birmingham. *On 29th May:* '[they] have been . . . modelling new figures for the Exhibition.'

A letter to a Birmingham newspaper reports having seen a young artist, 'yet a boy' (almost certainly G.B.), at work on 'miniature paintings, models in wax, rice paste, and plaster of Paris', in Bull Street, Birmingham.

1798

27th August: G.B. '[whose] age does not exceed twenty' is on the point of leaving Birmingham and 'returning to London'.

1799

24th March: A 'George Bullock', glass picture-frame-maker, married to Elizabeth Mansell, widow of Samuel Mansell, pawnbroker, of Coleshill Street, Birmingham (died 20th August 1798).

16th September: G.B. announces himself as 'G. Bullock, Modeller in Rice Paste' at no. 12 Ann Street.

Trade directories for 1800 and 1801 continue to list him as miniature painter and portrait modeller at this address.

1800

August-October: W.B.'s 'Cabinet of Curiosities' open at Portugal House, New Street, Birmingham.

September: G.B. exhibits portrait [wax?] of Mrs Siddons (no. 73) at W.B.'s Museum, Portugal House, New Street, Birmingham.

1801

From 16th March: W.B.'s Museum and business ('Silversmith, Jeweller, Toyman and Statue Figure Manufacturer') open at 24 Lord Street, Liverpool, where it remained until July/August 1804.

G.B.'s earliest surviving work, a signed and dated wax of Henry Blundell (no. 58) of Ince Blundell, near Liverpool, implies his presence in Liverpool (perhaps based at W.B.'s museum).

1802

21st June: Equestrian statue, Edward the Black Prince (no. 77), on show at W.B.'s Museum at 24 Lord Street, Liverpool.

1803

28th August: William Roscoe mentions Mr Bullock in a letter to J.E. Smith (*see no. 62*).

1804

G.B., describing himself as 'Modeller and Sculptor', lodges at W.B.'s Museum, 24 Lord Street, Liverpool.

27th June: G.B. announces move to William Stoakes's looking glass manufactory, 48 Church Street, Liverpool.

From about July: G.B. is in partnership with Stoakes as 'Bullock and Stoakes, General Furnishers and Marble Workers, 48 Church Street, Liverpool' (partnership dissolved October 1806).

G.B. of 'Liverpool, and at W. Stephenson's, Esq., 97 Pall Mall [The Royal Hotel]' exhibits six busts at Royal Academy (nos. 59, 61, 62, 78, 79 and 80).

From 8th August: W.B.'s Museum and business as jeweller, silversmith and chinaman at 25 Church Street, Liverpool (to 1807); then 27 Church Street (1807-09).

By December: G.B. designs drawing room and subsequently manufactures furniture and 'armour' (nos. 1-4) for the Marquess of Cholmondeley, Cholmondeley Castle, Cheshire (despatched September 1805).

1805

Bullock and Stoakes supply bronze figures to Stephen Tempest (Henry Blundell's son-in-law) at Broughton Hall, Yorkshire.

13th March: G.B. advertises his busts of 'The Young Roscius' and others; W.B. announces publication of [Lucius] Gahagan's bust, 'The Young Roscius'.

G.B. of '1, Southampton Street, Strand', exhibits three busts at Royal Academy (nos. 81, 82 and 83).

June: W.B. opens new 'Egyptian Hall' at Liverpool Museum, for the sale of ornamental furnishings.

4th September: Bullock and Stoakes open re-furbished 'Grecian Rooms' at 48 Church Street, Liverpool.

1806

Herculaneum Pottery founded in Liverpool.

15th January: G.B. invites subscription to his bust of the Duke of Gloucester.

12th February: G.B. announces closure of Grecian Rooms at 48 Church Street.

3rd-7th March: Sale of G.B.'s stock.

22nd October: G.B. announces reopening of Grecian Rooms at 13 Bold Street, Liverpool, and dissolution of his partnership with Stoakes. He also mentions, for the first time, 'specimens of his quarries in Anglesea'.

G.B. exhibits two busts at Royal Academy (nos. 84 and 85).

W.B. opens account at Herculaneum Pottery (ends 1808).

Colonel John Bolton, Liverpool merchant (*see* no. 88), employs J.M. Gandy, architect (G.B.'s partner 1809-10) at Bolton Hall, Yorkshire, 1806-10 (and subsequently at Storrs Hall Westmorland, 1808-11).

1807

G.B., 'Modeller, Sculptor & Grecian Rooms, 15 [sic] Bold Street; Yard [marble works] 55 Church Street, Liverpool.'

G.B. exhibits one bust at Royal Academy (no. 86) and designs a monument to Lord Nelson (no. 87).

3rd June: Sale of G.B's Bold Street premises announced for 5th June; this may not have taken place since G.B. still occupied 13 Bold Street in 1809 and 14 Bold Street in 1810-11.

G.B. opens account at Herculaneum Pottery (ends January 1811).

1808

30th April: G.B. is paid for 'designing the arrangements of the rooms' at the Herculaneum Pottery warehouse in Duke Street, Liverpool.

G.B. 'is to fit up' Hafod for Thomas Johnes (as of 15th March).

G.B. exhibits one bust at Royal Academy (no. 75).

G.B. supplies furniture and fittings to Thornhill, near Birmingham, until 1818, for James Watt Junior and (latterly) Miss Anne Boulton.

c.1808

Liverpool Assembly Rooms, Castle Street, by J.M. Gandy, erected (now demolished).

1809

G.B. modeller and sculptor, at Grecian Rooms, 13 Bold Street, and furniture rooms, at Hanover Street, Liverpool.

W.B. moves Museum to 22 Piccadilly, London.

Billiard Room (Rotunda), Bold Street, Liverpool, by J.M. Gandy erected (now demolished).

G.B. provides two bronze busts for James Watt Junior's sculpture copying machine.

By April: G.B. in partnership with J.M. Gandy as 'Bullock George, and Joseph Gandy, architects modellers, sculptors, marble masons, cabinet-makers and upholsterers, 55 Church Street, Liverpool' (dissolved September 1810). They collaborate at Storrs Hall (*see* no. 88).

c.1809

G.B.'s monument to the Rev. Glover Moore erected, St Cuthbert's Church, Halsall, Lancashire (no. 64).

1810

G.B. modeller, sculptor &c., 14 Bold Street, Liverpool (and in partnership with Gandy as above).

Liverpool Academy founded with G.B. as President, Henry Blundell of Ince, Patron, and William Roscoe, Treasurer.

At the 1st Liverpool Academy Exhibition, G.B. exhibits nine busts (nos. 59, 61, 62, 65, 83, 84, 85, 88, 89); Richard Bridgens, 'at Messrs. Bullock and Gandy's', exhibits 'Design for a Monument' and 'Screen in Sefton Church restored'.

G.B. exhibits one bust at Royal Academy (no. 90).

W.B. begins building new London Museum, the 'Egyptian Hall', at 172 Piccadilly, south side (completed 1812); architect P.F. Robinson.

1811

G.B. modeller, sculptor, &c. 14 Bold Street; counting house, 39 Hanover Street; yard, 55 Church Street, manufactory 79 Bold Street, Liverpool.

Prince Regent becomes Patron of the Liverpool Academy on death of Henry Blundell of Ince.

At the 2nd Liverpool Academy Exhibition, G.B. exhibits four busts (nos. 61, 78, 81 and 91); Richard Bridgens, 'at Mr. Bullocks', exhibits model of 'A

Nymph Attiring', and drawing, 'Chimneypiece, at Speke Hall'.

August: Geological lecture given by a Mr Bakewell in Liverpool; he identifies G.B.'s 'Mona Marble' as serpentine, and remarks on its resemblance to 'Verde Antique'.

G.B., working alongside William Atkinson, architect, for Stephen Tempest of Broughton Hall, Yorkshire, models '4 heads', and supplies 'Egyptian' chimney piece, etc.

G.B. restores hall at Speke Hall, Lancashire, and provides furniture, for Richard Watt (*see* no. 5). Work continues into 1812.

1812

G.B. resigns Presidency of the Liverpool Academy but remains a member; Richard Bridgens becomes an Associate. At the 3rd Liverpool Academy Exhibition G.B. exhibits one bust (no. 92); Richard Bridgens exhibits, from Bold Street, Liverpool, 'View of the entrance of the Ware Rooms of Mr. Geo Bullock's Egyptian Hall, Piccadilly, London'.

3rd February: Sale of G.B.'s stock in Manchester.

28th August: Sale of G.B.'s stock at Bold Street shop; G.B. 'is going to reside in London'.

1st-3rd September: Sale of contents of Speke Hall, including furniture supplied by G.B., 'which never has been used.'

11th September: Sale of G.B.'s pictures in Liverpool.

1813

G.B. listed in a Liverpool trade directory as modeller, sculptor, &c. Troughton Street; counting house and cabinet manufactory, 79 Bold Street, Liverpool (to 1814).

G.B. also listed in a London directory as upholsterer, Grecian Rooms, Egyptian Hall, Piccadilly, London (to 1814).

At 4th Liverpool Academy Exhibition, J.M. Gandy exhibits 'A Restoration of the East Window of Melrose Abbey, with the Tomb of Michael Scott'.

G.B. exhibits two busts at Royal Academy (nos. 92, 93).

23rd June: Payment made to G.B. by the 4th Duke of Buccleuch (*see* no. 36); another payment made on 16th November 1814.

Colonel Frazier – latterly Fraser [G.B.'s 'monied partner' at the time of his death?] at 28 Montague Place, Russell Square, London (until 1815).

W.B., Museum, 172 Piccadilly, London (until 1818).

Furniture by G.B. now at Gorhambury perhaps supplied to Harriet, Lady Grimston (who spent £400 on furniture in this year).

c.1813-14

G.B.'s monument to Anna Maria Bold erected St Luke's Church, Farnworth, Widnes (no. 66).

1814

At the 5th and final Liverpool Academy Exhibition,

Richard Bridgens, of '4 Tenterden Street, Hanover Square, London', exhibits two views of Richmant, near Bolton, seat of Joseph Ridgeway.

G.B. '4, Tenterden St., Hanover Square,' exhibits one bust at Royal Academy (no. 94).

About May: G.B. meets Jacques-Louis David in Paris.

21st November: Final sale of G.B.'s Liverpool stock and his Bold Street property; G.B. 'has removed to his manufactory, Oxford-street, London.'

December: G.B. casts copies of Shakespeare's effigy in Stratford church (*see* nos. 67 and 68).

Designs for furniture and fittings for Lord Macdonald, Armadale Castle, Isle of Skye, dated 1814-18.

Furniture supplied to Duke of Atholl at Blair Castle and Dunkeld, Perthshire (nos. 7-9), from 1814 to 1819.

1815

G.B. makes life mask of Sir Walter Scott, at breakfast (no. 95).

G.B. 'sculptor, 4, Tenterden street, Hanover-square; Mona Marble and Furniture Works, Oxford-street, London', a listing that continued into 1819.

22nd September: W.B. exhibits his London Museum (natural history collection) at Lillyman's Assembly Rooms, Castle Street, Liverpool.

Furniture and fittings for Napoleon's use at Longwood, St. Helena, designed and manufactured (nos. 18-21).

Designs for furniture and fittings for W. Nisbet, Biel, East Lothian, dated 1815-17.

1816

January-August: W.B. exhibits Napoleon's field carriage at London Museum, Piccadilly; then on tour (including a stop in December at 68 Bold Street, Liverpool).

G.B. exhibits one bust at Royal Academy (no. 69).

Furniture designed for Mrs. Barron [Barrow?]

Cabinets designed for Edmund Rundell [presumably the Edmund Rundell who was a partner in Rundell, Bridge & Rundell, and nephew of Philip Rundell].

From January: G.B.'s designs appear regularly in Ackermann's *Repository* (*see* no. 56) in 1816 and 1817.

Furniture and fittings supplied to Matthew Robinson Boulton at Tew Park, Oxfordshire (nos. 25-31). Delivery completed in 1818.

Furniture and fittings supplied to Sir Walter Scott at Abbotsford, Roxburghshire (nos. 15-17 and 68A), until 1819.

Payments made to G.B. and George Morant by 6th Earl of Cardigan, until 1819.

Furniture and fittings supplied to Sir Godfrey Webster at Battle Abbey, Sussex (nos. 12-14), until at least 1817.

1817

Furniture supplied to Mrs Ferguson (*see* no. 22).

Cabinets made, and two busts altered, for the Marquess of Abercorn (nos. 23, 70 and 71).

1818

Table designed for Lady Spencer [Lavinia, Countess Spencer, d.1831].

1st May: G.B. died.

8th May: G.B. buried at St. George's, Hanover Square, London, aged 35 according to the burial register.

1819

Bullock & Co., cabinet makers, 4 Tenterden Street, Oxford Street, London.

W.B., artist and naturalist, 172, Piccadilly, London.

Samuel Joseph exhibits bust of the late George Bullock at Royal Academy.

24th-25th March: Sale in Liverpool of G.B.'s pictures and library, and his shares in Liverpool's public institutions.

29th April-11th June: Sale of W.B.'s Museum collections, Egyptian Hall, Piccadilly, London.

3rd-5th May: Sale of G.B.'s 'finished stock,' Christie's, on the premises, 4, Tenterden Street, Hanover Square, London.

13th-15th May: Sale of G.B.'s 'unmanufactured Stock in Trade', Christie's, on the premises, 4 Tenterden Street.

1st July: The Times reports that several of G.B.'s workmen have been engaged by E.T. Cox, cabinet-maker, 13 Haymarket, London, who will manufacture oak furniture to G.B.'s designs.

Richard Bridgens begins work for James Watt Junior at Aston Hall.

Bullock's business still listed, as it had been since 1816, in *Kent's London Directory*: 'Bullock G. mona marble works, Oxford-str. & 4 Tenterden-st.'; this listing continued until 1821. The address then became '4, Tenterden-st.' (1822-25), and finally, '315, Oxford-street' (1826).

1820

W.B. auctioneer, Egyptian Hall, Piccadilly, London and (from 1821) 119, Sloane Street, London. A 'Jos. Bullock' was at the latter address in 1824.

1821

Three further designs associated with G.B. appear in Ackermann's *Repository* (*see* no. 56).

1822

5th August: Sale by 'Barker' of Bullock furniture, at Christie's, Pall Mall.

Publication of monograph by Richard Bridgens, *Sefton Church with Part of the Interior Decorations*, based on drawings made while in Liverpool.

Publication of second 'improved' edition of Richard Brown, *The Rudiments of Drawing Cabinet and Upholstery Furniture*, incorporating designs from Bullock's workshop.

1823

James Bullock, printer, 7 Lombard Street [now Lombard Lane], Fleet Street, London; printed several works of William Bullock, but his relationship to the two brothers is not known. He remained at this address until at least 1829.

1826

Publication of Richard Bridgens, *Furniture with candelabra and interior decoration*, incorporating designs from Bullock's workshop.